P9-BZS-667

THE NEW CHARDONNAY

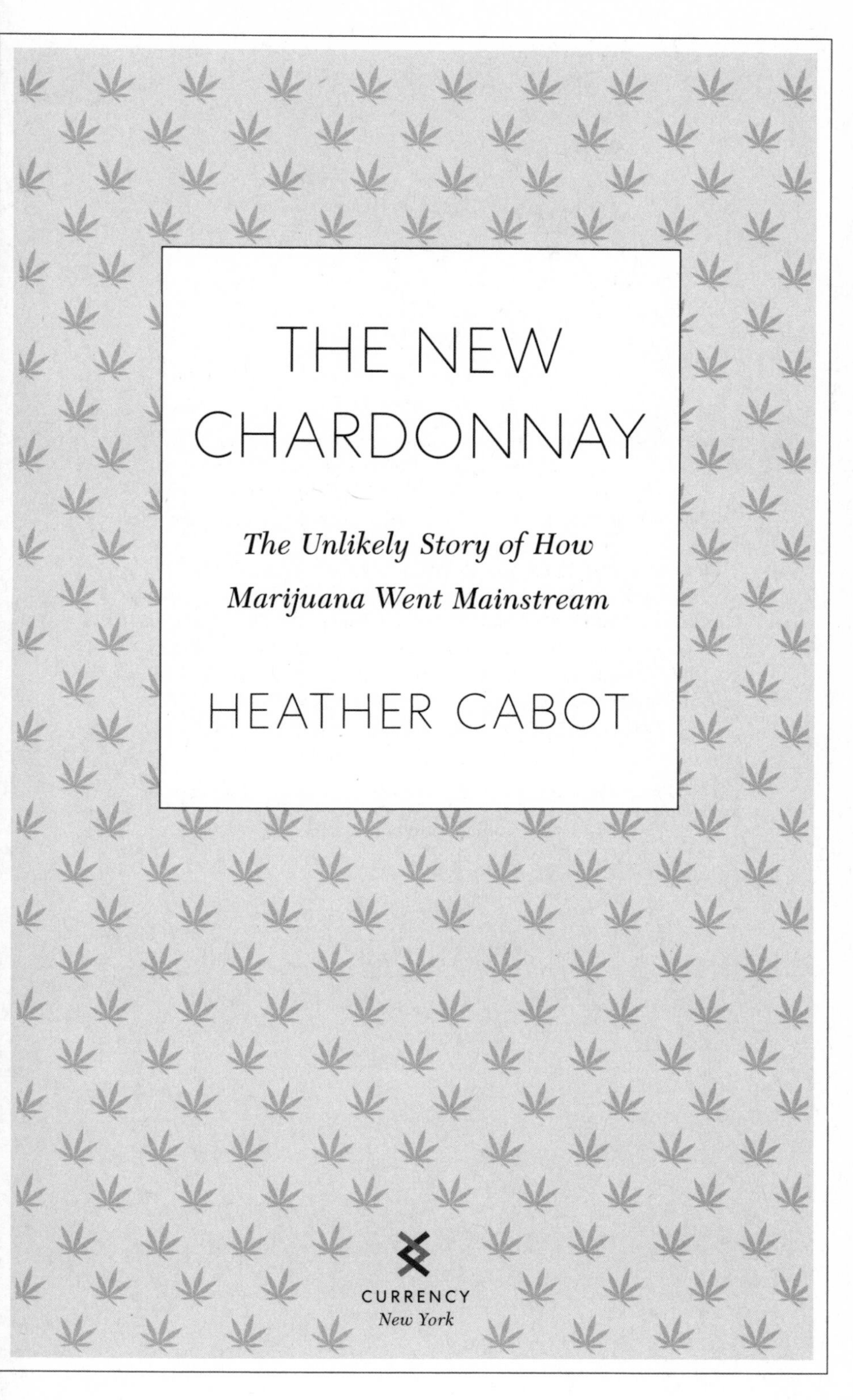

THE NEW CHARDONNAY

The Unlikely Story of How Marijuana Went Mainstream

HEATHER CABOT

CURRENCY
New York

Published in the United States by Currency, an imprint of Random House, a division of Penguin Random House LLC, New York.

CURRENCY and its colophon are trademarks of Penguin Random House LLC.

Library of Congres Cataloging-in-Publication Data
Names: Cabot, Heather, author.
Title: The new chardonnay / Heather Cabot.
Description: First edition. | New York : Currency, [2020] | Includes bibliographical references.
Identifiers: LCCN 2020007270 (print) | LCCN 2020007271 (ebook) | ISBN 9781984826244 (hardcover) | ISBN 9781984826251 (ebook)
Subjects: LCSH: Marijuana industry—United States. | Marijuana—Economic aspects—United States. | Marijuana—Social aspects—United States. | Drug legalization—Social aspects—United States.
Classification: LCC HD9019.M382 U6295 2020 (print) | LCC HD9019.M382 (ebook) | DDC 338.1/3790973—dc23
LC record available at https://lccn.loc.gov/2020007270

Printed in the United States of America on acid-free paper

randomhousebooks.com

2 4 6 8 9 7 5 3 1

FIRST EDITION

Design by Fritz Metsch

For Neeraj

CONTENTS

CAST OF CHARACTERS

Beth Stavola: Jersey Shore mother of six and former Wall Street executive who ventures to Arizona to strike it rich in medical marijuana

Ted Chung: Wharton alum and business partner of rap icon Snoop Dogg who spearheads Snoop's cannabis investment strategy

Jeff Danzer: Former fashion marketing executive and home cook who ditches his day job to become a cannabis chef and inventor

Dr. Raphael Mechoulam: Nobel Prize–nominated Israeli biochemist who identified the molecular structure of THC and CBD along with other groundbreaking discoveries that paved the way for modern therapeutic cannabinoid research

Bruce Linton: Founder and former CEO of Canopy Growth, the first publicly traded pot company in the world (NYSE: CGC; TSX: WEED), initially named Tweed Marijuana, Inc.

Chuck Rifici: Founding CEO of Tweed, charged with building a massive growing operation for one of the first licensed marijuana producers in Canada

Wanda James: First African American entrepreneur in the United States to own a marijuana business license and a prominent voice for racial justice in cannabis

Mel McDonald: Former U.S. Attorney appointed by President Ronald Reagan, fifth-generation Mormon, elder in the Church of Jesus Christ of Latter-day Saints (LDS), and unexpected supporter of legalizing medical marijuana

Tiffany Chin: Wharton grad, protégé of Ted Chung, and cofounder of Leafs By Snoop

Don Tucker: Former federal narcotics agent, twenty-five-year veteran of the U.S. Secret Service, and Beth's hired security consultant in Arizona

Sylvia Danzer: Jeff's mom, who raised him in an Orthodox Jewish home and inspires him to incorporate his heritage into his food

The Honorable Michele Fiore: Las Vegas mayor pro tem and former assemblywoman representing Clark County who cast the lone Republican vote in the Nevada legislature for medical marijuana legalization in 2013

Big Nanny: Kathie Beggans, Beth's mom and confidante

Julie Winter: Beth's youngest sister and chief operating officer of CBD For Life, one of the first CBD beauty and wellness brands in the United States

Jared Danzer: Jeff's middle son and business partner, who helps Jeff market his cannabis innovations

LEGALIZATION TIMELINE

August 1937: Congress passes the Marihuana Tax Act of 1937 and lays foundation for pot prohibition in the United States

October 1970: President Richard Nixon signs the Controlled Substances Act, designating cannabis Schedule I: a drug with a high potential for abuse and no accepted medical use

June 1971: Nixon declares drugs "public enemy number one" and formally launches the nation's "War on Drugs," spurring an upward trend of arrest and incarceration of black and brown citizens for low-level drug offenses

September 1986: First Lady Nancy Reagan unveils national "Just Say No" campaign

October 1986: President Ronald Reagan signs the Anti–Drug Abuse Act, establishing mandatory minimum sentences for specific drug offenses

September 1994: President Bill Clinton signs the Violent Crime Control and Law Enforcement Act (aka "the Crime Bill"), contributing to the disproportionate incarceration of African Americans and Latinos for marijuana possession

November 1996: Led by AIDS activists and gay rights advocates, California becomes first state in the nation to permit medical marijuana use

November 2012: Colorado and Washington voters amend state constitutions to legalize recreational marijuana and to regulate and tax it like alcohol

August 2013: The U.S. Department of Justice issues the Cole Memo, which guides federal prosecutors to deprioritize cannabis businesses operating legally under state law and to instead focus on drug cartels

December 2013: Uruguay becomes the first country in the world to legalize cannabis

January 2014: First recreational sales of marijuana begin in Colorado (Washington begins in July)

November 2016: California, Nevada, Massachusetts, and Maine voters approve recreational marijuana legalization

January 2018: California begins recreational sales, ushering in largest market in the world amid uncertainty about licensing, distribution, and competition from illicit market

February 2018: Cannabis swag bags gifted to celebs backstage at Academy Awards

June 2018: Canopy Growth lists on the New York Stock Exchange, the first "plant-touching" company to trade on that exchange

October 2018: Canada becomes first G7 nation to lift pot prohibition

November 2018: Massachusetts, first East Coast state to allow recreational use, begins sales to people twenty-one and over

November 2018: Michigan voters approve recreational sales of cannabis

December 2018: Farm Bill removes hemp from the Controlled Substances Act, opening door for interstate CBD commerce

December 2018: West Hollywood awards first licenses for pot lounges

May 2019: CVS, Bed Bath & Beyond, and Walgreens begin carrying hemp-derived CBD products

June 2019: Illinois becomes the first state to legalize the sale of recreational marijuana through its legislature and introduces major social justice initiatives

August 2019: Federal health officials and local health departments begin investigating nationwide outbreak of lung injuries from vaping

October 2019: Gallup poll finds 66 percent of Americans approve of legalization, the highest approval rating since pollsters began tracking the issue, a 30 percentage point increase between 2005 and 2018

INTRODUCTION

IT WAS A day that called for big, bold designer shades. The California sun warmed a throng of fresh-faced millennials in expensive athleisure ensembles as they waited in line to devour the latest advice on living their best lives—all carefully curated by their slender blond guru, the embodiment of all human aspirations: Gwyneth Paltrow. As the summer kicked off in June 2018, more than six hundred attendees had shelled out a minimum of $650 per ticket for the privilege of basking in the star's glistening essence at this wellness retreat in a sleek Los Angeles venue. In its third installment, the sprawling event featured a carnival of keynotes and classes aimed at devotees of the Oscar winner's digital media and e-commerce empire, the mecca of quirky health and wellness advice, goop. In the spotlight this year—along with B_{12} shots, mushroom coffee, and tantric sex tips—was the most popular federally illegal substance in America: marijuana.

It was at the "In goop Health" summit, where "G.P.," who has been known to smoke a little weed from time to time, announced to her fans that she was dipping a baby toe into the biz. Goop would curate a sampling of cannabis teas, bath bombs, vaporizers, and chocolates to be sold in a pot store like no other—the upscale retailer called MedMen, located on the trendy Abbot Kinney Boulevard in California's Venice Beach. MedMen's glossy candy-apple-red-themed chain of marijuana dispensaries in L.A., New York City, and Vegas were touted by the company as "the Apple Stores of pot" for the contemporary design of their retail spaces with sleek wood and glass display cases, plus a fleet of knowledgeable "budtenders" (sales associates) at the ready to advise curious customers. And because no exclusive event is complete without swag, G.P. highlighted the news by handing out red-and-white MedMen goodie bags to attendees of the "Future of Cannabis" panel hosted by her friend, the actress and former *Boston Legal* star Lake Bell.

Bell was well versed in weed. Her tattoo artist husband, Scott Campbell, had founded the luxury marijuana accessory company Beboe. Which explained why, along with her tasteful rose-colored pantsuit and nude heels, the actress modeled a shiny gold Beboe vaporizer—encased in a $50,000 Daniela Villegas jewel-encrusted pendant adorned with opals and pearls—as she led a discussion with several marijuana entrepreneurs and scientists on the ins and outs of cannabis. The goal was to educate this eager crowd on the array of trendy marijuana remedies touted to ease anxiety, relieve pain, and even boost libido—and to provide a primer on the difference between THC, the cannabinoid that gets you high, and CBD, the one that doesn't (but can be used to potentially reduce inflammation, muscle tightness, and nausea, among other ailments).

The room buzzed with questions during the hour-long event. The audience learned about the effects of the most well-known subspecies of the plant—indica and sativa—from UCLA cannabis researcher Dr. Jeffrey Chen. A marketing exec from the California cannabis wellness company Papa & Barkley revealed new innovations, like a cannabis "lube"—a product growing in popularity (especially among senior citizens)—and CBD-infused tampons to soothe menstrual cramps. *Really?* With the demeanor of a big sister schooling her wide-eyed younger siblings on the ways of the world, Bell concluded with a coy admission to the audience. She'd been "high as a kite" the whole time. Giggles ensued.

While you might expect that such a gathering would attract the stereotypical marijuana enthusiasts—stoners, burnouts, hippies, and deadbeats in tie-dye—that couldn't have been further from the truth. Instead, the room hosted a crowd of "Whole Foods shoppers and Equinox members," observed the cofounder of Lord Jones, a premium California brand of gourmet "edible" confections and infused skin lotions. These were curious, discerning consumers dedicated to a health-conscious lifestyle, with money to spend. These were women who might have ended the day with a glass of Chardonnay but craved an alternative, something that wouldn't leave them sluggish or add inches to their waistline.

And they were more curious than ever, now that pot was legal for medical purposes in thirty states, nine of them allowing recreational use for adults over twenty-one years old. By the summer of 2018, one in five Americans lived in a state where she or he could legally purchase marijuana—most located up and down the West Coast and in a few pockets on the eastern seaboard, with more states in the middle of the country considering legalization than ever before. Yet federal drug laws on pot remained stuck in 1970, when the Nixon administration and Congress assigned the plant to the most dangerous designation of the Controlled Substances Act, Schedule I, kicking off decades of aggressive law enforcement that filled up prisons with minor pot offenders, disproportionately people of color. But with the rapid acceptance of medical marijuana over the last decade, and the billions of dollars to be made from legal sale of the drug, activists and industry insiders optimistically predict that America's pot prohibition could fall away as soon as 2022, when either all fifty states will address it locally or Congress will act to reform federal drug laws. In the meantime, in towns and cities across the nation where weed is permitted and a lawful way to make a living, it has become a booming business that took in more than $12 billion in 2019 alone.

This wasn't just a West Coast thing. Across the country, in a leafy waterside enclave just outside New York City, a roomful of affluent middle-aged moms bubbled with queries, opinions, and personal stories about pot. It all started when one woman, an interior designer, confided that the roller-coaster ride of mood swings she had been experiencing thanks to the stress of raising three teenage daughters and juggling a full-time job was frustrating the heck out of her family. Another chimed in that she hadn't been sleeping much but was nervous about trying Ambien. Someone else complained that PMS and back pain were driving her crazy every month. That's when their friend, a physician with a holistic approach, gingerly mentioned a potential remedy: tinctures made from CBD. There was a pause, followed by some sheepish grins. Suddenly, the tastefully appointed den exploded with even more chatter than before. Everyone began to open up. They were all canna-curious.

Why not? Marijuana was making headlines right in their own backyard. Cynthia Nixon, otherwise known as the ambitious attorney Miranda Hobbes on HBO's *Sex and the City*—the show that practically defined these women's twenties—was now running in the Democratic primary race for governor of New York on an unapologetically pro-pot platform. Legalizing marijuana for adult use, she argued, was a social imperative to address the injustices wrought on black and brown New Yorkers arrested for low-level marijuana offenses at strikingly higher rates than whites were. This argument was so persuasive (or politically expedient, or both) that she successfully pressured her opponent in the primary, Governor Andrew Cuomo, to reverse his public stand against the drug.

Racial justice wasn't the only hot-button social issue to enter the discussion. By June 2018, as the opioid crisis ravaged the nation, even the New York State Department of Health had endorsed marijuana as an alternative to highly addictive prescription painkillers, and its commissioner had publicly thrown his support behind expanding the legal market. With Cuomo's new about-face and health policymakers' stamp of approval, Albany observers speculated it was only a matter of time before the Empire State would follow the lead of Colorado and California, where pot was supplanting alcohol as the new (legal) feel-good indulgence of choice.

In the months and years ahead, the governor (who went on to win a third term) and state lawmakers would find it wasn't so easy to come to a consensus on commercializing recreational cannabis, especially when it came to ensuring communities of color weren't left out of the potential fortunes to be made. In his 2020 State of the State address, the governor vowed once again to make adult-use marijuana a priority as elected officials in surrounding states New Jersey, Connecticut, and Pennsylvania also considered how to tap into the industry. They had watched as Massachusetts, which opened up over-21 sales in November 2018, now had lines around the block at some of its new lawful pot shops made up of out-of-towners who drove a few hours over the border to buy newfangled pot products.

The developments in progressive New York and up and down the East Coast coincided with a similar shift in some of Middle America's most conservative strongholds. Thanks to support from farmers who suddenly saw the benefits of "going green," and military veterans who saw pot as a promising alternative to psychotropic drugs and opioids as a way to manage residual pain from war injuries and PTSD, Oklahoma, one of the reddest states in the nation, had passed a ballot initiative to legalize medical marijuana with 57 percent of the vote—and even included a liberal provision that allows doctors to prescribe pot for any condition they see fit. Opposition groups reportedly outspent Oklahomans in support of SQ 788 by six to one. But the pro-pot campaign highlighted the kinds of stories money can't buy—stories of patients like U.S. Navy veteran Cody Barlow, who was prescribed nine thousand pills per year by his doctors at the V.A. for pain, PTSD, and depression, and instead found relief in medical marijuana.

The pace of change was positively head-spinning. When the fictional pot-dealing mom Nancy Botwin went legit and sold her legal marijuana cafés to Starbucks in the 2012 finale of the series *Weeds* on Showtime, it had seemed like a plot twist only Hollywood could cook up. Now there were real-life pot lounges, inviting shops in high-rent neighborhoods, and even big-box superstores complete with coupons and "buy one, get one free" promotions on the horizon. *O, The Oprah Magazine* was highlighting a tea party where the guests wore fancy hats and prim white gloves as they got high on THC-infused teas, while senior citizens were being bused from nursing homes and retirement communities to stores where they could peruse new cannabis-infused remedies to ease arthritis and insomnia.

Meanwhile, a whole new class of celebrity was getting in on the game. *Godfather* director turned winemaker Francis Ford Coppola announced he was now jumping into the weed business, and *The View* talk-show host Whoopi Goldberg was already teaming up with a California grower on a new brand of pot-derived period pain remedies. And to boot, Martha Stewart, arbiter of good taste and fine living, was now yucking it up with the ultimate O.G. stoner, Snoop Dogg, on prime-time TV in a marijuana "Munchie Snackdown."

All this as the investor class was listening to CNBC's Jim Cramer declare legal marijuana "the most disruptive force since Amazon" for sectors like beverages and Big Pharma. In 2018, Canada became the first industrialized nation in the world to legalize weed across its provinces. Pot companies were trading on the New York Stock Exchange and the NASDAQ, and the U.S. Food and Drug Administration had just approved the very first cannabis-derived drug, Epidiolex, to treat a rare childhood seizure disorder.

As a result, hundreds of millions of dollars in local tax revenue generated from sales of cannabis were going to schools and roads, creating thousands of jobs that were putting people back to work. Which is part of the reason why even one of the most ardent pot opponents, former Speaker of the House John Boehner, a Republican, stunningly reversed course. He joined the board of one of the largest U.S. cannabis-growing conglomerates, Acreage Holdings. If that wasn't enough of a one-eighty, the former Ohio congressman helped found a new K Street lobbying firm to push federal pot reform on the Hill. Plus, he was headlining a series of digital infomercials urging average Americans to invest in cannabis or risk losing their "once in a lifetime shot" at getting a piece of the "Green Gold Rush."

For most of the women who gathered in the suburban New York living room that afternoon, myself included, these new developments felt surreal. After all, we had come of age in the 1980s. We were the "Just Say No" generation. We all remembered the after-school PSA that warned us our brains would fry like eggs if we dared try drugs. Marijuana was something "other people" did. We may have experimented briefly in college. But now, as professionally accomplished suburban "supermoms," smoking weed conjured images of red-eyed truants devoid of ambition, scary drug dealers on seedy corners, or lazy couch potatoes wolfing down Taco Bell at midnight in their parents' basements.

What's more, as mothers of teens and tweens, cannabis was one of the many temptations we wanted our own children and their developing brains to avoid. We went to school meetings that warned us about the risks of edibles and vaping (and this was a full year before the fatal vaping crisis would send a chill across the weed industry and reignite parental concerns). We worried about our kids using marijuana behind our backs, or, God forbid, getting behind the wheel of a car while intoxicated—especially now that kids had new ways of consuming marijuana that were virtually undetectable, leaving behind no telltale smell, no trail of smoke, not even the incriminating "roach." On top of this, there were several women in the group who had been personally touched by drug addiction in their own families, and clung to the long-held warning and fear that marijuana was a "gateway drug."

And yet, the idea that it might be "okay"—socially acceptable, even—for mature adults to partake in something once so strictly forbidden was frankly mind-blowing . . . and deliciously intriguing at the same time. It was truly an Alice in Wonderland moment. And all of these developments prompted questions about whether the hype was real. Was lighting up really becoming as respectable as sipping a glass of wine? Would marijuana turn out to be the cash cow the industry portrayed it to be? Did the plant really possess the myriad of therapeutic benefits the glib marketers promised, even though clinical research was still emerging? Which of these products were safe for adults to consume, and in what quantities? How about the impact on kids? Or the risks of drug-impaired drivers on the roads? But for me, a veteran journalist and former ABC News correspondent, the most compelling question of the day was: How did we get here? How did marijuana manage to somehow shed its stigma, seemingly overnight?

The search for answers sparked the idea for this book—and the once-in-a-lifetime chance to ride along with a handful of ambitious entrepreneurs chasing their cannabis dreams. When I started reporting this book in the summer of 2017, the signs were everywhere that the taboo around pot was receding across age, race, and income levels in cities, suburbs, and rural areas nationwide. And it was happening fast, thanks to an unprecedented intersection of political, demographic, economic, and cultural forces driving marijuana into the mainstream.

Amazingly, at a time when the United States has never been more polarized politically, legalizing pot has become something both red and blue states can agree on. The potential riches to be made attracted a disparate group of fearless prospectors—people who were willing to risk it all while braving a rapidly evolving regulatory landscape in each state, even as pot remained illegal in the eyes of the Feds. These were people who could lose it all in an instant. And it's through their stories that we can begin to understand just how we arrived at this striking cultural and historical moment, what might be next, and what it all means for our communities, our families, and our society.

In the pages ahead, you will meet Beth Stavola, the blond, glittering Jersey Shore mom and former Wall Street executive with a ferocious drive to win, who tells her story of how she went out West to the land of El Chapo, battling unsavory characters in the illicit trade to compete against them by building a legal marijuana empire. You will go on the road with Ted Chung, the wiz behind one of the most famous rappers on the planet, Snoop Dogg, and find out firsthand how the two parlayed the entertainer's pot-smoking image into mainstream branded products and businesses. You will venture to Canada to meet the man known as "the Willy Wonka of Weed," who had big dreams of inventing an alcohol-free, calorie- and hangover-free cannabis drink of the future and along the way grew his company into the biggest pot producer in the world. And you will peek inside the kitchen of cannabis savant Jeff Danzer, the lovable gay dad of three, whose homespun culinary talents earned him comparisons to Julia Child and landed him a shot at opening a high-profile weed-themed restaurant like none other.

Of course, there would be choppy waters ahead. Volatile pot stocks would take a beating. The wily old-world drug dealers wouldn't be wiped out as promised. Efforts to pass banking reform on Capitol Hill that would free up capital for cash-strapped U.S. businesses would stall, along with hopes that New York and New Jersey would green-light their own Green Rush. Companies like MedMen, the one Gwyneth briefly curated products for, would lay off hundreds of employees, scuttle plans to open new stores, and teeter on the brink of insolvency as its brash CEO stepped down. The FDA would sound alarms about the overnight explosion of CBD and the safety of products on the market. And a slew of tragic deaths and injuries from THC vaporizers would unhinge both parents and prohibitionists alike. It would happen in the blink of an eye.

And yet, despite the headwinds, industry analysts predicted that legal cannabis could become a $28 billion business by 2023—rivaling healthcare, banking, and IT and spawning legions of modern-day prospectors determined to have their shot at building a fortune, and maybe even a legacy.

THE NEW CHARDONNAY

1 THE QUEEN OF CANNABIS

Monmouth County, New Jersey
December 2018

BETH STAVOLA WASN'T wearing a stitch of clothing. Clad in just her sparkly diamond studs and sleek black Bluetooth headset, she stretched out unselfconsciously on a cushioned massage table. As the afternoon sun streamed into her bay windowed boudoir overlooking the icy Navesink River, a few bucolic miles north of the Jersey Shore, Beth's "body fixer," Kathleen, discreetly released tension from her back.

While the therapist's hands expertly kneaded her client's aching muscles, the platinum blond business mogul propped herself up on both elbows. In her left hand she clutched two iPhones, leaving a free hand with which to occasionally slip her chunky black reading glasses onto the end of her nose as she quickly scrolled through text messages and returned an urgent call to a partner in Las Vegas. Time is money for any high-powered executive, but for one of America's most preeminent pot dealers, time moved at warp speed.

On this brutally cold winter day, two weeks before Christmas 2018, the multimillionaire named by *High Times* as one of the most influential "Women of Weed" was preoccupied with a big story playing out two thousand miles away. Beth and her tight-knit Jersey-based circle of analysts and marketers had just received an email telling them they had scored highly coveted licenses to open up four new retail marijuana shops in and around Las Vegas. This was a win that would expand her empire even deeper into Sin City, where anyone over twenty-one could now buy pot just by flashing an ID. With forty-two million fun-seeking tourists descending upon the desert city every year, this opportunity had Beth and her partners seeing green.

Beth's holdings in Nevada already included GreenMart, a high-tech facility in North Las Vegas the size of an airplane hangar, where a team of self-taught organic chemists in sterile jumpsuits, white lab coats, and surgical masks employed a proprietary method to carefully strip potent compounds from the genetically engineered crop of marijuana plants grown and hand-trimmed on-site. Using highly combustible gases and shiny pressurized gadgets worth hundreds of thousands of dollars, the technicians worked around the clock to delicately extract the molecules containing marijuana's chemicals in their purest form, and refined them into valuable oil. Those beakers of viscous amber liquid that lined the lab would ultimately fill cartridges for vaping or oral gelcaps; or, in the gentle hands of a professional pastry chef, the concentrates would be mixed into an array of gaming-themed edibles like dark, milk, and white chocolates molded into the shape of dice.

The news about the licenses hadn't yet leaked to the press. Nevada wouldn't disclose the names of the winners until the following week, when those who had lost out on the opportunity to get in the cannabis market were sure to be miffed. In the old days, encroaching on a rival's turf was an act of war that might end with a barrage of gunshots, a body tossed in a ditch in the dark of night, or some other gruesome consequence. But in the new landscape of lawful marijuana, an army of corporate attorneys on speed dial had supplanted the gang of *sicarios* available 24/7 to do the crime boss's bidding. And from what Beth and longtime lieutenant Tenisha Victor understood from their intel coming out of Vegas that afternoon, everyone seemed to be lawyering up.

"This is how things go. Every single state is a lawsuit. The losers just sue," explained Beth matter-of-factly when she hung up, her bare body draped by a sheet as Kathleen's hands continued to work their magic. Her legal fight ahead in Nevada typified the intensifying land grab happening across the country, as new states and cities opened up legal sales of the drug. Even as marijuana remained not only prohibited by the federal government, but actually classified at the top of the Drug Enforcement Administration's outlawed controlled substance list—along with heroin and cocaine—by the end of 2018, thirty-three states plus the District of Columbia had voted to legalize some sale of the cannabis plant. And ten of those states permitted marijuana sales for recreational use among adults over twenty-one, just like alcohol.

It was a whole new world. Marijuana businesses were now run by white-collar professionals who recruited new hires on LinkedIn, collected sophisticated customer acquisition data, and ran focus groups like any other consumer product company hawking toothpaste or energy drinks. More than thirty years after Nancy Reagan's "Just Say No" crusade demonized marijuana, and the zealous enforcement of tough drug laws jailed hundreds of thousands of low-income black and brown offenders, high-end pot was now being sold out in the open like a fine aged Scotch or a fancy anti-wrinkle serum—not on street corners or in dark alleys, but inside gleaming new storefronts called "dispensaries" and staffed by smiling sales associates with name tags.

Instead of clandestine handoffs in ziplock dime bags, newfangled legal cannabis products—both intoxicating and not—were proudly stocked under bright department store lighting with polished hardwood floors and eye-catching displays, or featured on inviting websites ready for delivery or pickup in every variety a cannabis connoisseur could dream up: Listerine-style breath strips, dark-chocolate-covered blueberries, gourmet fruit gelées, fizzy bath bombs, lemony tinctures, erotic oils, potent waxes, stick-on skin patches, carbonated beer-like beverages, sparkling wines, herbal teas, and even suppositories. There were hundreds of choices to consider. All of the pricey products were artfully wrapped in shiny cellophane, pretty glass jars, sleek pouches and boxes, and featured an extensive lab-tested ingredient list, dosing advice, and sturdy child-proof packaging. It was an extreme makeover. Weed was now marketed to an expanding audience of canna-curious customers, ranging from graying grandmas to weekend warriors to Chardonnay moms.

The American public had turned a corner and was increasingly embracing marijuana as an upstanding alternative to prescription pills, used to manage everything from chronic pain to chemotherapy side effects to seizure disorders in children to Parkinson's tremors to post-traumatic stress disorder. According to Gallup, 66 percent of Americans favored legalization, including more than half of Republicans polled. "The devil's lettuce" was quickly being rebranded as a magical elixir to bring about wellness to a wide cross section of consumers. Increasingly, the "high" was beside the point as savvy marketers seized on cannabidiol, also known as CBD, a compound that doesn't induce a buzz but was promoted as a treatment for stress, insomnia, and pain.

This was an era that someone like the drug lord El Chapo could probably never have imagined. Who ever would have predicted that the man the DEA called the "godfather of the drug world"—who once carried a monogrammed diamond-encrusted pistol, rode in an armored car, and whose death squad had taken hundreds of innocent lives—would someday be competing for market share with the likes of former Wall Street executive and mother of six Beth Stavola? And yet, when legalized marijuana quickly began to cut into the cartel's profits by 2014, he and his Sinaloa cartel were reportedly forced to shift the game away from pot to trafficking in even more heroin and methamphetamine, in an effort to maximize gains off America's deadly addiction to opioids.

Now, just a forty-minute high-speed ferry ride away from Beth's home office, the $14 billion don brooded in a high-security jail cell. Joaquín "El Chapo" Guzmán Loera was a prisoner awaiting trial in Manhattan's Metropolitan Correctional Center. The notorious kingpin, who had escaped maximum security prisons in Mexico not once but twice, using an elaborate network of underground tunnels—the same method he used to smuggle billions of dollars of illegal drugs over the border—was finally taken down when the DEA recruited his head of IT to secretly install spyware on his mistress's BlackBerry. If El Chapo typified the bloody ruthlessness of the sinister drug underworld, Beth Stavola personified the professionalism of the modern-day marijuana honcho operating strictly by the book and, increasingly, in the public eye.

Beth is the first to admit that she knew nothing about weed when she and her husband first decided to invest a million dollars in Arizona's fledgling medical marijuana market in late 2012. Back then, most of the big players in this newly legitimate market saw her as just some rich lady from back East with too much time and cash on her hands. The naysayers had no idea whom they were dealing with. Perhaps they couldn't see past her Chanel handbags, décolletage, and carefully coiffed hair—or the fact that she had six children at home. But what they didn't know was that Beth made a name for herself on Wall Street during the go-go '90s as one of the few women to hold her own in the notoriously alpha male world of high finance. Armed with the grit she developed early as a kid growing up in Jersey City in the 1970s, she rose quickly through the ranks of the investment bank Jefferies and Company to become a senior equities sales VP, covering some of the biggest fish, including Alliance Capital, OppenheimerFunds, and SAC Capital. It was a rough-and-tumble "eat what you kill" culture, mainly due to the fact that the sales team at Jefferies worked 100 percent on commission, as opposed to a more civilized salary and bonus structure.

On the other hand, the fact that her compensation was based entirely on the spoils of war from the month prior was essentially a form of "forced pay equality," as she called it, meaning that anywhere else on the Street at that time, she'd probably have had zero chance of earning as much as her male peers. But at Jefferies, if she closed a deal, the commission was all hers on the fifteenth of the month. And she needed that paycheck, especially after she divorced her first husband and became the sole provider for her two little kids at home, and was ordered to pay him alimony. Looking back, it's easy to see how Jefferies was like a training ground for her future foray into the largely male-dominated world of legal weed; the hypercompetitive culture only thickened her skin, cemented her resolve, and schooled her in the careful art of building strategic alliances with her adversaries.

Moreover, in the days before #MeToo, when testosterone-fueled Wall Street firms tolerated frat-house antics, she learned to prove she could pal around like one of the guys while still managing to firmly tell a supervisor to take his hand off her ass. During those *Wolf of Wall Street* days, she endured working in places so rowdy and full of machismo that when one firm closed a deal with Taser, the maker of the eponymous self-defense device, a portfolio manager thought it would be funny to hold a contest in which two coworkers would be paid $10,000 to be tased in front of their peers "to see what would happen." When a hulking analyst and a petite secretary took the dare, Beth just shrugged her shoulder pads and smirked at the spectacle.

Now, in her expansive home office—one flight above the tastefully decorated sitting room where she was receiving the first of her twice-weekly massage treatments—hung a framed black-and-white poster (given to her as a gift) that crystallized her approach to business and life:

> *Be a fucking wolf. Be a fucking lion. Take no shit. Set goals, smash them. Eat people's faces off. Be a better person. Show people who the fuck you are. Never apologize for being awesome. Stay the mother fucking course.*

And she had stayed the course, despite all of the risks and uncertainties involved in starting a business still deemed illegal by the federal government. Since the dawn of the commercialized pot industry in America, when Colorado and Washington voters legitimized the marijuana trade by ushering in recreational programs in November 2012, the intrepid entrepreneur had skillfully charmed politicians, local police chiefs, and even the most ardently opposed community leaders to help expand her ventures from Arizona to Nevada to California to Maryland to Massachusetts and, most recently, to her home state of New Jersey, evolving her business into what is known in industry-speak as an "MSO," or multistate operator. As more states opened the door for over-21 use, Beth's well-oiled on-the-ground operations, artfully cultivated relationships, and wolf-like ambition positioned her to cash in on fresh markets.

Yet she would often say she felt like she had a target on her back. The industry was only growing more competitive, and it was clear that to succeed in this rapidly evolving legal landscape required two things. One, an unwavering commitment to following the rules as assiduously as possible (even though they were just being invented and constantly revised), and two, quick access to an infinite amount of cash. Millions at the ready. You needed it to secure real estate where you could set up shop (even before you got the green light to open); to hire the right lobbyists, fixers, and license application writers; for political campaign contributions; and of course, for the endless number of palms to grease along the entire supply chain. When people learned you were in the marijuana business, there was always a premium to pay. Couple that with the fact that the Feds still had the power to shut down your credit cards and bank accounts at any time—a headache Beth had experienced firsthand when the account containing all of the gifts from her youngest daughter's First Communion was frozen. On top of all those hurdles, with pot still being federally illegal, you couldn't get a bank loan to start a business; and thanks to Section 280E in the tax code, the IRS didn't allow you to write off most expenses on your tax returns.

And, of course, there was the thriving illegal market to contend with; the drug dealers and self-proclaimed "master growers" who weren't slinking back into the shadows any time soon and who all wanted a piece of the action, too. It was hard to know who were the good guys and who were the bad guys. Everyone was taking a cut.

With all these hidden "startup costs," it was no wonder the only people who could take advantage of the early opportunities were largely those with deep pockets of their own. By the close of 2018, most of the people running the largest multistate "plant-touching" operations were wealthy white men—with Ivy League degrees, Wall Street pedigrees, and country-club connections to an elite network of private investors—who could both finance these speculative ventures while offering warm introductions to the local officials whose blessings you needed to smooth the way.

Beth and her scrappy team broke this mold. Operating on the sunny third floor of her striking 20,000-square-foot waterside mansion in Red Bank, they secretly looked forward to 3:00 P.M., when, like clockwork, three of Beth's five daughters would shuffle in from school. Nearly buckling under the weight of their backpacks, thirteen-year-old twins Ava and Julie, and the baby of the family, eleven-year-old Elle, would be greeted by hugs and high-protein snacks set out by their kindly Indonesian housekeeper, Annie, smiling in her scarlet lipstick. Annie always laid out a generous spread of grilled chicken strips, cheese cubes, and sliced hard-boiled eggs for the girls—and for Beth's staffers, who often meandered downstairs for a midafternoon break. It felt like family. And for good reason. Two of Beth's first employees in the cannabis venture had once been live-in nannies for the Stavolas and cared for her children since they were tiny. So why wouldn't everyone linger at the ample kitchen island for a bit before Elle was whisked off to a riding lesson with Diamond, the new pony she'd recently received for her birthday, while the twins rushed off to algebra tutoring?

Down the hall from the kitchen, her husband, Jack, ran Stavola Companies, a massive collection of enterprises that dated back to when his grandfather Joseph arrived on Ellis Island from Naples, Italy, to seek his fortune in 1904. Joseph Stavola would have done anything to make a dollar. He hauled trash seven days a week to put food on the table for his wife, Carmela, and their eight children, and, through sweat and sheer will, turned it into a lucrative business. By 1948, his son Frank, Jack's dad, founded what would grow into the empire Jack oversaw today. Seventy years later, the family business, which Jack managed with his partners, included garbage collection, recycling, gravel mining, asphalt plants, road construction, contracting, and shopping malls spanning the Garden State.

Jack had designed and built this dream home himself, with its white marble columns, sweeping walnut staircases, two-story windows, full spa, and infinity swimming pool. It was an opulent setting worthy of a backdrop on Bravo TV's *Real Housewives*. Beth, who friends said was occasionally mistaken for the movie star Cameron Diaz (and even asked to sign autographs on the street from time to time), had in fact been approached to appear on the New Jersey installment of the popular reality show, but she turned it down to stay focused on her new career in cannabis.

Despite their luxe lifestyle, Jack, fourteen years her senior, was still in many ways a traditional Italian husband—just like his grandfather. He was down-to-earth, hardworking, and fiercely loyal to his family. He was also intensely private and known affectionately around Beth's office as "Mr. Hollywood" for his habit of rarely taking off his dark designer sunglasses. It was rare that you even heard his low voice. But Jack didn't hesitate when asked to characterize his wife's insatiable drive to win. He called her a pit bull.

"She's like a dog with a bone. She won't let go," he said. And then he added, with a kidding/not kidding hint of a smile, "Just don't get her mad."

In truth, Jack's somewhat old-school values were actually the reason Beth ended up in the marijuana business in the first place. It was a second marriage for them both. After the birth of their twin girls, the fourth and fifth of six in their blended family, Beth had gone back to work in the city. Up at dawn every morning to take the hydrofoil across the Hudson from Jersey, and often working late into the evening with clients, Beth's marathon hours were becoming a sticking point in the marriage. She loved her work, and had a loyal staff of nannies and housekeepers to manage her life at home like clockwork. But, as Jack tells it, he wanted his wife "right here," tapping his index finger to emphasize that he meant at his side. This arrangement wasn't working for him. He wanted Beth home, and after several years of grumbling about her grueling schedule, he gave her an ultimatum. It was him or the job. They didn't need the money. She had babies at home. Beth reluctantly gave in.

During her first few months as a stay-at-home mom, she missed the office so much that she continued to dial in to the daily 7:00 A.M. conference call. She couldn't let go.

By the time she gave birth to their sixth child, she was hungry for a new challenge. So when a deal broker approached the Stavolas about a chance to invest in a risky yet exciting emerging industry, Beth couldn't resist. She and Jack got on a plane to Arizona to meet with a potential new partner, and in a matter of weeks the deal was sealed and Beth had begun a new (if unconventional) chapter.

NOW IT WAS December 2018, and Christmas had come early for Beth this year. The Stavola home was decked out with a shopping-mall-sized lighted wreath, suspended from a balcony over the house's columned front entrance, and shimmery pinecones dangled delicately from gold ribbons on crystal chandeliers in the spacious kitchen and dining room, accented by matching metallic centerpieces in ornate goblet-shaped vases on tables throughout the first floor. A perfectly trimmed Christmas tree stood in the marble entrance bedecked in gold and ivory. Professional decorators scurried around, unpacking seasonal accessories and moving the furniture in preparation for a holiday party Beth was hosting for the New Jersey Cannabis Industry Association (NJCIA) later that week. Beth and her younger sister, Julie Winter, were NJCIA trustees, and this event would attract some of the most influential lobbyists, lawmakers, and entrepreneurs involved in the efforts to make New Jersey the eleventh state to legalize recreational pot. (Illinois would beat Jersey to the punch in the summer of 2019.)

The Stavola manse stood inside a gated compound just a stone's throw from the private residence owned by New Jersey's recently elected Democratic governor (and pot proponent), Phil Murphy, and his wife, Tammy. Things looked promising. The week after he was inaugurated eleven months earlier, Murphy was seen on camera smiling and handing Beth the official pen he had just used to sign an executive order expanding the state's medical marijuana program, a move many believed would lay the groundwork for over-21 sales in short order. Legalizing marijuana had been a signature issue of his campaign, and Beth had been a generous donor. Tammy also happened to be a friend of Beth's, and the two still occasionally caught up over mani-pedis at a power salon nearby. Multitasking was how Beth got shit done.

As she flipped over onto her stomach for the waning moments of her massage, Beth couldn't stop thinking about how far the industry—and she—had come.

Now, nearly seven years since Beth first staked her claim in weed, she had another megadeal on the horizon. If she pulled this one off, the year ahead would see her biggest windfall yet. If all went as planned, the opportunity would be worth more than half a billion dollars. Hard to believe it had all started with a chance conversation that led her to the high desert of Arizona and into the Wild West of weed.

PLAYING TO WIN

Six Years Earlier . . .

Scottsdale, Arizona

November 2012

LOOKING OUT FOR the very first time at the towering saguaros dotting the rocky mountainsides and the spectacular flamingo-pink sunset above, Beth Stavola felt the electric rush that often came with chasing down a new challenge. There was something about Arizona, with its otherworldly copper-hued boulders and spiny succulents, ancient tribal lands, and mystical New Age tourist attractions contrasted by the steeples of megachurches, gun-toting sheriffs, and firebrand family-values politicians. It was a place of stark contradictions where a maverick like Beth could feel right at home. She sensed the desert could be a new frontier for her, a chance to make a fresh start. The mom of six had been out of the rat race for a few years now, having left her high-powered Wall Street job to spend more time raising her family. Who knew what would happen once she tried to put her professional skills back to work? She was the kind of person who looked for signs. After all, the psychic she had consulted for years had predicted she would one day run a business bigger than her husband's. Perhaps fate had brought the Jersey Shore to the Valley of the Sun.

Even so, the business of marijuana was far from an obvious path. She wasn't a pot smoker. Never had been. She recalled sampling it once or twice when she was in college in the late '80s, and that she hadn't liked the way it made her feel. Since then, she really hadn't given marijuana a thought at all.

That is, until she met Vince Diorio* at the bar of the Kierland Westin Resort and Spa in North Scottsdale, an oasis of turquoise swimming pools and emerald green fairways in the shadow of the McDowell Sonoran Preserve. She and her husband, Jack, had been introduced to their future business partner by a deal broker who'd brought them promising investment prospects in the past, and now—just a few days after they had first heard about this particular venture and decided they were curious enough to fly out West to learn more—here was Diorio making a very convincing pitch. In short, he was looking for backers to help finance the hefty startup costs of launching a "grow" and sales operation in Arizona's newly legal medical marijuana program.

Diorio explained that Arizona, the fifteenth state in the United States to legalize medical cannabis, was a potential bonanza. If neighboring Colorado, where pot had been permitted for medicinal use since 2000, was any indicator, they could be getting an early jump on an untapped market poised for explosive growth. The Rocky Mountain State had sold $199 million worth of medical marijuana to a consumer base of just 100,000 patients in 2012 alone. Now that Colorado voters had given the thumbs-up to legalize recreational sales, there were estimates Colorado's cannabis industry could one day balloon to more than $2 billion in revenue per year.

The thinking was that Arizona would follow a similar path in a matter of years. Although the state's early attempts in 1996 and 1998 to end pot prohibition were repealed by conservative lawmakers, in 2010 voters finally passed Proposition 203, which allowed chronically or terminally ill patients to possess small amount of cannabis with a doctor's approval. Hard-line opponents led by Republicans Attorney General Tom Horne and Governor Jan Brewer sued to block the program before it even got off the ground, alleging it conflicted with federal law. But by the time Beth and Jack met with Diorio, the courts had allowed medical marijuana to proceed.

The pent-up demand for pot was evident among the tens of thousands of patients already clamoring for medical ID cards, and from April 2011 to June 2012 the number of patients registered had shot up by 82 percent to more than 40,000, according to Arizona's health department. Though chronic pain was the top reason people sought relief from cannabis, there were thirteen other approved conditions, including cancer, AIDS, MS, and Crohn's disease. The implications of these numbers were clear: the licenses Arizona had just awarded the previous summer to ninety-six entrepreneurs to open dispensaries were hot commodities. If Beth and Jack partnered with Diorio, he told them, they would get in on the ground floor.

Cocksure Diorio touted himself as a seasoned serial entrepreneur and claimed to be one of the biggest weed growers in Colorado. At six-two and 250 pounds, he certainly commanded the Stavolas' attention, as he promised them he had the contacts and the know-how to make this work. If they loaned the Arizona project a million dollars, he assured them, they would recoup their money in three to six months, and more cash would continue to flow in from the pot sales of a new dispensary that would open within a year.

The following morning, Diorio took Beth and Jack on a road trip, venturing about two hours north of the sprawling subdivisions and strip malls, which over the last thirty years had pushed the border of Greater Phoenix into the open swaths of sand and stone once covered only by tumbleweed. They rode north on I-17 out of Phoenix, past the once picturesque foothills now overrun by tidy ranch homes and SUVs, where the elevation gradually climbs and the temperature dips, as the tans and browns of the desert give way to thickets of tall evergreens. Once in Yavapai County, they rolled through the ponderosa pines of the Prescott National Forest, eventually passing through a handful of old copper mining towns and cattle ranches and into the verdant Chino Valley. That's where Diorio proudly showed them his field of dreams: two hundred acres for sale. With its unique climate and easy zoning restrictions, he claimed, Chino Valley would be the perfect spot to construct a 12,000-square-foot greenhouse in which to cultivate medical-grade marijuana. He introduced Beth and Jack to Don Giotto,* a colleague from Colorado, and his fiancée, who Diorio said would help operate the farm. On the surface, it was an impressive proposition. Plus, the opportunity came along with the chance to buy a valuable license for a soon-to-be-developed dispensary in southern Arizona. If all went according to plan, the Stavolas would be vested in a vertically integrated business—meaning they would control both the supply chain *and* the distribution channels. True, they knew precious little about the medical marijuana business. But they walked away from their meeting convinced Diorio and his team had the expertise to manage it all on the ground. It seemed as if they had stumbled across a winning Powerball ticket.

In a sense, they had. Arizona actually held a real lottery to hand out the first sought-after dispensary licenses, and anyone who wasn't a convicted felon and could cough up the $5,000 application fee, plus show they had $150,000 in the bank, could enter. After Arizona regulators reviewed the applications over several months, there were 426 entities vying for a golden ticket. But by law, only a handful of stores would be allowed to open in each section of the state. Competition was cutthroat; there were 126 separate geographic regions and multiple contestants for each one. Under pressure to give everyone a fair shot, state regulators decided to try something novel.

At 9:00 A.M. on August 7, 2012, three bureaucrats wearing serious expressions and black polo shirts with ARIZONA DEPARTMENT OF HEALTH SERVICES logos emblazoned on the front, carefully pulled numbered white bingo balls from a machine called an Atomic Table Top Bingo Blower. The state had purchased three machines, each costing $10,000, specifically for this momentous event—one for practice, one for the lottery day, and one for backup, just in case.

Applicants weren't allowed to attend the televised drawing at state offices in downtown Phoenix. They had to tune in online for four hours to watch the livestream and wait patiently as the lucky numbers were drawn for each region, one by one.

The Salari* brothers, sons of Iraqi immigrants, were among the hopeful applicants who couldn't take their eyes off their laptops that sweltering morning. If they won, it would be the beginning of a new chapter for their family. In the late 1970s, their parents had fled the rise of Saddam Hussein in search of a better life in the United States. The family had recently relocated to sunny Arizona from Michigan, where they had first settled and made their living for two decades running a local fish market. But once they heard about the chance to bid for a marijuana license, two generations of Salaris pooled their savings so they would be eligible to apply—which they did. Arash, the younger brother, had been growing marijuana on his own for some years to treat debilitating back pain after suffering a serious car accident in 2008. He had since graduated from growing a small amount in a closet to cultivating plants inside a warehouse he leased in South Phoenix. He and his family decided to leverage his experience to make a real go at a large-scale legal operation.

When the family heard their numbers called and learned they had won licenses permitting them to open three dispensaries, they were over the moon. Yet it was clear startup costs would be massive. Had they been opening a couple of clothing boutiques or a chain of bakeries, for example, they could have simply gone to the bank. But with marijuana federally illegal, early entrepreneurs couldn't get a small business loan, and institutional investors wanted nothing to do with them. It would take hundreds of thousands of dollars or more to get up and running. For this reason, partnering with wealthy individuals for private capital was a common strategy of the day. Vince Diorio brought them all together. He thought he had found a perfect match in Beth and her husband. He helped the Salaris sell the management rights of one of the licenses in a sophisticated deal that took advantage of murky new rules about making money off the supposedly nonprofit ventures.

After three days of meetings with Diorio and the brothers, Beth and Jack sat down with Ryan Hurley, a senior partner of a Phoenix law firm that specialized in cannabis, and began to hammer out a joint venture with Diorio that would be called Green Gems.* First order of business was a $250,000 payment to Arash Salari in exchange for the rights to open the dispensary in Douglas, about four hours south of Phoenix. This was much more money than any other investor had gambled to get into the nascent market in Arizona, and after the sale, word on the street was that Beth had vastly overpaid. The deal obligated her not only to put up the money to finance all of the startup costs of the grow, build out a suitable location for the store, and lease the space, but also to prepare it for state inspection within seven months, install a myriad of high-tech security equipment, establish security protocols for handling large volumes of cash and marijuana, and find trustworthy staff to run all of it.

Back home in Red Bank, Beth embarked on a crash course in cannabis, learning about everything from plant genetics to grow cycles to potential crop-killers like mold and pests. One day, she found herself on the phone with a gentleman named Aubrey Bradley, a ginger-haired salesman with a surfer's drawl and a wealth of information to offer. He had founded a company called Growlite, which specialized in high-tech lighting for indoor horticulture. His primary customers had traditionally been marijuana bootleggers: criminals running underground grow houses who were quite skilled at hiding from the law. Naturally, many people who had made an illegal living growing and selling weed in their basements, sheds, or in tents outdoors now wanted to come out of the shadows and cash in on the new legal market. But because of their shady dealings (and in some cases, criminal records), few of them could fulfill the basic requirements for owning a license. This set off a frenzy of shotgun marriages where illicit growers trying to go legit sought out so-called suits, or people with upstanding jobs and assets, to finance and sometimes front their license applications. But these unions were often fraught with volatility, as Phoenix-based marijuana industry consultant Nicholas Russo observed, looking back at the early days. "You had a lot of subculture marrying the new industry . . . and that's why you saw a lot of groups implode," he explained.

Aubrey could tell right away that Beth was a different sort of client. For one, Beth wasn't just a suit; she had actual business credentials. Even more notably, her purchase order for 222 lights was the largest one he had every received, and unlike most of his customers, she wasn't paying cash. He took her credit card number over the telephone for a $200,000 sale and marveled at the scope of what she planned to build.

"Back then, a big grow was fifty lights. A hundred lights, that was unheard of," he recounted. The message was clear: this self-proclaimed Jersey Girl was playing to win.

The large sale tipped him off that big players were taking Arizona's new market more seriously than he'd realized. Aubrey would help install the lights inside the greenhouse Beth's team was building on the forty acres she had purchased in the Chino Valley. When she met him in person, Beth immediately had a good feeling about him. He was a handshake guy who stood out as someone she could trust. It was a friendship that became invaluable sooner rather than later.

About six weeks later, while attending her brother's beachside wedding in Naples, Florida, Beth saw an Arizona area code pop up on her mobile phone. She reluctantly picked up. Don Giotto was on the line, and he shared shocking news. He told her that Diorio had been stopped for driving under the influence near Bisbee, Arizona, about twenty minutes north of the Mexican border. Cops found a marijuana grinder in the car, which was owned by the company, and threw him in jail. Even worse, she learned Diorio had been driving with a suspended license and that the Porsche Cayenne had been seized—a clear sign that this was not his first brush with the law. Giotto told Beth he had driven south nearly five hours from Prescott to bail him out.

Then she heard that Diorio wouldn't let anyone else take the wheel for the long ride back to central Arizona and insisted on smoking pot in the car. The arrest alone could have put their operation in jeopardy, but even more troubling was the fact that it seemed highly suspect for a man who claimed he was an expert in navigating the legal marijuana industry. Further, she learned that Diorio had been bragging to Giotto and the rest of the team about his plans to smuggle plant cuttings—otherwise known as "clones"—from Colorado to Arizona so he could begin cultivating certain sought-after high-THC strains. They all knew that transporting marijuana across state lines—even from one "legal" state to another—was absolutely forbidden, and could have landed everyone under arrest by the DEA. Not only that, they all knew that over the past year, the Feds had been cracking down hard and raiding state legal marijuana grows and dispensaries in California and Washington that they suspected of violating these interstate laws.

All Beth could think about at that moment was the fact that her million-dollar investment was about to blow up. She immediately dialed Aubrey Bradley, who tried to calm her down, telling her in his laid-back voice, "Don't worry. I got you, girl." He would personally check out what was going on up at the grow.

In the meantime, Beth wasted no time and hired a private investigator to do some digging on Diorio. What the detective found made her blood run cold. She found out her business partner was actually a convicted felon who had served time for conspiring to rob a local businessman at gunpoint as he made a bank deposit, and for domestic abuse to boot.

Although this was news to Beth, it turned out Diorio had been bragging about his violent past to employees, even lording it over them as a sign of his "street cred." He told them he had ties to all five

New York Mafia families, and that he had killed people but had never been caught. He shared detailed memories of the grisly murders he'd supposedly committed and threatened anyone who crossed him that he would make them pay for their mistake. And he claimed that if they didn't do what he said, he could "make a call" and something might happen to their families. Evidently, Diorio was known to ride around with an automatic weapon in his car and slept with one under his pillow. He was later arrested again for aggravated DUI in Prescott, the closest city to the grow in the Chino Valley.

As Beth learned more about his past, she began to closely scrutinize recent company expenses and became incensed to find dozens of questionable charges on the debit card she had set up for company use. There were purchases at Sunglass Hut, several spas, a men's clothing store, nail salons, and hotels, as well as airline tickets. *Someone* was brazenly stealing from the company, and in light of recent events, Diorio was a reasonable suspect. When she saw a charge for Diorio's daughter's bridal gown on the account, she was livid. Then it became clear that her so-called partner had been writing himself checks made out to cash, and making almost daily ATM withdrawals, for months—with nothing to show for the supposed business expenses. In a period of two months, Diorio had gone through $47,000. By the time Beth caught wind and cut him off, the loss was $65,000. She had to figure out how to dissolve the partnership before she lost it all.

But before she even had time to hatch a plan with her lawyers, she received another distraught call from Giotto. Apparently, Diorio was on a rampage. He had shown up at the grow screaming about how he was strapped for cash, and had ordered Giotto to hand over all of the firearms that been had purchased to secure the cultivation area, so he could sell them. He flew into a rage when he was told the guns were not on-site. In a panic, Giotto, who lived on the property, had quickly snuck away and called Beth, telling her he was terrified for his family and his own life. Beth filed for a restraining order against Diorio in Prescott Junction Court the next morning, and made quick arrangements for a security guard to protect her own family in New Jersey.

Beth's next phone call was to her lawyers in Phoenix. She needed some answers about how to disentangle herself from this nightmare partner, Diorio. And then suddenly the firm told her they could no longer represent her. They felt the case was shaping up to be too dangerous, and they didn't want to have anything to do with it. She would have to find someone brave enough to go to war with this gangster.

Luckily, one of her employees at the Chino Valley cultivation area named James White knew of just the man for the job. He'd been following the news coverage about a respected former U.S. Attorney who had gone up against some of the most vicious criminals in his career, including the Poland brothers, who had infamously hijacked an armored van, kidnapped the guards, and, while the victims were still alive, forced them into canvas bags filled with rocks, then dumped their bodies into Lake Mead. The brothers were sentenced to death in a case that made national headlines. And now this steely prosecutor was suddenly one of Arizona's most vocal advocates for medical marijuana. White called Beth in New Jersey and told her, "You have to find this attorney Mel McDonald. He's the guy who's going to get you out of this."

* "Diorio," "Giotto," "Salari," and "Green Gems" are pseudonyms. To protect Beth's privacy and her safety, these names have been changed. Information about their involvement comes from public affidavits, confidential sworn depositions, court filings, and interviews conducted by Cabot.

3
SNOOP AND TED'S EXCELLENT ADVENTURES

Mumbai, India

January 2013

IN A FIVE-STAR hotel room, high above the swirl of India's most populous city, with its beeping army of auto-rickshaws, buzzing mopeds carrying a crush of commuters in vibrant saris, and Bollywood beats pulsing from tiny tea shops on seemingly every corner, Ted Chung needed space to think. The air-conditioned suite provided a brief respite from the sensory overload on the smoggy streets below. But the ambitious entertainment executive had little time to waste. He was on a mission. He was on the hunt for weed.

But not just any hookup would do. He and his team needed to track down the finest-quality bud in this vast city. Never mind the fact that in Mumbai, as in most places in the world at the time, the plant was prohibited by law. He was procuring it for one of the most discerning cannabis connoisseurs on the planet—his longtime business partner and friend, Snoop Dogg.

This was the way it played out everywhere the hip-hop icon and his trusted manager traveled on tour. In the most far-flung places, from St. Petersburg to Durban to Beirut, if you were on the road with Snoop, you became fluent in the illegal markets of marijuana: analyzing the origins of the local supply, navigating the stealthy distribution channels, and, of course, homing in on the most reliable dealers from whom to score the best product. After all, smoking weed every day was a hallmark of Snoop's enduring persona. His prolific odes to 420 filled his music catalog. No matter where the double-platinum-album-selling singer-songwriter found himself, nothing disrupted his daily routine of getting his "lettuce" so he could light up. And to that end, Ted's extensive Rolodex of cannabis contacts was legendary in the music industry. In fact, he often fielded urgent calls from the managers of other big acts—or even the stars themselves—scrambling for similar intel when they touched down in cities across the globe.

Touring for two years with Snoop had been like going to grad school for cannabis. But this was the first time he and the entertainer had visited this corner of the world. Cannabis had long been outlawed in India, though its use had flourished underground for literally thousands of years. As they had repeatedly in other locales, Snoop's resourceful team, including Karan Wadhera, the kid brother of Ted's college roommate, hustled to acquaint themselves with the folks who ran the illicit networks. Without fail, they always closed the deal.

Mumbai was kicking off the affable star's much-anticipated inaugural trip to the region, where he was beloved for introducing West Coast G-funk to the masses, spawning a new generation of rap fans among the burgeoning millennial middle class. After Mumbai, the soft-spoken performer would take the stage at two sold-out shows in Pune and Delhi, filling out his schedule with numerous publicity appearances.

Snoop, born Calvin Cordozar Broadus, Jr., and recently rechristened "Snoop Lion," had just returned from a life-altering journey to Jamaica and was about to release his first reggae album. His was a formidable run that began in the spring of 1992. He burst onto the music scene at age nineteen when Dr. Dre discovered the young rapper from Long Beach and invited him to lend his languid style to "Deep Cover," the first track Dre dropped after the breakup of the seminal West Coast gangsta rap act N.W.A (Niggaz Wit Attitudes).

The eponymous title song for the action thriller starring Laurence Fishburne featured a young Snoop repeating the ominous refrain "1-8-7 on a undercover cop," referring to the California Penal Code term for murder. It came out just twenty days before Los Angeles erupted in violence following the stunning acquittal of four white cops accused in the brutal beating of black motorist Rodney King. The song's release also coincided with an escalation of "broken window" policing of black and brown neighborhoods across the country, which would ensnare thousands of young men in the criminal justice system for pot possession. The obscenity-laced song quickly led to many more notable collaborations with Dre, including his 1992 triple-platinum album *The Chronic;* a year later, Dre's Death Row Records would launch Snoop's slew of *Billboard* chart–topping hits by producing *Doggystyle,* his very first solo album, complete with a white Parental Advisory Warning emblazoned on the cover. In time, Dogg, as his friends call him, would trade his menacing image for a decidedly more accessible, fun-loving persona. But one thing the celebrity didn't shed, as he evolved into "Uncle Snoop" and began to appeal more to Top 40 music fans, was his professed love for the ganja. From his earliest days, weed played a starring role in his lyrics, his videos, and his ubiquitous TV and radio appearances. And it only grew more prominent in his work over time, as the United States and the rest of the world moved closer to legalizing cannabis.

By 2013, the Doggfather had become a certified Bollywood star without ever setting foot in India, thanks to a cheeky cameo appearance via green screen in Chicago for the wildly popular 2008 movie *Singh Is Kingh*. The film featured Snoop dancing to Punjabi pulses and dining on a plateful of traditional Indian naan and saag paneer while Indian heartthrob Akshay Kumar dug into fried chicken and waffles. Alongside Kumar, he rapped, "What up to all the ladies hanging out in Mumbai!" in an irreverent video for the film's title track. *Singh Is King* went on to become India's number one movie that year, and according to *Variety*, the title song sold five million copies in less than two weeks.

Now, five years after the film debuted, the storied performer graciously rolled in two hours late to greet an exuberant press corps in Rastafarian red, green, and yellow sunglasses, a matching crocheted cap, and an Adidas tracksuit, while Ted, his stoic handler, stood by in Malcolm X glasses, black suit and T-shirt, and red kicks. The two made for an odd pair as reporters shouted a barrage of questions while cameras clicked and flashed incessantly. While the charming hip-hop legend preened for photos with his typical swagger, his cool business partner silently scanned the scene to ensure it all unfolded seamlessly, and on brand. What few outsiders would have realized—unless they spotted the golden UPenn class ring Ted proudly sported on his finger—is that Snoop's most trusted adviser had attended one of the most prestigious business schools in the country. With a level of precision and discipline that would have made him a coveted hire for any of the white-shoe consulting firms, this Wharton grad had instead become the mastermind behind the franchise of one of the biggest music personalities in the world. And their visit to this nation of 1.3 billion people was the culmination of Ted's diligent work to bring Snoop a truly global audience.

"It's going to be an emotional roller coaster," the entertainer told a fawning TV interviewer when asked what to expect from his upcoming shows, before being whisked away from the media frenzy by his entourage for a stop at "Uncle Louie" (aka the Louis Vuitton store), then ferried to his hotel to kick back and blaze up with his posse.

Back at the ritzy hotel, with room service on the way, the TV was tuned to the only thing on at midnight, a kitschy Tarzan-inspired show in Hindi. But no matter. It was just something mindless for Snoop and Ted to have on in the background while the singer lit a fat one. "Tarzaaan," the singer crooned in a bluesy tone at the television, as he lounged on the ample couch and Ted puffed nearby. It was just another night in the excellent adventures of Snoop and Ted.

It was hard to believe their relationship had begun with a cold call. Back in 1999, Ted was a scrappy entrepreneur hustling every which way to get his marketing agency off the ground. He had come a long way since his freshman year in Philly, when a young Theo, as he was called back then, had struggled to figure out how to fit in with his buttoned-up blue blood classmates. A first-generation Korean immigrant from Long Beach, California, Theo/Ted felt a sort of otherness the moment he set foot on Penn's historic campus. When he graduated, armed with his degree in economics, coursework in African American studies, and a deep admiration for hip-hop and the way it could meld diverse cultures through music, Ted set his mind on pursuing what he saw as the literal white space in the marketing industry—a gaping hole in the way brands spoke to young black, brown, and LGBTQ audiences.

"There was chocolate ice cream, vanilla ice cream, strawberry ice cream. But we wanted to be the rainbow sherbet," he would reflect years later.

For one of his very first campaigns, he set his sights on partnering with a fellow Long Beach native, the one and only Snoop Doggy Dogg. He wanted to secure a product placement for a client in one of the rapper's videos but didn't have any contacts at the label. So he relentlessly worked the phones for weeks, cold-calling and charming his way up the Universal Music food chain. He finally got through to someone involved in videos and managed to talk that person into giving him the once-in-a-lifetime chance to show up on set and pitch D-O-double-G himself. The pitch led to a deal that ultimately sealed their partnership and ignited their roller-coaster bromance. The partnership, initially under Snoop's label, Doggystyle, soon spurred a run of hit collaborations with artists including Wiz Khalifa, Pharrell Williams, and Katy Perry. And by 2013, Ted had orchestrated the launch of many successful television appearances and film projects, while growing Snoop's social media following so massively that by the time they arrived in Mumbai, Snoop was reaching tens of millions of fans around the world.

Enterprise was in Ted's blood. He was the son of an engineer—a self-made entrepreneur who had built a successful business selling casters, or swivel wheels, for a range of heavy industrial uses. Every day of his childhood and for many years thereafter, his industrious dad got up and drove to his forty-foot shipping container turned office in Compton, an industrial city south of L.A., where Ted and his brother would spend hours after school running around the warehouse that stood out back, playing hide-and-seek among the towers of cardboard boxes and shipping crates. Ted loved the smell of the steel and the oil, and especially the unforgettable pungent odor of rubber. Its intensity permeated the space, a comforting reminder of his dad's work ethic and his determination to provide a good life for his family. He had never seen his father work a day in his life for anyone but himself, and this endowed Ted with a fierce desire to make his own luck.

Growing up, Ted developed an early love of music, learning to play the saxophone and piano in grade school. He gravitated to hip-hop as a teen and matured into a talented DJ. By high school, he was applying his admiration for diverse genres of music by spinning tunes for under-eighteen parties he organized that drew Asian, black, Latinx, and white kids alike. But arriving at an Ivy League university was his first encounter with the New England prep-school elite and the type of exclusivity that comes with old (white) money. Los Angeles had lots of rich people, to be sure, but it lacked the entrenched social constructs of East Coast wealth. And with his laid-back L.A. vibe, which didn't fit the stereotype of the typical Asian American guy portrayed in American pop culture, he recalls, his classmates didn't quite know what to make of him. If he wanted to have a social life, he would have to decipher how to traverse this exclusive new landscape. In time, he fell in with a tight-knit band of equally smart, unique students who didn't have family legacies to rely on and who socialized on the margins of the more established cliques. The group, including a not yet famous John Legend, would go on to build their own powerful network—one that would prove indispensable long after the late-night dorm parties ceased and real life began.

To be sure, his wasn't the traditional path for a child of Korean immigrants. But it made sense that a kid obsessed with dreaming up innovative ways to weave everything from a blues baseline to a Bollywood chorus into a memorable dance track wasn't going to go slave away in a suit and tie on Wall Street or apply to med school—or even go into the family business. So after college he took a low-paying job scouting talent for a boutique record label that was ultimately acquired by Universal Music Group. This led to a stint "mining the vault" of the archives of Polygram Records, where he was tasked with uncovering memorable choruses or refrains from hit songs and offering them up to DJs and hip-hop artists to blend into their creations. Meanwhile, he and his cousin Seung were gearing up to launch what would become Cashmere Agency, the multicultural marketing firm that would ultimately lead him to Snoop.

Like music, cannabis had always been part of Ted's DNA. His passion for the plant endeared him to Snoop immediately. They loved the way smoking unleashed creativity, rolled back inhibitions, and fostered deep, authentic conversations. Snoop had long said he used it medicinally for his migraine headaches and had even gotten a state-issued medical marijuana card in California. Both believed in the healing powers of cannabis and railed against America's longtime racially charged marijuana laws. Seventy-six years after the infamous *Reefer Madness* propaganda film first warned citizens about "the burning weed with roots in hell," every forty-two seconds a person was arrested for cannabis in the United States, according to 2012 FBI crime statistics. Most of those detained during the uptick of marijuana crackdowns in the early '90s through 2012 were black or Latinx, according to the ACLU, which in an explosive report declared, "The war on marijuana is a war on people of color." The civil rights organization revealed that a black person was nearly four times as likely as a white person to be arrested for marijuana possession, even though usage among black and white people was virtually the same. Between 1998 and 2012, 39 percent of drug offenders federally incarcerated for marijuana-related crimes were Hispanic and 37 percent were black, reported the Bureau of Justice Statistics. Once released from prison, they would not only be barred from voting and face challenges finding jobs and housing, they would also be shut out of the new legal cannabis industry—and the potential millions it held—because their felony convictions prevented them from working in the field (a point of contention that would begin to be addressed in the future, through record-expungement initiatives). Snoop himself had been arrested for marijuana possession multiple times, and personally experienced how the disproportionate profiling of black and brown cannabis users was endemic to the enforcement of U.S. drug laws. In many ways, the star's constant flaunting of his smoking as he rose to worldwide fame was his own personal protest against the racial injustices of cannabis prohibition.

Ted and Snoop had long fantasized about a time when smoking weed would no longer be a crime, and now, in the first weeks of 2013, the dream seemed closer to reality than ever before. Colorado and Washington voters had just approved recreational marijuana use, and even from halfway around the world, Ted's entrepreneurial mind was racing. The genie was about to pop out of the bottle, Ted thought, and who better than him and Snoop to capitalize on this moment in history? This was a sleeping giant they could not afford to miss. It was a "moment of arbitrage," in business school parlance, or in other words, a window in which to seize on an opportunity before the rest of the world catches on.

But beyond the potential for personal gain, Snoop and Ted believed that a legal marijuana industry could provide a once-in-a-lifetime chance for so many Americans to create generational wealth. You didn't need to be a Kennedy or a Rockefeller to strike out on your own in this new industry. You didn't need a degree from an Ivy League university, or access to the right networks of people; there was no legacy architecture—like what Ted and his friends had encountered in college—that could keep minorities or outsiders from gaining a foothold.

And music had long helped marijuana counterculture seep into the mainstream with conspiratorial lyrics that referenced getting high.

"Way back in the days of the jazz era, they were speaking on the plant, because the plant was something that was a way of helping them find their groove, find their mind and find their mental, to create some of the most classic music that was ever written," Snoop Dogg explained in *Grass Is Greener,* a documentary about 420 history.

From Louis Armstrong to Bob Dylan's refrain "Everybody must get stoned" to the legions of Deadheads lighting up as they followed Jerry Garcia and, of course, to the gangsta rappers like Snoop, who memorably sported a white baseball cap with a prominent marijuana leaf in the iconic "Nuthin but a 'G' Thang" video with Dr. Dre, the drumbeat for getting blazed thrummed on. Snoop and Ted were already insiders who could leverage their insights and contacts to help people in their orbit take advantage of the fast-moving shift.

The two friends saw legalization as an opportunity to begin to right the wrongs of the drug war while simultaneously introducing new, potentially massive economic opportunities for the disenfranchised. And they felt strongly that their team needed to have a seat at the table. But they knew they had to move quickly. It wouldn't be long before corporate America would be nipping at their heels.

In one of Snoop's most memorable hit songs of all time, "Gin and

Juice," he famously raps, "With my mind on my money and my money on my mind." As he and his business partner first hatched a plan to take legal marijuana by storm, the lyric could not have been more on point.

The race was on to cash in on cannabis.

A CHEF IS BORN

New York, New York

August 2012

As the hour crept past midnight and the din of the city quieted into a late-night lull, Jeff Danzer kicked back on his couch in his Manhattan apartment and settled into a mellow high. Once again, the successful fashion-marketing executive couldn't sleep. With his feet up and his mind open, he listened to the upbeat voice of billionaire self-help guru Tony Robbins in the hope that the recorded lecture given to him by a friend might spark a new direction for his life.

So much had already changed for Jeff over the last ten years.

A decade earlier, he had been just another straight white dad riding the crowded morning train to the city from his home in leafy New Rochelle. The following year he was divorced, on his own, and adjusting to life as an out-and-proud gay man. Now he was living in an apartment on Wall Street and counting the days until the weekends when it was his turn to see his three young sons.

In his former life, he'd rushed home each evening to his wife and their growing family, who observed the strict Orthodox Jewish traditions Jeff had always known. They kept kosher, clinging to the age-old dietary laws that prescribed never mixing milk and meat, and prohibited pork and shellfish, but despite these culinary limitations Jeff seemed to always be in the kitchen or at the grill in the yard, making his sons smile as he whipped up all of their favorites. They would gather around the dinner table every Friday at sunset to usher in Shabbat, the Sabbath, lighting the candles, blessing the wine, and tearing off thick, crusty pieces of the challah that Jeff sometimes baked himself. They held fast to their insular community with whom they celebrated births and bar mitzvahs, and had observed countless Jewish holidays and rituals through the years.

But when the Twin Towers fell on September 11, 2001, the horrific tragedy pushed Jeff to finally face a truth about himself he had hidden most of his life. The terror attack made him realize he didn't want to die without his sons knowing who he really was. He told his wife he was gay. He moved out. They divorced, and suddenly the father of three with the ready smile and infectious sense of humor was shunned by friends. Jeff was nearly forty years old by the time he made the courageous choice to no longer conceal who he really was. Now, as he stared at the ceiling of his bachelor pad, he was pushing fifty and once again questioning his life's purpose.

Lilly Rivera-Steinberg, a divorced mom of four, was going through her own major life transition when she first noticed Jeff in the marble lobby of 45 Wall Street. She thought he was good-looking and wondered to herself if he was single. Smiles and small talk by the mailboxes and crowded elevator bank quickly turned into long dinners in their apartments and late-night hangouts, especially once they discovered they lived right next door to each other—and that there was no romantic chemistry to complicate things. They became instant friends, and eventually so did their kids. Jeff would affectionately call his tall brunette neighbor with the bright red lipstick his "swife" (*straight wife*), and she referred to him as her "gusband" (*gay husband*). They saw each other through all of the trials and tribulations of single parenthood, keeping each other company on lonely evenings and making comfort food for each other and their children. There were Thanksgiving dinners where Lilly, who is Puerto Rican, taught Jeff how to make her famous turkey with *sofrito,* an elaborate family recipe. There were even Passover seders, with Jeff's teenage sons sitting around the table in matching royal blue yarmulkes, listening to their father retelling the Exodus story from the Haggadah while Lilly snapped photos of the occasion. It was their version of *The Brady Bunch,* Lilly would recall fondly, years later.

But cooking and child-rearing weren't the only recreational activities they shared. Lilly lived in apartment 422, and they often joked it should really be called "apartment 420," given the amount of weed they smoked when the kids were with the exes. (For the uninitiated, "420" is a kind of secret handshake for pot smokers that originated in 1971 when a group of San Rafael, California, high school friends decided to meet up to smoke after school one day at 4:20 P.M., according to Ryan Grim, author of *This Is Your Country on Drugs: The Secret History of Getting High in America.*)

"We [each] survived a divorce, [raising] seven kids in total, heartbreaks, ups and downs, and even Hurricane Sandy together among so much more. But in the end it was the laughter, the love, and the bond we have, that made it seem easy," she explained.

When they first met, Jeff confided that after years of working in the fashion branding business, during which he took 2(X)IST underwear from a fledgling $2 million company to a $30 million megabrand, he was aching for a new chapter. In truth, with his fiftieth birthday on the horizon, he was ready for a major career change.

"I said to myself, 'What am I going to do in my next fifty years?' " Jeff wanted to do something big. Something that would have a positive impact on people's lives. He just didn't know what.

It was Lilly's new boyfriend, Danny, who introduced Jeff to Tony Robbins. One night, after another long conversation about what Jeff wanted to do with his life, Danny lent him an old set of Robbins cassette tapes: all twenty-five hours of them. The tapes were so old, Jeff remembers, that he had to track down a Sony Walkman so he could actually listen to them. *What do you like to do that makes you feel happy and fulfilled?* asked the voice piping through his headphones.

That was easy. He loved being in the kitchen. Always had. His mom, Sylvia, still remembers her dark-haired toddler, the eldest of her four boys, peeking over the counter in the kitchen of their Los Angeles ranch-style home, peppering her with constant questions about what she was kneading or simmering or stirring as she prepared for the weekly Shabbat meal. She bought him his first cookbook at age six, and even though he was just learning to read, it wasn't long before he was following the kid-appropriate recipes for cinnamon French toast and English muffin pizzas. But what he loved to do most was improvise.

"He would come up with a recipe in his own mind: 'Let's see how this goes together.' He would put it together and the next thing we knew it was there. He made something," Sylvia remembers with pride.

Having left his strict religious dietary observance behind in the divorce, Jeff was now relishing all kinds of new tastes and textures that had previously been off-limits. Suddenly, pork belly, lobster, calamari, and other previously forbidden ingredients were on the menu, and his mind was full of new culinary ideas.

Beyond concocting delicious dishes for friends and family, Jeff unapologetically loved smoking weed and how it made him feel. Recently these two passions, cannabis and cooking, had converged for him, if quite by accident. A friend's mom, who was battling ovarian cancer, had been written a prescription for medical cannabis in the hope it might ease her pain and help stimulate her appetite, and she'd reached out to Jeff asking if he might try baking her some of his famous toffee cookies with some marijuana mixed in. Like many of her generation, she was intrigued by the idea of marijuana as a less addictive option to many of the prescription drugs she might have been prescribed for pain relief, but couldn't imagine lighting up a joint and smoking the stuff. Jeff was surprised by the request at first, but figured, "Why not?" Looking back, he admits, he didn't really know what he was doing. He threw the ground-up dried cannabis into a Crock-Pot with some butter and left it to sit overnight. Then he strained it through cheesecloth, put it in the freezer, skimmed the residue off the top, and used the greenish "canna butter" to make the cookies. They were barely edible.

"They tasted horrible and my friend's mom said, 'You ruined your cookies. But I feel great.' And then she said, 'You really have to try to get rid of that taste,'" recalled Jeff.

He took her request seriously and attempted to bake them again, along with some fudgy brownies for a young relative who had recently been diagnosed with a malignant brain tumor and was struggling with extreme nausea from chemotherapy. But the herbaceous taste of the cannabis was still too strong and, frankly, unappetizing. Still, Jeff observed, while his baked goods may not have been tasty, they did seem to work. Both his relative and his friend's mother reported that after consuming them, their appetite would return, they would sleep better, and their headaches seemed to disappear.

Jeff desperately wanted to find a way to make the treats taste good. But he also wanted to understand *why* cannabis seemed to have all these medicinal benefits, and began reading whatever research he could find online about the healing applications of the plant. Jeff knew that cannabis had been used for thousands of years in ancient societies across the world to numb pain, ease nausea, quell anxiety, and decrease inflammation. But despite the fact that by 2012, twenty-one states allowed marijuana for medical purposes, federally funded clinical research on the efficacy of it was scarce, as it remained a Schedule I drug on the government's list of banned substances. That designation labeled it harmful and with no proven medical benefits, so U.S. scientists who wanted to research it needed to apply for permission from the DEA and FDA, and were only allowed to study the cannabis grown at the one government-approved farm at the University of Mississippi.

Then Jeff stumbled onto a video of the Israeli biochemist Dr. Raphael Mechoulam. A Holocaust survivor who emigrated from

Bulgaria to Israel as a teen, Mechoulam is widely regarded as "the grandfather of cannabis" for his groundbreaking academic and clinical research into cannabinoids, the more than one hundred powerful compounds found in the cannabis plant, including THC and CBD. Specifically, the Nobel-nominated scientist was looking at how these compounds work with matching receptors in our brains and bodies to produce the plant's intoxicating and therapeutic effects.

In 1964, when Mechoulam first began procuring seized hashish from the Jerusalem police department for his studies, he became the first researcher in the world to isolate and map the molecular structure of the chemical in cannabis that gets you high: delta-9-tetrahydrocannabinol, commonly known as THC. But what really intrigued Jeff was the academic's research into cannabidiol, aka CBD, a cannabinoid that doesn't bring on a high but seems to play a role in soothing suffering.

Jeff had already been seeking out strains with higher levels of CBD, which were not easy to find, when he learned the Hebrew University scientist was the first to discover that CBD, THC, and other cannabis compounds can be more effective and therapeutic when they are consumed together rather than in isolation. Mechoulam called it "the entourage effect."

Later, the scientist would turn his attention to one of his most important discoveries to date: he discovered the endogenous compounds that activate the endocannabinoid system, a series of receptors in the brain that regulate bodily functions in mammals, including mood, appetite, sleep, bone growth, and inflammation. He believes the research on endogenous cannabinoids, those made in our bodies, holds the most promise for curing disease in the future.

"The compounds that we make, the receptors that we have, and these [endogenous] compounds are involved in a huge number of disease states," Mechoulam explained to this reporter in a telephone interview in the summer of 2019. He went on to describe his latest theory for how endocannabinoids might one day be used to mitigate the effects of brain trauma, osteoporosis, and drug addiction.

At the age of eighty-eight, "Rafi," as he is known to his friends and family, still continues to collaborate with notable scientists across the globe and oversees research at Hebrew University's Multidisciplinary Center for Cannabinoid Research, which he founded. Inside the university's School of Pharmacy, thirty-five researchers in fields ranging from agriculture to chemistry to drug development to pharmacology are still working to discover and test new treatment modalities using cannabinoids, as well as those using the body's own pathways.

While none of Mechoulam's clinical research has ever delved into cannabis-infused edibles (and the scientist remains skeptical about CBD being added liberally to everything from soft drinks to smoothies without more clinical study and government oversight), his life's work and the promise of how it could really help people was swirling in the back of Jeff's mind in 2012. As he reclined in his living room, listening to Tony Robbins encourage him to take stock of his passions, divine inspiration finally hit like a lightning bolt.

By now it was 2:00 A.M., but Jeff and Lilly always had an open-door policy. He ran next door to her apartment, bursting with the news that he had finally decided on his next act.

"Oh my God, I've figured it out," he announced. "I am going to be a cannabis chef!"

5 THE WILLY WONKA OF WEED

Smiths Falls, Ontario

September 2013

THE AROMA OF milk chocolate once wafted across this humble hamlet, delighting scores of schoolchildren and tourists alike who journeyed to the backwoods of Eastern Ontario to behold Hershey's largest factory outside the United States. Sadly, the delectable scent of cocoa was long gone by the autumn of 2013. In its place, a whiff of despair had settled over the town. Like many other manufacturing hubs across North America, a swift and unexpected wave of layoffs had rippled through tiny Smiths Falls, leaving blighted buildings and broken spirits in its wake.

An hour's drive southwest of the capital city of Ottawa, down a country road dotted with maple syrup and Christmas tree farms, past a narrow main street and beyond the grassy banks of the burbling Rideau Canal, 1 Hershey Drive once bustled nonstop. Railcars delivered cocoa beans and peanuts by the ton and fresh locally farmed milk by the gallon, at all hours of the day and night, keeping the giant mixers whirring, the long conveyor belts humming, and the automated packaging machines working full tilt. Lines of wide-eyed visitors snaked through the popular "Chocolate Shoppe," gleefully stocking up on armloads of kisses and candy bars. They particularly loved the broken remnants you could buy at a discount, and some locals even flocked to the store once a month to replenish their cupboards with treats.

Now the buildings stood vacant and eerily silent. Forgotten. The towering corn syrup tank, massive cocoa butter extractors, and deep copper bowls used to submerge crunchy roasted almonds and peanuts in melted milk chocolate that would harden into a shiny shelac—they all stood suspended in time. In the old distribution center, abandoned desks, rotary telephones, and whiteboards scribbled with black marker still stood, gathering dust. The Smiths Falls water tower, which used to greet travelers to Canada's "Chocolate Capital," had been hastily painted over, erasing its forty-five-year marriage to the beloved confectioner. This real-life embodiment of Willy Wonka's chocolate factory had become nothing but a ghost town.

But for two entrepreneurs on the hunt for the perfect spot to build their crazy new medical marijuana business, this empty chocolate factory was filled with promise. All they needed to do was convince the townspeople that cannabis could be their golden ticket.

By the time Bruce Linton, a charismatic middle-aged tech CEO, and Chuck Rifici, his earnest politically connected cofounder, stumbled upon the 470,000-square-foot plant, the two had already been scouting real estate around their home province for months without much luck. Their hopes of redeveloping the empty Playtex plant in Arnprior, a nearby old logging town, hit a snag before they could even present their big plans. After some initial discussions, several local leaders found the potential stench, let alone the topic of pot, so repugnant that the town rejected the deal overnight. The partners found themselves pounding the pavement yet again. No matter how respectable these two businessmen in suits and ties came off, or how many jobs they might one day create, weed was not an easy sell. Even though medicinal cannabis had been legal in the country since 2001 and the Canadian government was preparing to overhaul the way its citizens accessed it, not everyone wanted a pot factory on the next block.

But they weren't giving up. Bruce was the sort of guy who liked to win and rarely backed down. Even as a small-for-his-age ten-year-old junior hockey player, he'd lobbied hard to be the team captain. He loved being the one calling the shots. And even though he was usually the smallest guy on the ice and not the most gifted athlete, he skated hard and wasn't afraid to throw elbows, proudly racking up the most minutes in the penalty box during his last season.

Although his height eventually caught up to that of his peers, he never outgrew his hard-charging impulses and appetite for risk, both of which propelled him to the highest echelons of the Canadian business world over the course of his impressive career. The chatty entrepreneur, with his gap-toothed smile and mop of blond hair, never went after the obvious or the easy. His attraction to counter-intuitive opportunities grew in part from his knack for devouring thorny public policy issues. He actually enjoyed reading thick, wonky reports and dissecting dry government stats. A self-proclaimed nerd, he had majored in political administration and economics at Ottawa's Carleton University and was outspoken as a student rep on the school's board of governors. That was when he caught the attention of his future mentor, the Welsh Canadian tech mogul Sir Terry Matthews. After college, he went to work for Matthews's data networking giant, Newbridge Networks, at what happened to be the dawn of an era of deregulation and restructuring in the telecommunications sector across North America. He then went on to launch various information technology and infrastructure ventures in developing nations.

Finally, in the late summer of 2012, Linton, who was working to tame his youthful competitiveness as he edged closer to his fiftieth birthday, was chomping at the bit for his next challenge. The married father of two boys remembers sitting at the kitchen table in his suburban Ottawa home one morning with a pile of newspapers spread out before him. It was rare that he actually had the time to do more than skim the headlines, but on this day he was enjoying the luxury of reading the papers cover-to-cover. That's when an in-depth story about medical marijuana caught his eye.

THE CONSERVATIVE GOVERNMENT under Prime Minister Stephen Harper was facing a backlash from Canadian police chiefs after tough mandatory-minimum sentences for marijuana possession had gone into effect the past winter. One of the sticking points of the controversy was the fact that since 2001, tens of thousands of Canadians were already allowed to legally grow as many as four hundred marijuana plants at home for personal use. All they needed was a doctor's note that said they needed 100 grams per day to treat any one of a wide array of medical ailments, ranging from chronic pain to cancer. For perspective, the average joint contains less than half a gram of dried cannabis, which meant that patients could grow many times more than they could consume. According to veteran marijuana rights attorney Alan Young, the poorly written laws gave way to a huge surplus and a massive underground, or "gray," market, as the excess pot that people cultivated in their basements and garages was being sold to not quite legal "compassionate care clubs" popping up in cities across the provinces and, increasingly, online.

It was lucrative. At CA$7.69 per gram of the highest-quality bud, a pound could fetch close to $3,500. And while only about forty thousand Canadians were legally permitted to use the drug for medicinal purposes by 2013, the real number of consumers was estimated to be between two and three million people. This made for an increasingly frustrating cat-and-mouse game for police who were struggling to enforce the vague drug laws. They just couldn't keep up.

"The medical and recreational user was blurred. And so, police would be making these small-time busts, and people would say, 'I'm growing it for my arthritis.' It just became a pain," explained Young, whose early court challenges to Canada's drug laws paved the way for medical marijuana legalization. "We kind of overgrew the government. We just normalized it by having so many of the grows all across the country."

All of this was news to Bruce Linton at the time.

"I was like, 'Shut up! You can grow cannabis at your house?'" he recalled in the folksy manner he still retains from his upbringing on a small farm in Southwestern Ontario.

This was a lightbulb moment; an idea completely out of left field. Unlike Ted Chung or Jeff Danzer, the only experience he'd ever had with pot was once getting too high in college. Cannabis just wasn't something he encountered in his everyday life. But its economics of supply and demand tantalized his inner wonk. His entrepreneurial antennae sensed something big was about to happen if the government was going to change the way it handled medical marijuana and begin to regulate its sale. Marijuana had been gaining credibility as medicine for some time—just like in the United States, where Colorado and Washington voters were on the cusp of ending cannabis bans altogether. Right here in Linton's own backyard, the nation's capital, the complicated politics of an antidrug prime minister and his need to appease police on this issue made it clear to Bruce that Canada had hit an inflection point. He smelled a fruitful opportunity in the making.

He dug into the political chess game with gusto as he learned of government proposals being floated to revamp the entire medical cannabis market by shifting it from private home growers to corporate licensed producers, or "LPs," within the next year. The Canadian government would essentially be flipping an underground commodity market and legitimizing it, giving a few businesses the exclusive first-mover advantage in an industry Bruce estimated could potentially be worth $100 to $200 billion. If things took off the way he thought they might, a handful of lucky entrepreneurs would end up winning the proverbial lottery by securing one of the very few licenses for growing and distributing medical marijuana across the nation.

Struggling to contain his enthusiasm, the veteran executive started quietly calling old colleagues and friends to see if they wanted to partner or invest with him to make a run at this burgeoning industry. But as he reached out to his high-powered network to pitch them on this opportunity, he found that nobody wanted anything to do with it. Getting rich off medical marijuana would be "a lot easier than inventing the next-generation Google," he told his friends. And yet, they didn't seem interested.

"They were like, 'What's wrong with you? You got money. You got a good reputation. This sounds sketchy. Why would you do that?' " he recalled seven years later.

But for a person like Bruce, who prides himself on skating to where the puck's going, those negative reactions were far from a deterrent. In fact, they only spurred him on. If 99 percent of the most capable people he knew weren't even going to step out onto the ice because they were worried about tarnishing their reputations, he thought, then surely he had an even bigger shot at winning. But even as a guy who admitted he never went to a meeting he didn't want to chair, he knew he couldn't run or finance the new venture entirely by himself. He needed a partner.

By the spring of 2013, Bruce had finally found one in Chuck Rifici, a serial tech entrepreneur himself who had founded his first startup before graduating from college, and who had worked for Bruce early in his career. By now, he was considered a political insider, and was at the time volunteering as chief financial officer of the Liberal Party of Canada, the opposition political party. Chuck, too, it turned out, had been watching the political machinations around marijuana in the nation's capital. He knew the opportunity for medical cannabis in the Great White North could be big—especially if Canada ultimately decided to leapfrog past America's patchwork of state-by-state ballot initiatives and make recreational marijuana legal on a national level—becoming the first G7 nation to end pot prohibition after nearly a century.

For that to happen, the political control in Parliament would have to shift from the harsh stance of Harper and the antidrug Tories to the pro-pot Liberals—an outcome that seemed increasingly plausible given polling that suggested 66 percent of Canadians favored marijuana use, and the fact that Justin Trudeau, the youthful, newly installed leader of the Liberals, was becoming the party's rising star.

Bruce and Chuck decided to call their company Tweed (the *T* stands for "therapeutic"), in part because the name sounded reliable, durable, and of course upstanding. Chuck signed on as chief operator, as Bruce took on the role of chief evangelist and fundraiser. After all, this was a business that demanded serious infrastructure, and they knew they would need millions to get a major new agricultural venture like this one off the ground.

But in the fall of 2013, as the crisp air settled over the province and the sugar maple leaves began to turn from green to gold, the Tweed team still wasn't sure where it was going to begin growing its product. That is, until they got a serendipitous tip about the abandoned Hershey's property, and with it, a glimmer of hope that due to the existing zoning laws for the manufacture of agricultural products (e.g., chocolate), they might be able to circumvent local opposition. The truth was that by then, Smiths Falls needed cannabis as much as these founders needed a place to get their business off the ground.

It had been five long years since the maker of kisses and peanut butter cups had pulled its stakes out of Canadian soil and headed to Mexico, taking five hundred jobs with it. At the time, the close-knit community of Smiths Falls was already reeling from the loss of two other well-paying employers—Stanley Tools and a government-run facility for the developmentally disabled—and Hershey's exodus struck the dizzying third blow. Forty percent of the town's workforce and 20 percent of its 8,800 residents had already been laid off, and even those lucky enough to find work struggled to make ends meet. Some commuted an hour each way to Ottawa. Others were forced to leave town altogether. And those who stayed were turning in rising numbers to food banks and public assistance in order to care for their families. Incidents of domestic violence, burglaries, and addiction were also increasing at alarming rates.

"At one time it was a booming town and then it just died. And we had nothing here, absolutely nothing. There was no work, no place to shop, nothing," recalled Linda Spencer, a mother of three, who had lost her job at the government agency. Her family had lived in the town for generations.

"Our confidence is built on our ability to look after our families and feed our families and [on] the houses we live in, the cars we drive. And when all that gets turned upside down, it can be horribly devastating," explained Shawn Pankow, a blue-eyed, white-goateed financial planner who was serving on the town council and would later go on to become mayor. For him, too, this was personal. His family's roots in Smiths Falls dated back to the beginning of the twentieth century, when his grandfather arrived from Ukraine with five dollars in his pocket and knowing not a word of English. Two of his cousins had lost their jobs at Hershey's.

The town politicians had tried desperately to lobby government officials in Ottawa to help lure a new employer to the sprawling space, but to no avail. With its ready access to power, water, and labor, it seemed like quite a bargain. But no one had snapped it up just yet.

"It was the largest building for the cheapest price," recalled Mayor Pankow, who took office in 2014. In fact, the massive size of the site had initially deterred Bruce and his partner from even considering it. But by now, the race for Canada's medical marijuana market was truly on. In June 2013, the national government confirmed that it would officially begin the arduous process of evaluating applications for the country's first legitimate medicinal marijuana licenses. With potential rivals now coming out of the woodwork,

Linton and Rifici faced a major time crunch. They needed a home base to anchor their operations, and they needed it fast.

They persuaded the owner of the property to let Tweed take over a third of the Hershey's factory on the promise that they would invest millions to retrofit the building first; then, once they had raised more money, they would buy the whole thing. The structure of the deal avoided a potentially contentious local hearing. The iconic landmark that once housed a veritable playground of confectionary delights would be transformed into a hub for hydroponic cultivation of medical cannabis before anyone had a chance to raise a stink. And in the end, jobs were jobs.

Up to eighty jobs would be created at first. It wasn't much, but the news set off a hopeful buzz around town. Residents got a giggle out of headlines that proclaimed Smiths Falls was now "Spliff Falls," but the snarky media coverage fizzled fast once Tweed broke ground and secured one of the first coveted licenses in the nation.

In a few months, light and life would return to the abandoned old chocolate factory. But the sweet ending for Smiths Falls was really just the beginning of an even more delicious story. Never in their wildest dreams did the residents of this beleaguered community imagine that in just a couple of years, their town would be home to the biggest cannabis company on the planet.

6 WHAT'S BOOZE GOT TO DO WITH IT?

Denver, Colorado

November 2012

INTREPID CANNABIS ENTREPRENEURS Beth Stavola, Ted Chung, Jeff Danzer, and Bruce Linton had never crossed paths in 2012. They didn't possess the same backgrounds or professional experiences. They didn't travel in the same circles or even share the same views about casual drug use. Ultimately, the same spark would ignite these visionaries on that historic election night when Colorado and Washington became the first states to legalize marijuana for recreational use. They heard the boom of the starting gun and knew that if they didn't move quickly, they might miss out on the prize of a lifetime.

The opportunity was fraught with unknowns. Pot would remain federally illegal. It was unclear how the Justice Department would respond to new state-legal enterprises and customers in this new political climate. President Barack Obama had just won a second term, and his administration had sent mixed signals about how it would cope with the clash between federal and state laws on cannabis.

Despite the uncertainties, a new intellectual argument for legalization took hold in the birthplace of the Libertarian Party, where a frontiersman mentality that spurned government overreach ran deep from the ruddy foothills to the craggy Western Slope. Colorado would provide fertile ground for a feisty group of pot proponents to recast marijuana as both a medicinal product *and* a recreational one, framing the debate in a fresh way that helped move the needle like never before. Their tactic took direct aim at weed's shady stigma by pitting it against alcohol, the most widely used and accepted legal intoxicant. The question at the ballot box wasn't whether cannabis was the pernicious vice the federal government had made it out to be for nearly eighty years, but, rather, whether it was in fact *less* harmful to society than beer, wine, or spirits. And if a majority of voters could wrap their heads around this dichotomy, pot activists reasoned, citizens would see the logic of amending Colorado's constitution to tax and regulate marijuana just like booze. If passed, Amendment 64 would create the world's first legal over-21 marketplace and with it millions in tax revenue to fix crumbling schools. And thanks to medical sales already booming in the state, a well-funded campaign with cash from outside donors, and a series of colorful publicity stunts, that's how it played out.

The message that weed was "safer" than alcohol took eight long years to craft. It was controversial. It not only troubled marijuana opponents concerned about teen use and drugged driving, but it even flummoxed some longtime advocates at first. When it came to recreational marijuana, national drug policy leaders had always focused their talking points on the merits of wiping out violent drug cartels and solving the racial injustices of the War on Drugs, not promoting the virtues of smoking a joint over drinking a stiff cocktail.

"The argument was all about how the criminal market is bad, not that marijuana is good. Right? So, the last thing anybody wanted to do was get into the business of promoting cannabis use or attacking something that is as American as apple pie, which is alcohol, right?" recalled longtime legalization advocate Troy Dayton, an early investor in the industry.

This strategy was even more implausible in Coors country, where cracking open a cold one was part of the local identity. After all, the

Coors Brewing Company was the first brewer in the nation to sell beer in an aluminum can, the emblem of an American tradition. Established in 1873, the storied brewery nestled at the foot of the mountains along Clear Creek in the Denver suburb of Golden was one of a handful of beer makers that managed to survive Prohibition. It went on to merge with Miller to become one of the largest in the world.

Beer's role in the local economies of the region only grew when Colorado's first craft brewpub opened in Denver in 1988. Founded by an out-of-work geologist named John Hickenlooper and three of his buddies, Wynkoop Brewing Company breathed new life into a forgotten ghost town of abandoned Gold Rush–era warehouses and ugly parking garages in lower downtown. Hickenlooper—a serial restaurateur who went on to become a highly popular two-term mayor of the Mile High City, two-term governor of Colorado, and 2020 Democratic White House hopeful—had big plans for the redevelopment of this neglected neighborhood, which would soon be renamed "LoDo." (Hickenlooper declined to be interviewed for this book, but as of this writing he had dropped out of the race for president and was embarking on a bid to oust Colorado Republican senator Cory Gardner.) As soon as his celebrated brewery opened in the cavernous J. S. Brown Mercantile Building, it would pave the way for world-class sports arenas, gourmet restaurants, luxury lofts, and a whole new generation of microbreweries and trendy watering holes across a state dependent on tourism.

With beer as the backdrop, Colorado provided an unexpected setting for this new take on marijuana reform that was set in motion in September 2004, in the shadow of the alcohol-overdose death of a former homecoming queen. It was the weekend of the big football game between rivals Colorado State University (CSU) and the University of Colorado (CU) Boulder, and a popular sophomore from Beatrice, Nebraska, named Samantha "Sam" Spady was out party-hopping at fraternities around the CSU campus in Fort Collins, consuming copious amounts of beer, tequila, and vanilla-flavored vodka shots. Spady was barely able to stand by the end of the night and eventually passed out around dawn. According to news and police reports, the nineteen-year-old honors student was discovered the next day lying stone-cold in a back room on the second floor of the Sigma Pi frat house. She had a blood alcohol level of 0.436 percent, more than four times the legal limit for driving.

Two weeks after Spady lost her life, another Colorado college student named Lynn Gordon "Gordie" Bailey, Jr., an eighteen-year-old former varsity football captain and freshman at CU Boulder, tragically died of alcohol poisoning during a fraternity hazing ritual. According to the Gordie Center, a foundation his parents created to help prevent future deaths, "Gordie and twenty-six other pledges, dressed in coats and ties for 'bid night,' were blindfolded and taken to the Arapaho Roosevelt National Forest, where they were 'encouraged' to drink four handles (1.75 liter bottles) of whiskey and six (1.5 liter) bottles of wine around a bonfire in 30 minutes." He was brought back to the Chi Psi frat house, stumbling and incoherent, to "sleep it off," and never woke up.

These tragic deaths spurred nationwide calls to address an epidemic of excessive underage drinking at colleges and universities. It was a heart-wrenching made-for-TV story about two telegenic all-American kids that the twenty-four-hour cable news channels and the network morning shows gobbled up. Spady's parents made tearful appearances on *Good Morning America* and *Dr. Phil,* and both families founded nonprofits and produced documentaries to sound their warnings.

Amid the hand-wringing and calls for change, marijuana reformers were watching closely from Washington, D.C. In the months leading up to the media frenzy over college binge drinking, Steve Fox, the federal lobbyist for the Marijuana Policy Project (MPP), had been sifting through polling data looking at voters' beliefs and opinions about weed versus alcohol, and noticed a promising trend suggesting that some citizens might be swayed to legalize marijuana if they were presented with a case that showed how pot was less damaging to society than alcohol. From domestic violence to date rape, and now to this spotlight on deadly alcohol poisoning among young people, he believed statistics about the perils of alcohol worked in marijuana's favor. He wasted no time dispatching a young mentee to Boulder with a small grant to begin an experiment on the very college campuses where Spady and Bailey had died.

Enter twenty-two-year-old Mason Tvert, a garrulous University of Richmond political science grad and the perfectly cast spokesman to reach college kids who spent their weekends partying hard. He was close to their age, funny, a bit rumpled, and loved to talk. An avid debater who grew up privileged amid the resort lifestyle of Scottsdale, Arizona, Mason could strike up a conversation with just about anyone. He had also nearly died from alcohol poisoning as a high school senior and was more than happy to share the story. After drinking heavily at an outdoor country music festival, he'd ended up in the ER with no memory of how he got there. Somehow, he says, no one asked him how or where he got the beer. The police weren't called, and he wasn't ticketed for underage drinking. He was sent home from the hospital the next morning in a taxi.

It was a completely different situation a year later when he was rounded up along with more than twenty other college classmates on suspicion of marijuana use and summoned to the Richmond police station for questioning as part of a wide-ranging grand jury probe. No charges were ever filed, but the stark contrast between the two experiences smelled of hypocrisy to him.

"I almost drank enough to die and no one asked me where I got it," he marveled years later. "[And in college], I'm using marijuana. It's not causing any problems to me or anyone else, and [there is] a multi-jurisdictional task force [investigating]. So, it's like every level of government from the DEA down wanting to know where I'm getting this marijuana. And it's like, 'How crazy is this?' "

In January 2005, with startup funding from MPP, Mason and Steve launched an organization called SAFER, which stands for "Safer Alternative For Enjoyable Recreation." Armed with a grant for $32,000, SAFER began to organize students at CSU and CU to vote for nonbinding resolutions to roll back university penalties that were more severe for pot possession than for underage drinking. Under the current policy, students could be kicked out of the dorms or suspended for smoking weed. But if they were under twenty-one and got caught with booze, the punishments amounted to a slap on the wrist and an admonishment to "drink more responsibly"—a directive difficult to take seriously amid a beer-soaked culture that promoted tailgate parties and keggers, recounted Mason as he sat in his Denver office crammed with marijuana campaign memorabilia. In truth, the initiatives had no power to change university policy. But the local media ate them up anyway. Soon, Mason's youthful face and shoot-from-the-hip sound bites started making Denver's evening news, while SAFER was getting covered by the local newspapers, the *Rocky Mountain News* and *The Denver Post*. Of course, the push at the colleges was really just a taste of what was to come. Within six months, in the summer of 2005, Mason turned to the people of Denver and gathered the five thousand signatures SAFER needed to get on the November ballot with Initiative 100—a proposal for police to deprioritize marijuana arrests of adults carrying less than one ounce of pot.

Now that SAFER was getting traction for its message about the hazards of drinking, it was no surprise that Mayor John Hickenlooper and his brewpub would find itself in the campaign's crosshairs. Looking back in 2019, Mason would characterize the mayor as "an angel sent to us from Heaven" for the politician's unwitting role as a foil for the brazen young activist. SAFER first grabbed the spotlight with controversial billboards and lawn signs promoting the idea that domestic violence and crime would go down in Denver if people traded in their pints of craft brew for bong hits. But a month before election day, when the mayor told reporters he was against decriminalization because he believed marijuana to be a "gateway drug," that was all the prompting Mason needed to go after the Democrat with guns blazing.

By this point, the young campaign director had traded his T-shirt and jeans for a respectable suit and tie. He used a morning television appearance to fire a direct shot at Hickenlooper by telling an incredulous interviewer, "The mayor happens to be a drug dealer. He just sells his drug [alcohol] in a legal market and is lucky enough that our laws allow it." The TV anchor quickly wrapped up the *Good Day Colorado* segment, but Mason wasn't done.

The following afternoon, he and a small group of I-100 advocates unfurled a red-and-white banner outside the City and County Building that asked rhetorically, WHAT IS THE DIFFERENCE BETWEEN MAYOR HICKENLOOPER AND A MARIJUANA DEALER? THE MAYOR HAS MADE HIS FORTUNE SELLING A MORE HARMFUL DRUG. Once again, local TV cameras captured it all. When city hall brushed off the small rally with a dig from the mayor's acting chief of staff about sending the campaign a shipment of Doritos and Oreos (the implication being to dismiss them as a bunch of stoners prone to "the munchies"), Mason was ready once again with another sensational photo op. This time, he raced to a local costume store called the Wizard's Chest and found the perfect props to make his point. On the steps of the columned municipal building, he laid a body bag with a gruesome fake foot hanging out of it, tagged the toe with the words ALCOHOL POISONING, and placed a poster next to it that proclaimed THE POTENTIAL HARM OF ALCOHOL. For good measure, he set some of Hickenlooper's Wynkoop Brewing Company's branded coasters and jugs next to the "corpse," and a few feet away he piled a mountain of Doritos and Oreos and, above the packages, posted a sign that read THE POTENTIAL "HARM" OF MARIJUANA. Naturally, reporters from Denver's news stations and daily papers swarmed the spectacle. Councilman Charlie Brown, a vocal opponent of SAFER who had made headlines for admitting to taking down pro–I-100 lawn signs, told reporters Mason's tactics were "deceptive and misleading." Even some longtime marijuana rights activists were concerned Mason had gone too far by attacking such a well-loved mayor.

In the end, no one was more surprised than Mason that the gimmicks actually worked. On November 1, 2005, Denver passed a bill to decriminalize the use of marijuana with nearly 54 percent of the vote: the first city in the nation to do so. But Mason and his band of supporters weren't ready to celebrate this victory just yet. They wanted more. They set their sights on taking their SAFER message statewide.

That was when they hit some bumps in the road. Denver and its mayor maintained they would continue to enforce state law, which still criminalized marijuana and, they argued, superseded a city ordinance. And true to their word, city arrests for pot possession ticked up in the year following the vote. A 2006 effort to pass a statewide measure making it legal for adults over twenty-one to possess up to an ounce of marijuana, known as Initiative 44, fell short. Meanwhile, marijuana activists continued to torment the mayor of Colorado's largest city and jumped at any chance to call him out. During Hickenlooper's easy reelection campaign, for example, they sent an advocate to his public events dressed up in a bright yellow chicken suit and a sign that read CHICKENLOOPER. WHY WON'T YOU DEBATE MARIJUANA? The attacks were widely covered by the media but didn't hurt Hickenlooper's high approval ratings. He was reelected with 87 percent of the vote and was already being courted to run for governor.

"As far as real-life political fairy tales go, it was just about impossible to trump Mayor Hickenlooper," wrote Denver's *5280* magazine several years later.

The stalled attempts to expand pot reform gained fresh momentum in 2009 in the immediate aftermath of a lawsuit brought by a mild-mannered attorney named Brian Vicente and his medical marijuana rights organization, Sensible Colorado. While Mason specialized in hijinks and hyperbole to make headlines, Brian's approach was decidedly more understated. Fresh out of the University of Denver's law school, Brian had spent five years quietly carving out a niche for himself educating the sick and dying about the state's tiny medical marijuana program. The avid snowboarder first got interested in medical marijuana after clerking for the outspoken U.S. district court judge John L. Kane, who inspired him to build a small practice advocating for patients who got entangled in the criminal justice system.

"I was tired of having medical marijuana patients call me and say they've been beat up in a public park, in the back alley. They were scared to buy medicine. And they wanted to buy it from stores. They thought that that would be the dignified and safe way to buy it. And I agree. So my concern was making sure that patients were able to access medical marijuana from a pharmacy-like setting instead of buying it from a garage or an alley," explained Brian of the case that paved the way for the first state-approved retail stores to open.

Marijuana retailers—medical or otherwise—did not exist in the state at the time. Patients suffering from cancer, HIV, and other ailments could procure marijuana from small-scale collectives called "caregivers" under Amendment 20, which had passed in 2000, but the caregivers were only allowed to service a total of five patients. In a case he brought on behalf of an AIDS and hepatitis C patient named Damien LaGoy, Brian argued in Denver District Court that the number set by the Colorado health department was arbitrary and violated patients' rights by limiting their access to medicine. Further, the patient limit was not even written into the state constitution; health officials and members of the DEA had come up with the policy in backroom meetings. When the judge ruled in his client's favor in November 2009, it threw open the door for Colorado to allow the first dispensaries to open. Now caregivers could sell to as many patients as they could handle. And there were indications that the Feds would allow these businesses to proceed unhindered. The Obama administration had just come out with a memo from Deputy Attorney General David Ogden reiterating a holdover policy from the Bush White House that advised federal prosecutors to stay focused on drug cartels rather than state-sanctioned medical marijuana patients and caregivers. A booming industry was born overnight.

"Entrepreneurs came out of the shadows and rented strip mall storefronts throughout Colorado to meet the demand. Persons considered 'drug dealers' the night before became 'small business owners' by morning. Soon, there were more marijuana shops in Denver than there were Starbucks coffee shops. There was no turning back. An entirely unregulated network had taken root," explained former Colorado deputy attorney general David Blake and Jack Finlaw, who served as a top aide to Governor Hickenlooper, in a 2014 article published in the *Harvard Policy and Law Review*.

On the corners of major Denver thoroughfares, commuters would be greeted by giant green spinning arrows pointing them to medical stores selling half-price joints. And the smell of pot seemed to be everywhere. On some days, you couldn't help but notice it drifting toward I-70 as soon as you pulled out of Denver International Airport twenty-four miles away from downtown.

In the midst of the explosive growth and complaints, in 2010 the state began to work quickly to bring the wild marketplace under control. The first step was educating legislators on both sides of the aisle, most of whom had never set foot in a marijuana grow or a dispensary, and many of whom had never even met any real live patients who used cannabis to manage pain, nausea, or other conditions. Working groups were established to set the rules for operating these new businesses, like where they could be located, what time they could open and close, how they would vet customers, and what kinds of products they could sell. This tangle of questions brought together a motley cast of characters. One of the strangest moments, Brian Vicente recalls, was sitting around a table in a sterile conference room inside the state's Department of Revenue building in Golden, alongside criminal court judges, child welfare advocates, police, and illegal marijuana growers alike.

"It was really this pinch-me type moment, where we would be talking about what should the font be on the warning label of the marijuana brownie. It was a conversation that never occurred in history, right? Prior to that, you know the only conversation was how long should these people go to jail for," he recalled of the notorious federal mandatory-minimum sentences that led to the mass incarceration of tens of thousands of nonviolent marijuana offenders every year. "Now here we're agreeing, 'No one wants marijuana in the hands of kids. No one wants people driving under the influence. No one wants the illegal market anymore, now that there's the opportunity for a legal market.'" The stakeholders found common ground, and through 2010 and 2011 formalized the first regulations to bring the marijuana trade out of back alleys and onto Main Street. The efforts set the stage for the next attempt to legalize recreational pot statewide.

One of the cannabis entrepreneurs on the front lines was Wanda James, a respected former U.S. Navy officer, local Democratic campaign manager, and appointee to President Obama's National Finance Committee. She and her husband, ex-Marine, chef, and restaurateur Scott Durrah, first founded the Apothecary, a medical pot cultivation facility and dispensary, in 2009, and later went on to establish Simply Pure, a line of THC edibles and a popular dispensary. She was the first African American woman to own marijuana business licenses in the United States, and had a strong point of view on why it was critical that the new cannabis industry not leave communities of color behind. The racial injustices of the drug war cut close to home. Wanda's own brother had served eleven years in federal prison in Texas after he was arrested at age seventeen for carrying four ounces of marijuana. While he was incarcerated, he spent four years of his sentence picking cotton in the fields near the prison. As her national profile grew, she was passionate about sharing his story and explaining the hypocrisy of black and brown people still being thrown in prison for marijuana offenses while others—mostly white men—were making millions off the industry.

But even while she advocated fiercely for more opportunities in cannabis for minorities, she was also well aware of the risks involved for anyone striking out in this new world.

"It was few and far between, the people who really supported this. It was unknown territory. Back then, stepping out and saying that you were . . . opening a dispensary, working with cannabis, you were putting yourself in massive legal jeopardy. People were going to jail. They were being arrested," she said, looking back a decade later on the risks she and her husband undertook.

Fears ran deep. Anyone who wasn't an insider and came around asking questions was suspected of working for the Feds—and was often viewed with even more skepticism if he or she declined a hit when offered, recalls Chris Walsh, a no-nonsense former *Rocky Mountain News* reporter who would go on to become founding editor and the future CEO of *Marijuana Business Daily*, later dubbed "the *Wall Street Journal* of weed" for its objective coverage of the burgeoning business. He distinctly remembers a leery marijuana executive sidling up to him in the men's room after a meeting to say under his breath that he still wasn't convinced Walsh wasn't with the FBI. It would take years for trust to build among the pioneers who once ran their businesses in the shadows, activists who fought for patients' rights to access cannabis, social justice advocates, and the new generation of white-collar professionals and MBAs hoping to capitalize on the Green Rush.

But somehow, these strange bedfellows all managed to come together in the spring of 2011 to put another statewide referendum on the ballot for the presidential election the following year. A diverse group of entrepreneurs, investors, medical marijuana and racial justice activists, and others convened in the barebones Sensible Colorado headquarters, a shoddy basement office that looked a bit like a college dorm room. It was there that Brian and Mason revealed their plans to use the SAFER message comparing weed to booze to break through to voters. Amendment 64, co-authored by Brian and MPP's Steve Fox, would be called the "Act to Regulate Marijuana Like Alcohol." Despite a shared passion to address the harms of the drug war on communities of color, polling showed they had to be pragmatic about what would resonate most with voters at the time.

"We found that 'It's safer than alcohol' was the easiest message for people. Nobody's going to tell you that someone should go to jail for selling beer or for being caught with a beer on them or even an open beer. You didn't go to jail for that. The goal was, 'Let's link this to beer and alcohol,' because that was something that people in Colorado really understood," recalled Wanda.

But beyond this messaging, the group also had another argument up their sleeve, and this one involved dollar signs. Legalizing recreational weed meant tax revenue, and tax revenue meant new money to repair leaky roofs, remove asbestos, and fix aging bathrooms, among other much-needed repairs for the public schools.

Of course, there were also plenty of Coloradans for whom the number one priority was keeping kids off drugs; after all, what was the point of fixing up the schools if it meant the kids were showing up high? Colorado's largest teachers' union, which had been part of the initial planning for the proposition, came out firmly opposed just two months before the election, citing concerns about marijuana use among children. Most of the state's elected officials, including three former governors and Denver's mayor, vehemently opposed the measure, as did Governor Hickenlooper, who by now was running for his second term, and who invoked children's safety as a reason to block recreational legalization.

Public health policymakers raised alarms about the high THC

potency of the latest generation of pot products, and asked questions about the risks to people with a history or predisposition to substance use disorder. Others worried that the streets would be overrun with drugged drivers. After all, there was no Breathalyzer or other roadside technology invented yet that could test for THC and reliably link it to impaired driving, especially if a driver had been drinking alcohol, too. And Dr. Kathryn Wells, who served on a state substance abuse task force and oversaw Denver's child welfare office, cited fears about blurring the lines between medical use and recreational use. She felt full-scale legalization would confuse consumers and, more important, convince young people that marijuana was "no big deal."

"Recreational use of marijuana is recreational use of marijuana. I don't say, 'Go home and have a glass of wine at the end of the day because it's medicine.' If you want to do that to relax or whatever, that is substance use. Okay. That is what it is; it's not a medication," the child abuse specialist underlined in an interview at the Denver Health clinic.

OF COURSE, IT would be years before the impact on Colorado's children would be known. But the world would be watching, just as it was on election night 2012 when Amendment 64 passed with 54 percent of the vote. Governor Hickenlooper joked that Coloradans shouldn't "break out the Cheetos and Goldfish too quickly," since pot was still illegal under federal law. But he also conceded that his administration intended to respect the will of the voters. Commercialization in Colorado was about to take flight. It was game on.

7 MORMONS FOR MARIJUANA

Gilbert, Arizona

January 2013

CRIMINAL DEFENSE ATTORNEY Mel McDonald hesitated before picking up the telephone to dial his wife. He knew she would be devastated by the urgent news he needed to share with her. As a former federal prosecutor and the youngest superior court judge ever elected in the state of Arizona, McDonald had been an insider in the state's Republican circles for more than thirty years. He had served on President Ronald Reagan's War on Drugs task force with fifteen other notable U.S. Attorneys in the 1980s, including future New York City mayor Rudolph Giuliani and future Oklahoma governor Frank Keating. McDonald, now in private practice, still kept an ear to the ground at the statehouse through his tight network of conservative cronies.

Now he had a lump in his throat upon hearing that a state assembly member from Fountain Hills, an affluent suburb northeast of Phoenix, had introduced a bill that could overturn the state's medical marijuana program. Approved (albeit narrowly) in 2010, the program was just beginning to be rolled out by the health department when Representative John Kavanagh called upon lawmakers to put the contentious issue back on the ballot once again. This was a Hail Mary intended to kill the program once and for all.

McDonald's sources told him it looked like Kavanagh had the votes he needed to get his proposal through the legislature and onto the governor's desk, and that all of the local prosecutors were lining up to support a repeal.

"The marijuana lobby wanted us to believe the law was about compassion for sick people, but the data shows that the pot goes almost entirely to recreational use," Ed Gogek, a physician and addiction psychiatrist who sat on the board of Keep AZ Drug Free (an antidrug group backed by the Arizona Cardinals), told the *Phoenix Business Journal* at the time.

McDonald was a fifth-generation Mormon and elder in the Church of Jesus Christ of Latter-day Saints (LDS), who had grown up in a devout household near Salt Lake City and published a book about his missionary work. He clung to his faith and religious observance so strongly that he had never touched a drop of alcohol, let alone Diet Coke or coffee, as caffeine and booze were traditionally eschewed by early LDS church leaders. His wife, Cindy, a petite blonde with an impish smile, had converted to Mormonism when they wed: a second marriage for both. She threw herself into the tight-knit church community near their home in Gilbert, a Phoenix suburb of grand, Spanish-style ranch homes set amid glimmering man-made lakes and rolling golf courses. Still, after more than twenty years of marriage, she couldn't give up her morning jolt of caffeine. Mel regularly joked about her habit when he came down for breakfast and smelled the familiar aroma of her small coffeepot brewing. "I smell sin," he would sing with a twinkle in his eye, as they laughed at their inside joke. It was clear that their lives revolved around their large extended family and the Mormon temple as soon as you stepped into their home in a pretty waterside subdivision called Val Vista Lakes; the walls were adorned with framed photos of their children and grandchildren, interspersed with biblical quotes. Given his law-and-order background and strong religious conviction, Mel probably was the least likely person to question whether marijuana should be against the law.

But he and Cindy had a secret.

For more than a decade, Cindy had been buying marijuana on the street. Not for her own consumption, but for her son. She would do anything to keep him alive.

One afternoon in 1997, the McDonalds' world was turned upside down when fourteen-year-old Bennett (Ben for short) was riding on his GoPed electric scooter and was hit by a car going forty-five miles per hour as he crossed a busy intersection near their home. He suffered a traumatic brain injury, which eventually caused grand mal seizures that would leave him debilitated and his family desperate. Two years after the tragic accident, his epilepsy had gotten so bad that paramedics were being called to the house a few times a month, as he would involuntarily injure himself when the seizures struck.

Ben was prescribed powerful drugs to keep the seizures at bay, but the medication caused such intense nausea that he had no appetite. He would sometimes go six or seven days without eating and couldn't keep his medicine down. Cindy watched in horror as her boy wasted away. At one point, the teen's weight dwindled from 189 pounds to 119. They were losing him.

"I'm watching my kid die. He's not eating. He's whittling away. He's seizing on the floor. His head's getting cut open," she recalled, as her eyes welled up.

One day, an elderly neighbor named John, who lived at the end of their block, struck up a friendly conversation with Cindy as she unloaded groceries from her car. He was in a motorized wheelchair, and explained he had been in a car accident that shattered two of his vertebrae. Cindy asked him what he took for the pain. He smiled and replied that he had started using marijuana as medicine, and that it also helped with his nausea. With an empathetic smile, John told her that if she ever wanted her son to give it a try, she could knock on his door.

As she writes in her memoir, *The Least Likely Criminal,* which she published in 2018, it took her a few more weeks before she got up the courage to take John up on his offer. In that time, Ben had more seizures, and she was at her wit's end. Mel was at work the day Cindy finally invited her neighbor over to show Ben how to roll a joint. She was so nervous, she had to leave the room. Amazingly, after a few minutes of inhaling, her son said he was hungry for sandwiches and went into the kitchen to start making them. She was floored. He continued to smoke cannabis with John, and within weeks the color returned to Ben's cheeks. He could eat without vomiting and he began to put on weight.

For the first time in months, Cindy was hopeful. But procuring the marijuana her son needed was still very much a criminal endeavor in those years. Simply possessing weed could have landed her in jail and most likely would have destroyed her husband's career. Not to mention, what would their church friends think? She couldn't tell her husband what she was doing.

When her supply ran out she would trade her modest mom-wear for tight ripped jeans, a beat-up leather jacket, and dark lipstick and sneak away to buy a few ounces from anyone who would sell it to her. It was dangerous putting on a different persona to blend in with the drug-dealing crowd, but she says she wasn't scared.

"There is a part of me that's a real badass, that I don't really give a shit. You know? I'm a little bit of a rebel anyway. It only comes out when I really need it to," she explained years later, as she sat next to her husband in their sunny den and shared the story. "I wasn't afraid or anything like that . . . I was like, 'I'm going to do it. I don't really care. If I have to spend a night in jail, I'll spend a night in jail. I'm going to see if I can keep my kid alive.'"

For a time, she was able to keep her clandestine outings to some of the seediest areas of Phoenix under wraps—until one day her husband asked her why Ben was looking better and, miraculously, eating again.

She couldn't lie. Cindy told him what she had been doing behind his back. Mel exploded. This went against everything he had stood for in his long career, not to mention his deep-seated Mormon values. He wouldn't have it.

A few days later, when his famous temper cooled down, Cindy presented him with stacks of research she had gathered showing studies of the potential efficacy of medical marijuana on epilepsy. The fact was, Mel couldn't argue with what he had seen with his own eyes. Ben *did* seem to be getting better. He would never be cured, but cannabis did seem to improve his quality of life. So he agreed that Cindy could keep doing what she was doing, on the condition that she would have to keep the pot in a locked safe, and Mel could never hear or see anything about it again.

"I said, 'I can't be a part of it, because I don't want to get in trouble with the bar. If you get caught, I'll represent you, but your name is going to be in the headlines because you're married to the former U.S. Attorney,'" he said. "I would tell her, 'If you ever get busted, you know, don't be driving the Mercedes. They'll forfeit it. You've got to be super cautious. You've got to keep it separate and apart from me. If there's a search warrant on the house or something, I can't be involved.'"

And so they lived with this family secret for more than a decade.

There were many close calls. One time, Ben had locked his bedroom door and didn't respond when his mom called to him. Thinking he was hurt or worse, Cindy frantically phoned the police for help. When she agreed to let the cop kick in the door, her teenager wasn't even there. But his pipe and a marijuana grinder were lying on a nightstand in plain sight. Cindy broke into tears and told the officer the drug paraphernalia belonged to her. He let her off and she breathed a heavy sigh of relief.

These kinds of events went on until November 2010, when the issue of medical marijuana went back to Arizona voters for a third time and they passed a referendum to legalize it by a hair, with a 4,000-vote margin. Mel remembers coming home from work that evening to find Cindy in tears. She was watching the coverage on the ten o'clock news. Through her sobs, she told him she was so relieved that she and Ben would no longer have to hide.

More than two years later, despite foot-dragging on the part of the state, dispensaries were finally opening. Ben had a medical card, and Cindy could purchase the pot he needed without worry. But now, as Mel dialed his wife's mobile number, he had to break it to her that the medicine they believed had saved Ben was in jeopardy once again. He knew this time he could not stand by and let it be overturned. He had to do something bold.

His next call was to Ryan Hurley, a well-known partner at Scottsdale's Rose Law Group, who once described his mission as "defend[ing] the medical program from shortsighted and closed-minded prohibitionists."

The red-haired attorney, with a neatly trimmed beard and mustache, was one of the first lawyers in Arizona to make a career out of cannabis law. Hurley could hardly believe what he was hearing when the former judge revealed his personal connection to the debate over medical marijuana. They talked about the odds of Kavanagh's bill succeeding; at the moment, it seemed likely it would. Mel decided it was time to go public. He would lend his name, his reputation, and his political currency to the fight. He would speak out against Kavanagh's measure at a state capitol hearing where local prosecutors were expected to argue for it.

"The idea was to take these folks on at the legislature, head-on. I would go testify at the legislature, so you get the prosecutors on one side of the room, and I would go up, and as the former U.S. Attorney," Mel explained.

He wasn't just any prosecutor. In the 1980s, McDonald was the face of Arizona's fight against drug trafficking across its rugged 370-mile border with Mexico, handpicked to help draft Reagan's War on Drugs policies at the height of America's efforts to go after the cartels and stem the crack cocaine epidemic. This was during the days that "Just Say No" public service announcements flooded the three broadcast networks and became a household phrase, as First Lady Nancy Reagan traveled the country to evangelize supporters of her antidrug crusade. It was also the era when LAPD police chief Daryl Gates—who once infamously testified on Capitol Hill that "casual drug users ought to be shot," and was later ousted in the wake of outrage over Rodney King's beating—first introduced Drug Abuse Resistance Education, known as D.A.R.E. The popular program, in which uniformed police officers talked tough to teens about the perils of pot, and through which the term "gateway drug" came to be the ultimate warning, would eventually be implemented in 75 percent of America's high schools. This was the world in which Mel McDonald had staked his crime-fighting career. How could a man in his shoes switch sides?

But the way Mel and Cindy saw it, how could he *not*? Next, Hurley said it was time to call the press. They decided to give an exclusive to a well-respected columnist at *The Arizona Republic,* a writer named Laurie Roberts.

Cindy was nervous. They had no idea how the Mormon community would react to the news that they had been breaking the law for so many years. They worried about Ben and how he would be perceived by his peers at church. And, of course, they wondered if Mel's career would be over.

On the morning of February 2, 2013, they slept in a little later than usual and steeled themselves as they gingerly picked up their newspaper from the front steps of their home.

And there it was.

The banner headline "An Unlikely Appeal for Medical Marijuana" was splashed across the front page of Arizona's largest newspaper, along with a beautifully written account of the heartbreak, worry, and shame they had felt for so many years. The column made a strong case for the compassionate use of cannabis. After reading it, they prayed it would make a difference.

Then they checked their voicemail and were stunned.

Judges, lawyers, friends, and even the state president of the Mormon Church—the religious institution that didn't even allow coffee and tea—had privately given their support to Mel and Cindy. There were so many uplifting messages. But one of the most surprising came from one of Mel's most prominent and controversial clients. Yes, even Sheriff Joe Arpaio—the cowboy-boot-wearing Maricopa County lawman who once proclaimed himself "America's Toughest Sheriff," notorious for making prisoners wear pink underwear and housing them in canvas tent cities in Phoenix's 100-plus degree summer heat, and who would later be pardoned by President Donald Trump after he was convicted of contempt for defying a 2011 federal court order to stop racially profiling Latinos—had picked up the phone that morning to say he was behind them. Mel was suddenly everywhere telling his and Cindy's dramatic story.

"There are plenty of folks in Arizona like me—who don't fit the profile of a medical marijuana advocate. We are here and we will use our voices to fight for people like my son. Because to take away my son's marijuana would be like taking insulin away from a Type 1 diabetic or taking pain medications away from a cancer patient because there are some out there who abuse pain medications," he wrote in a February 2013 op-ed in the *Arizona Capitol Times.*

Seventy-five years old and full of passion, he traveled the state speaking on behalf of medicinal marijuana. And, of course, the skilled litigator made the rounds on all the local TV news shows, where he pressed his case. Kavanagh's bill swiftly died. Soon, Mel had a brand-new client who hailed from the Jersey Shore and desperately needed his help.

8
THE NEW CANNA CONSUMER

Playa Vista, California
Spring 2013

JUST A FEW traffic-clogged miles away from L.A.'s star-studded hills and breezy Pacific views sat a plain beige building nestled among other plain beige buildings in a commercial district called Playa Vista. Located on the fringes of Los Angeles International Airport, this area was quickly shedding its blue-collar roots as YouTube, Microsoft, Electronic Arts, and The Honest Company moved in, accompanied, predictably, by luxury apartment buildings and $4 million single-family homes. But even before the area had begun to transform into "Silicon Beach," one nondescript structure, buffered by a high-security fence, had long been home to Cashmere, formerly known as Chung & Associates, the marketing firm Ted had founded with his cousin. In less than a decade, it had quietly amassed a roster of high-profile clients that read like a who's who of corporate America: Nestlé. PepsiCo. Adidas. BMW. Google. Netflix.

The headquarters was far from flashy. It operated under the radar, a bit like Ted himself, whose low-key office was crowded with Snoop memorabilia and a prodigious collection of hip-hop action figures. An autographed photo of the cerebral Korean entrepreneur shaking hands with President Barack Obama sat sandwiched between a boxed T-Pain toy microphone set and a camo-clad talking Master P doll. On the walls hung a framed black-and-white photo of a stone-faced Snoop in a do-rag and Ted's Wharton diploma. A cluttered coffee table in front of a quilted white leather couch was home to a cluster of hot sauce bottles representing every ethnic tradition under the sun: sriracha, Cholula, Louisiana, Frank's, even sambal oelek chili paste. They symbolized the cautionary tale of Tabasco, the peppery condiment ubiquitous in restaurants all across the United States when Ted's dad emigrated from South Korea in the 1950s to study engineering at the University of Oklahoma. According to Ted, in a story he often shared, Tabasco had lost a chunk of its market share because it hadn't paid attention to the changing tastes of a diversifying America. The company's missed opportunity crystallized his own mission.

"In 2042, this country will be majority multicultural. So every brand has to think about it," he explained of his drive to always be one step ahead of emerging trends. And he was convinced the next major trend—and budding business opportunity—was going to be in cannabis. He believed legalization efforts were just getting started and would soon spread across the country—and the world.

The two-story space also doubled as home base for Stampede Management, the nerve center of Snoop Dogg's business development operations. The reception area was sparse, except for the walls, which displayed an array of colorful canvases that the entertainer had painted during the rare downtime when he wasn't on tour.

Managing e-commerce deals from a small first-floor office, next door to Ted's, was a ponytailed young woman who had started with the company as an intern only eighteen months before. Like her boss and mentor, Tiffany Chin had attended the prestigious undergrad program at Wharton; and, like Ted, she couldn't have been less pretentious. After a stint as a Wharton teaching assistant, Tiffany had tried her hand at consulting and found it utterly unfulfilling. She knew she had to be honest with herself. What she really wanted to do was work in showbiz. She scoured the Web for opportunities to break in and finally applied for an internship at Stampede. Three days and two short phone interviews later, she packed up all of her belongings and hopped on a flight bound for the West Coast—and hadn't looked back since. With instincts, tenacity, and a confident smile that belied her twenty-three years, Tiffany quickly rose through the ranks to a full-time job overseeing Snoop's work with brands like G Pen, Colt 45, and Adidas. And now that Ted and Snoop were eyeing big investments in legalized weed, she was poised to take charge of a key piece of the business.

It had all been set in motion the moment Ted and Snoop returned from the India trip. Ted was convinced that legalization efforts were just getting started, and now he was looking at the future of cannabis through the Wharton lens of supply chains, revenue modeling, margins, and ROI. It was a B-school case study like none other. As soon as he had recovered from the jet lag, he immediately got to work.

He and Snoop were determined to get in on the ground floor. But the fast evolution of the laws around cannabis presented a steep learning curve. If they were going to go for the green in a big way, they needed real-time intelligence and analysis with scholarly depth. Why not form a cannabis "think tank" to keep them apprised of all the latest research?

And so, amid the action figures and the hot sauce, they convened a sort of Brookings Institution for weed. Ted recruited a brain trust of friends with regulatory, legal, and finance prowess to supplement what he already knew about the illicit market for marijuana. Tiffany stepped up as a key lieutenant, as did Nick Adler, an entertainment lawyer who was working with her on Snoop's branding and business development. Evan Eneman, who was by then the president of the Wharton Club of Southern California, signed on, too. A trained pastry chef who grew up on Long Island, Evan had spent more than a decade at PricewaterhouseCoopers advising Fortune 100 clients on assurance, operations, strategy, cybersecurity, and privacy.

Over several months, the tight-knit group set off on a fact-finding mission to investigate every aspect of the legal framework that would shape the new marijuana businesses on the horizon. They visited dozens and dozens of indoor and outdoor grows, and toured dispensaries of every shape and size across North America, Asia, Africa, and Europe. They were on a quest to track down any and all investment opportunities that might exist once state bans began to fall away.

The clock was ticking. Rocky Mountain State voters had approved a constitutional amendment to end the ban in November 2012, and pot would be legally available for over-21 sales like alcohol on January 1, 2014. This made for a frenzied waiting period as everyone anticipated the new rules and regulations, which would most likely differ from the oversight of medical marijuana that had been in place since 2009. Mostly, this was guesswork. Recreational marijuana was a whole new ball game. And ironically, one of the most steadfast opponents of legalization—Governor John Hickenlooper—was now charged with overseeing the launch of the program he had fought from its earliest days.

It would be a crucial time for Ted and his team to gear up and eventually put boots on the ground. To decipher which business opportunities were most promising, they needed to try to understand the complex intersection of politics and commerce in Colorado and other potential new markets. This new hyper-local industry would be highly regulated; that much was certain. But because it was all still being invented in real time, there was no playbook for how it would work. They would have to write their own. After three months, the think tank convened in Playa Vista to lay out a battle plan. It read like a corporate mission statement on your typical PowerPoint deck.

Number one, the experts agreed that Snoop and Ted should get into the cannabis content business. It was clear the counterculture was going mainstream, and they were in the right place at the right time to pounce.

"Like *Rolling Stone* had captured the moment for the rock and roll community when rock and roll evolved into a mindset and a generational moment," Ted explained of the idea behind launching a cannabis media company, which would come to be named Merry Jane.

They could leverage their Hollywood know-how and contacts and start creating compelling TV shows, documentaries, digital media, and more that would resonate with audiences beyond old-school stoners. No one needed another *Harold & Kumar* movie. They had to create story lines beyond college kids jonesing for their next White Castle run and instead produce compelling content for the tastemakers of Middle America. With Snoop's global platform, they reasoned they could drive the conversation to help normalize marijuana use. And they had some unconventional ideas about whom to partner with. That part of the story would evolve over time.

The second recommendation was that Ted and Snoop raise a "modest" investment fund of $25 million to take advantage of the early deals that were already coming their way—like the startup founded by an ex–U.S. Army Special Forces soldier who created odor-resistant packaging, made from the material used for body bags. Or the company that was formulating a new kind of vaporizer pen whose cartridge wouldn't get clogged by thick cannabis oil. Innovation was exploding, and they had an inside track. But as long as marijuana remained federally unlawful, they decided, they would stay away from owning stakes in companies that were directly "touching the plant"—meaning no grows, no extraction or manufacturing operations, and no dispensaries. Instead, they would focus on getting a piece of ventures that operated "around the plant": that is, those offering solutions for navigating this highly regulated industry, like compliance- and inventory-tracking software, agricultural technology, packaging, and scientific lab equipment. It was far from sexy. But it was potentially lucrative. Plus, no one was going to get arrested for producing plastics or writing code while they waited for the U.S. government to end the prohibition on pot. For now, they figured, the fund would be the vehicle to mine their fortunes from the "picks and shovels" of the emerging sector, rather than seeds and soil.

And third, even if they weren't going to grow the plant themselves, the think tank determined that the time was right for Snoop to explore licensing: that is, putting his name on someone else's product. (Again, they didn't want to touch flower, so this would keep them one step removed.) But before finding a partner, they needed to see if Snoop's brand would have weight in the marketplace, and how best to showcase it. Tiffany took the lead on that one. She consulted with major talent agencies William Morris and CAA to assess Snoop and the degree to which people associated him with cannabis. At the time, there were three major celebrity players in the marijuana game: country music legend Willie Nelson, the late reggae star Bob Marley (or more accurately, his estate, which decided to lend his name to a new marijuana startup), and comedian Tommy Chong of Cheech & Chong fame. When the analysis came back to Tiffany, it showed that Snoop's brand recognition trumped all three combined. Plus, he already had a formidable platform to promote the products. He was still making music. He was still touring. He physically embodied the brand and could call it out everywhere—from live onstage to his multitude of media appearances to all of his social media channels.

"We were like, 'We have a real moneymaker here,'" Tiffany recalled.

The team decided the brand needed to evoke luxury, a California laid-back feel of blue skies and palm trees, while incorporating the singer-songwriter's iconic style and, of course, his famous West Coast street lingo. *Fo shizzle,* as Snoop might say. But most important, it needed to appeal to the average consumer, the person who wasn't a regular marijuana user like the rapper. Their initial research showed that women would be prime customers in the era of casual cannabis use. And to that end, the artist once known for lyrics that objectified women enlisted the creativity of a female-led design team from Pentagram to help shape the brand. The highbrow design firm already had a prestigious roster of clients that included Shake Shack, Samsung Galaxy, and *Saturday Night Live,* for which the company produced the opening sequences for several seasons, including the show's fortieth anniversary.

The designers set off to create sleek, clean, white Apple Store–like packaging with pops of eye-catching purple, red, and orange to form a distinct brand identity: one that would set the products apart from the hippie-dippie packaging with giant marijuana leaves and tie-dye reminiscent of the old-school head shops. This needed to feel new and upscale. And yes, legit. The result was what would come to be named "Leafs By Snoop," or LBS. In a wink to the stoner set, LBS is also shorthand for *pounds,* as in "moving pounds," aka selling marijuana.

The final LBS logo evolved into a more angular version of a golden marijuana leaf. Inside each package, memorable lyrics and Snoopisms—such as *Ooouuuweeee* or *Puff, puff pass*—would be playfully commemorated on brightly colored stickers, adorned with Snoop's loopy handwriting in gold. On the back would appear directions from the master himself for how to use each product, like *Now, grind it, roll it, light it.*

Because Colorado was the first place the products could be legally grown, manufactured, and sold (to the over-21 market), the team needed to find a local partner to license their brand. It would have to be someone with the expertise and the scale to produce a wide range of white-label goods in Snoop's name—and someone who would meet the entertainer's high standards. Tiffany and Ted quickly homed in on a fearless serial entrepreneur named John Desmond Lord, who had relocated from New Zealand to Denver.

A fifty-four-year-old father of three who gave off a rugged adventurer's vibe with his Kiwi accent, head of silvery blond hair, and goatee, Lord had spent his youth tending dairy cows on his family's farm in a tiny town near Auckland, and made his first fortune manufacturing and selling baby seats and crib accessories to retailers like Walmart, Toys"R"Us, and JCPenney in more than thirty countries, including the United States. Ever since he'd sold his global baby supply company in 2013, he'd been ostensibly retired. But a life of leisure didn't suit him for long. He grew restless and started looking for a new entrepreneurial challenge. He knew the ins and outs of running a business under tight government scrutiny, given his past expertise with baby products and their rigorous consumer safety standards. Cannabis intrigued him, plus he was already living in Colorado when the state launched its medical market. So Lord began by renting out some of his commercial real estate property to marijuana growers and learning the business from the inside out. By the time Colorado voters passed Amendment 64, he was well on his way to building out a massive growing, processing, and retail operation.

According to projections, by 2019 Desmond's brand, Enlightened Health (LivWell), was expected to amass fifteen retail stores, with each store selling $20,000 in products per day. That extrapolates to $2.1 million a week, or $109 million per year. It was big-time. Tiffany was impressed by the company's footprint, trajectory, and professionalism. The deal they struck over two years of negotiations was the very first arrangement to lend Snoop's name to what would become one of the widest-selling products across Colorado.

From the start, they had worked furiously on the consumer experience, trying to figure out which products would sell the best. It was well known that Snoop was a flower smoker, so it was a given that LBS would offer premium bud to grind and smoke. However, the entertainer was not a fan of edibles, and according to Tiffany, this was common knowledge.

This presented a challenge, given that industry analysts including their own think tank had reason to believe that for many novice consumers, especially the Chardonnay moms who represented a key customer target, eating a gummy or chocolate would be much more palatable than rolling a joint, puffing on a vaporizer, or hitting a "dab rig," a pipe that holds a waxy and highly potent THC concentrate. If they wanted to appeal to the growing canna-curious market and especially the female one, edible marijuana needed to be in their plans. They would have to approach it thoughtfully.

But once Colorado's recreational market launched in January 2014, edibles had begun to spur controversy as news reports of children getting rushed to the ER after eating marijuana-infused candies alarmed parents and politicians alike. Then, *New York Times* columnist Maureen Dowd brought a national spotlight to the issue when she penned a harrowing personal account of what happened when she ate too much of a medicated chocolate bar and got violently ill. "I barely made it from the desk to the bed, where I lay curled up in a hallucinatory state for the next eight hours," she wrote of having had one too many nibbles of a candy that was meant to contain sixteen servings but wasn't labeled properly.

By October of that year, the Associated Press reported that the state health department was proposing to ban all forms of edible marijuana, "to make it easier to keep kids from overdosing." But not long after, the *Times* followed up with a story that "the proposal had not gained much traction." After all, edibles were big business, making up half the state's recreational sales at the time, according to *The Denver Post*. To regulators, it seemed easier to demand that purveyors fix the packaging than to ban this popular category.

Tiffany and the branding team she hired from Pentagram were closely watching all of this unfold. Given the spike in ER visits and two untimely deaths that had occurred that spring, they knew they needed to ensure that LBS containers for any THC-infused edibles met the strict and fast-changing standards imposed by the state. They also knew that in order to assuage the anxieties of the inexperienced consumer, particularly the moms worried about their kids breaking into their secret stash, the pristine white packages would now also have to include precise dosing directions and clear warnings, along with dependably tamper-proof containers.

In December 2014—after months of curating the strains worthy of Snoop's name, and experimenting in the LivWell kitchen for the right flavors for his LBS edibles—Tiffany and Ted thought it was time for Snoop to experience the fruits of his team's tireless labor firsthand. So Tiffany arranged to bring Snoop to Denver for the big reveal—a tasting like none other. But it had to be top secret. Tiffany wanted to keep the LBS launch quiet until just the right moment, and the official unveiling of the brand was still eleven months out.

This trip had to be stealthy and speedy. Somehow, the rap icon arrived in the Mile High City with his entourage and a few close friends in tow—including his cousin and fellow cannabis connoisseur, rapper Daz Dillinger—undetected by the news media and the paparazzi. This was no time to do press; Snoop was here to inspect every aspect of his new partner's business, a job he appeared to take seriously. Tiffany and Ted captured Snoop on video studiously taking in the rows and rows of maturing cannabis plants, with their delicate conical buds flowering under the bright lights of LivWell's massive commercial indoor cannabis farm. And once Snoop had finished inspecting the plants themselves, he asked questions about the growing techniques and genetics.

When the sun went down, he smoked. It wasn't for fun. This was work . . . quality control. He tried LivWell's wide array of indica-dominant strains, a category of cannabis that induces a mellow, sleepy high. Each one offered a unique effect, potency, flavor, and aroma with notes that ranged from earthy to piney to vanilla to lemony. With the help of his friends, eventually he narrowed down his favorites to five. As a connoisseur, Snoop had very distinct preferences and only enjoyed smoking indica varietals. Which meant he needed someone with an objective point of view and a critical palate to try the sativa-dominant choices, the strains that bring on a more energetic, creative buzz. He turned to Tiffany, the former intern turned branding maven, to weigh in. Suddenly she had become a cannabis tester for one of the biggest superstars on the planet. She was on the hot seat to smoke up in front of the star and his posse and decide which three sativas would bear Snoop's name. And if all that wasn't surreal enough, next she had to present to him the proposed flavors for his edibles, which they had affectionately branded "Dogg Treats." The pièce de résistance was an array of fruit chews that had the same full mouthfeel as the drugstore candies Snoop loved—like fruity Starburst and Skittles, and Now & Later taffy—and came in familiar flavors like lemon cherry, strawberry, and raspberry. (According to Tiffany, the chews would go on to become so popular, dispensaries couldn't keep them on the shelves.) Snoop also loved Jolly Ranchers and all kinds of gummy bears, so the team of culinary experts set to work on a prototype of a hard candy with the consistency of a sucker, as well as a gummy. And because the Doggfather was also known to have a weakness for Reese's Peanut Butter Cups, the chefs whipped up something they called a "peanut butter gem," shaped in Snoop's signature LBS angular logo and dusted with golden cocoa powder. All of these were carefully prepared in virgin versions at first, so the singer-songwriter could sample the flavors without getting high. In the end, he loved them all.

LBS finally made its public debut the following fall. It had been two years in the making by this point. But instead of a big blowout bash at a hip nightclub to unveil their top secret project, Tiffany arranged for an intimate yet extravagant private party at LivWell owner John Lord's suburban Denver mansion. She kept the exclusive guest list short and upstanding, inviting reporters from *Rolling Stone* and *Time* along with the local news media, a handful of state lawmakers, bureaucrats from Colorado's Marijuana Enforcement Division (the oversight agency for cannabis in the state), and attorney Brian Vicente, one of the co-authors of Amendment 64, the constitutional amendment that legalized recreational weed.

When it was time for the big announcement, Snoop personally greeted the VIPs on a small stage, then showed a brief video (narrated by Tiffany) that introduced all of the LBS products, including the eight flower strains, and explained how those strains would be infused into oils for the fair-trade chocolate bars, peanut butter gems, fruit chews, and gummies, as well as two types of concentrates called shatter and wax.

"Since I've been at the forefront of this movement for over twenty years now, I'm a master of marijuana. So naturally, my people can trust that I picked out the finest, freshest products in the game," Snoop proudly told the room, and then grinned as he invited them to join him in the festivities. "Let's medicate, elevate, and put it in the air."

That's when the party really started. Snoop beckoned his curious guests into the next room, where the walls and windows were draped in gold lamé fabric from floor to ceiling. Three pretty, young women in white T-shirts with shiny golden LBS logos presided over long tables lined with glass jars filled with LBS buds; trays of hand-blown glass pipes, grinders, and rolling papers; and a colorful array of the new edibles. They began rolling joints and packing pipes, which Snoop happily puffed and passed as he mingled with those who eagerly partook; he even graciously posed for photos with them. About thirty minutes later, the rapper emerged as "DJ Snoopadelic," and began spinning a set of Prince, Tupac, and Rihanna tunes for the revelers. When Snoop's familiar refrain, "La da da duh-dah"—the opening notes of Dr. Dre's 2000 hit "The Next Episode" with its famous final line, "Smoke weed every daaaay!"—came on, the crowd went wild as the star rapped along with himself on the track.

The next morning, the products were already lining LivWell's dispensary shelves, ready for purchase. The rollout had been a success. It had been a make-or-break moment for Tiffany, the dutiful daughter of Taiwan-born immigrants, who had not long ago veered off of her respectable career track: a teaching post at an Ivy League business school and a cushy management consulting job. She had traded it all for the Hollywood high life. Literally. And now she had secured her place at the company, inside Snoop and Ted's exclusive inner circle, and in the annals of marijuana history.

9 THE MAGIC SEEDS

Smiths Falls, Ontario

November 2013

THE OLD HERSHEY'S factory looked "like something out of a zombie movie" when Tweed moved in. In the wake of a 2008 union dispute, the candy maker had returned all the "top secret" equipment back to the mother ship in Pennsylvania. Anything that wasn't auctioned off was left behind to gather dust. Bruce Linton and Chuck Rifici would redesign the front entrance and office areas later. For now, they were focused on the Herculean task of figuring out how to grow massive amounts of marijuana. One thing they did know: the first thing they needed to do was to buy the seeds to get them started.

Fortunately, seeds were not in short supply. Just like in the fairy tale "Jack and the Beanstalk," it seemed as if every medical marijuana grower in Canada and his granddad had magic seeds to sell to these new purveyors of pot. As soon as the founders of Tweed Marijuana found out they had been selected by the government to be one of the first twelve firms to supply cannabis to all of Canada, there was no time to waste. The government was already predicting it would be a $1.3 billion industry by 2024, before the legal harvests even started. So they ran out to buy the best seeds from the only legal source they could—the home growers across the nation who had been allowed to harvest a certain quantity of pot lawfully in their basements or backyards since 2001. Those tens of thousands of private micro-grows would soon be outlawed, and pot production would be turned over to a handful of new commercial enterprises like Tweed. The twist was that the home growers were the only ones with the keys to unlock their successors' future profits. They owned the intellectual property—the genetic formulas behind the most potent and popular cannabis strains—and, of course, the seeds themselves. Naturally, some of them wanted to cash in on this Green Rush, too.

Then there was the matter of honor. From Vancouver to Quebec, growers who for years had tended to their plants under bright lights in their garages and backyard greenhouses were so fiercely proud of their progeny, it often sounded as if they were boasting of their very own family lineage. They touted their hearty personal stock and spoke of "mothers"—the female plants that had been bred to birth future generations of unique cannabis cultivars, each with its own distinct and sought-after traits passed down from its forebears. They promised tall stalks, wide leaves, and bulbous blooms thick with trichomes, the tiny crystals containing the sought-after mind-altering and anti-inflammatory cannabinoids THC and CBD, the most well known of the 100-plus botanical compounds that determine the end product's aroma, flavor, and intended effect.

Whether you wanted something to make you feel sleepy, hungry, giddy, or any other desired sensation, these self-educated botanists claimed to have bred the very best one for that purpose, designating each type with funky names like OG Kush, Girl Scout Cookie, and White Widow. It was foreign nomenclature to the uninitiated, and there was no official registry or database by which to confirm the lineage or authenticity of the claims. Did these growers really own the secret sauce? And would they truly be willing to sell these hard-won trade secrets? The only way Tweed's cofounders could be sure about the seeds they had purchased was by planting them all, watching them grow, and then testing them for potency in a lab. And they only had four months to do it, before the Feds would close the window for purchasing the necessary "starting materials." So they bought up as many strains as they could and brought them back to the old chocolate factory—all under the watchful eye of Health Canada bureaucrats, who themselves were feeling their way in the dark as this new way of doing business took shape.

Among many things the Hershey's plant didn't have at the time was a vault to stash the seeds. This presented an unforeseen hitch when Chuck first arrived back in Smiths Falls with five thousand seeds in hand. He had never planted anything before in his life. He had downloaded to his Kindle a couple of how-to books on growing pot, and, after about thirty minutes, determined that the agricultural operation he needed to build out required sophisticated expertise. But suddenly, on this night, as he recalls, he had no choice except to roll up his sleeves and get started. He found out the new regulations mandated that if there was no safe, the seeds would have to be planted on the spot. The naïve CEO and three other employees on the payroll, including a recently hired master grower from the United States, were barred from leaving the premises until every last seed was in the soil. So they pulled a dizzying all-nighter burrowing each and every one into careful rows. Luckily, as Chuck would joke later, "there's a reason they call it weed." The seeds quickly started sprouting.

Bruce and Chuck managed not to kill any of their very first plants. But there were so many other missteps. And they were costly. By the end of 2013, after only one month of operations, Tweed had already lost close to a million dollars, according to its unaudited reports. The stumbles were fast and furious as Chuck and the team tried to figure out the proper amount of light, the optimal temperature and humidity of the grow rooms, how much water and fertilizer the plants needed, and so on. In the first few months after getting off the ground, Tweed lost its most delicate harvests to powdery mildew and mold; it turned out that these rookie growers had allowed visitors to touch the plants without taking proper measures against contamination.

On top of everything, the factory itself needed lots of work, including a new industrial roof, which ended up costing a million dollars, and the air-conditioning system and ductwork they installed in one of the first grow rooms ended up costing nearly five times what they had expected. And the self-anointed "experts" from the marijuana underworld, whom Chuck and Bruce had imported from the United States to offer their sage advice, only added to the confusion. The problem was, there was no consensus on best practices. Every consultant had a conflicting point of view, often informed by superstition, tribal practice, or folklore. The more Chuck and Bruce tried to sift through all of the advice, the more time and money they wasted trying to crack a code that didn't exist.

But even though they made so many painful mistakes in the early years, Bruce later said he was grateful for having learned that trial and error was the only way to get ahead in this business. They couldn't be afraid to fail. The LED lights they thought would be more cost-efficient in the grow rooms ended up not giving off enough heat. They at first hired any hourly workers they could find to trim the mature buds off the plants in preparation for drying, and quickly figured out the delicate job required more than just any pair of hands. They realized burly, tattooed guys didn't trim nearly as fast as the nimble beauticians they ultimately recruited, who were well versed in wielding a pair of scissors while holding a conversation at the same time. Another invaluable lesson emerged when the affable founders discovered, a little too late, that the trusted CFO they had recruited, with his crusty personality and sensible work boots, didn't really like to use computers and preferred to write out the ledgers in scrawling longhand instead of plugging expenses into software-powered spreadsheets. They had to let go of one of their first key hires and start all over again. And on and on.

"It's a bit like becoming the 'most improved' hockey player on the team. If you start really bad, you can move up," Bruce quipped years later.

Case in point, he gestured to rows of potted plants through a large glass window, explaining how propagating the next generation works best when the cuttings are taken from the top leaves.

"How do we know we want to do that?" he rhetorically asked a group of fifty visiting investors trying to keep up with his breakneck explanations and stories. "We ask the plants. So we did an A-B comparison on 'Is it better?' Everybody has a theory. Chop part of the plant off, decrease photosynthesis, less risk on the plant, more energy to the roots. Some say, 'Never cut a plant, it's the worst thing you could ever do.' I don't give a shit, just try them both! And so, we try them both and all of a sudden it turns out you actually get faster, higher concentration, better rooting, by doing these steps."

Taking risks was something he'd learned growing up on his family's small farm, where breaking and fixing things kept him and his brother out of trouble. According to Bruce, the company had probably made more mistakes than any other cannabis producer in Canada, but that wasn't a bad thing. The team *needed* to mess up in order to learn which plants were best to grow and how to keep them healthy, and to solve the biggest and most lucrative puzzle of all: which varieties would yield the most product in the least amount of time.

"When you start breeding, you don't try to just breed for like 'How could I make it purple or smelly or super-high THC?' You might say, 'How can I, on an annual basis, get an extra turn per year per room?'" Bruce explained. This was the crux of growing cannabis at scale. And there were no models to turn to, given that no grower in Canada had yet turned a legitimate crop of this size—and certainly not in the United States, either. And yet, here in Smiths Falls, Bruce and Chuck's original plan had been to harvest and dry 15,000 kilograms, enough to supply all of Canada's 39,000 patients, as Bruce would later tell famed *Shark Tank* investor and commentator Kevin O'Leary in an interview on the CBC.

As the March 2014 deadline approached for Tweed to get its

hands on whatever seeds it could, the company was running out of cash. At the same time, its harvests were not yielding what they had hoped.

"We were spending money like drunken sailors," Chuck would later admit. But the grand plan to take the company public was still racing ahead.

The only way to raise the millions they needed to keep going was to go to Bay Street, the Wall Street of Canada, and offer shares of the company to investment banks willing to take a gamble on Tweed in the hope that, ultimately, they would be able to resell its stock to everyman investors. This wouldn't be a typical IPO. Instead, they would list Tweed on the Toronto Venture Exchange (TSX-V) by taking over a defunct company that was already listed. The strategy, called a "reverse takeover," or RTO, would chart a course for other Canadian cannabis ventures. And later, U.S.-based companies, including Beth Stavola's, would follow Tweed's lead to tap into cash from the public markets up north.

But perhaps more than money, what this startup really needed to survive was brand recognition. Tweed needed to stand out from the pack, but because the new Canadian cannabis corporations were barred by the government from advertising, their only hope of gaining market share was to earn some major publicity to help educate patients and doctors who would be writing recommendations for the new pot products that could now be obtained through the mail. Bruce and Chuck knew from the start that selling the company's stock to the public would make an instant media splash and lend credibility to the fledgling brand, without running afoul of government rules—and without spending a penny on PR.

It worked.

"Bruce knew that as a public company, he could advertise by talking about his company. He also believed getting support from the marketplace early was key," said Steve Ottaway, managing director of GMP Securities, the first investment bank to organize institutional funding of the company.

The spotlight on Tweed going public raised its profile, and Bruce emerged as its chief pitchman, evangelizing the promise of Big Marijuana to patients while simultaneously tantalizing investors eager to get in on the Green Rush. The nerdy former tech CEO, with his folksy Canadian accent and plainspoken manner, suddenly became the new face of legalized cannabis. On April 4, 2014, the day Tweed debuted on Canada's stock exchange, it was valued at $89 million. And that valuation only continued to climb as the months went by, making some of its very first employees overnight millionaires and bringing unexpected prosperity to the formerly downtrodden hamlet of Smiths Falls.

But behind the scenes, with its call center buzzing with orders, Tweed was still struggling to produce enough cannabis to supply the demand. Expenses were mounting daily, along with the pressure to perform now that the company had attracted the media spotlight. As if that weren't enough, the company even had a run-in with the Royal Canadian Mounted Police the very week it went public, when the Mounties seized a cache of 700 kilograms of marijuana stashed in fifty hockey bags and boxes in the belly of a plane at the Kelowna airport in British Columbia. When it turned out the bags were bound for Tweed and another company (Mettrum) that Tweed would later acquire, the *National Post* reported, it raised questions about whether the cannabis producers had been transporting illicit product to make up for the shortfall, even after Tweed immediately issued a statement saying it believed it was complying with Health Canada's rules.

In the boardroom, things were about to hit a boiling point.

All of it came to a furious head in the summer of 2014 during a reported clash between the two founders. It seemed that Smiths Falls wasn't big enough for the both of them, and Chuck was ultimately fired by the board over allegations of mismanagement, including "consistently missed targets and milestones" in the construction of the original factory, and a potential conflict of interest in taking a loan from a contractor, according to a 2018 report in the *Ottawa Citizen*. He was shown the door in August 2014, and vacated his seat on the board shortly after.

"I knew I was never going to win the battle of the younger CEO entrepreneur making all those mistakes versus the more senior chairman who does the raising of the money for the company. One looks like a much better bet than the other, if you have to choose. And it became clear that we weren't going to be able to continue on together," he would reflect five years later, after both sides had dropped their lawsuits against each other.

With Bruce at the helm, the company continued to expand. Health Canada was suddenly inundated with hundreds of applications from entrepreneurs who also wanted their own shot at a billion-dollar market, and Canadian marijuana stocks heated up like never before, with average Joes and Janes betting their retirement savings on the promise of pot.

But the frenzy fueled by Green Rush dreams had only just begun. In October 2015, a progressive candidate for prime minister bested the Conservatives on a popular platform that included ending pot prohibition once and for all. The telegenic Justin Trudeau, son of a former prime minister, won handily and quickly announced plans to legalize marijuana across the country—making it the first industrialized nation in the world to allow adults to lawfully buy cannabis for recreational use. The idea that smoking marijuana out in the open would one day be as socially acceptable as drinking a Molson wasn't a pipe dream anymore. It was the future, and it was coming soon. Sooner than anyone could have thought. And now more than ever, companies like Tweed, which was renamed Canopy Growth Corporation in 2015, would be jockeying for position both at home and abroad, as Canada was signaling to the global investment community that it was open for business. While America dragged its feet on legalization with political infighting and puritanical debates, Canada positioned itself as a pot superpower, the first developed nation to export cannabis across the planet.

As all of this unfolded, Ted Chung and his team were busy launching Leafs By Snoop in Colorado, and making their first investments in canna tech. But they were paying attention to the news north of the border. Snoop's tenacious business partner felt in his gut that Canada held big opportunities they couldn't afford to miss.

10
NEW SHERIFF IN TOWN

Prescott, Arizona
April 2013

As she made her way to the century-old courthouse to face down the bandit threatening to destroy her business, echoes of the Wild West greeted Beth Stavola with every *click-clack* of her Chanel heels. On the tidy square of lawn leading to the columned Yavapai Superior Court stood an imposing bronze monument of a macho mustachioed cowboy tugging on the reins of a whinnying horse: a memorial to Sheriff William Owen "Buckey" O'Neill, the heroic militiaman and mayor of Prescott, who fought on the front lines of the legendary fire that torched the mining town's infamous Whiskey Row.

On July 14, 1900, a blazing fire originating from a candle that had fallen on a mattress in an empty hotel room, leveled the town's busy saloons and brothels—along with the rest of downtown Prescott. But the cowboys, gamblers, and painted ladies who frequented the busy establishments didn't let a few flames interfere with a good time. As the story goes, they pulled a twenty-four-foot carved oak bar from the wreckage of the Palace Saloon and lugged it across the street to keep the revelry going while the fire burned through the night. Now, more than a hundred years later, behind the courthouse plaza, it's tourists rather than local cattle ranchers who are more likely to belly up to the refurbished bars on Whiskey Row. But the associations with sin and vice—and the memories of crime-fighting posses led by men like Sheriff Buckey, chasing down desperadoes in the pine forests of old Prescott—lingered everywhere you looked. It seemed a fitting scene for Beth and her own posse, led by the unimpeachable former prosecutor Mel McDonald, as they marched into the courtroom to take on Vince Diorio, an outlaw so brazen he had even signed his own name when he illicitly purchased a cache of automatic rifles and pistols at a local gun show.

It was a cool, dry morning, and as Beth tentatively stepped inside the entrance of the Yavapai courthouse, her eyes widened at the sight of a sign pointing to a spot for gun-carrying visitors to hang up their holsters. *I can't believe I'm going into court to face off against a derelict and convicted felon in a place where they're hanging their guns on the wall,* she thought to herself. She sure wasn't in Jersey anymore.

Everything leading up to this moment had been a blur. Beth and her husband, Jack, had decided to invest in Arizona's nascent medical cannabis industry only a few months before. It had been a bumpy ride from the very start, culminating with the recent news that the man leading the venture on the ground had hidden his true identity and his criminal record with a false Social Security number. It turned out, after a private investigator uncovered his ruse, that Vince Diorio was a violent criminal who had served time in federal prison for attempted robbery, and had been stealing tens of thousands of dollars from their business. In the last two weeks, Beth had been dropped from her original law firm because the partners were concerned that taking on Diorio, who claimed to be connected to New York organized crime families, imperiled them all. In desperation, she had enlisted the help of a lawyer and high-profile medical marijuana advocate to help push Diorio out of their partnership.

She remembered dialing former U.S. Attorney Mel McDonald at his home office not knowing if he would even take her call. He had just helped sink the last-ditch attempt in the Arizona legislature to repeal medical marijuana, and was now traveling around the state testifying at local zoning hearings and doing media interviews reiterating his support for medicinal cannabis. But as soon as McDonald heard what Beth was facing, he felt compelled to get involved. He knew all too well that medical marijuana in Arizona was in its infancy and still very contentious. In his view, Beth's situation could become a scandal that would give ammunition to politicians who would like nothing better than to see the program wiped out.

"Beth, I don't know where it's going to land, but we got to get rid of this guy. He's going to not only hurt you, but he's going to hurt the entire industry," McDonald recalled telling his new client. All he could think about was what would happen to his son, Ben, if the law was overturned once again. He couldn't let that happen. So he signed on to represent Beth in her suit against Diorio, in hopes of getting him out of the picture for good.

Suing Diorio flew in the face of the sober advice Beth initially received from her husband's lawyer, who told her the fight wasn't worth it, especially if Diorio really did have ties to the mob, as he had bragged. Whatever his connections, Jack's lawyer had said, it was clear that Diorio himself was volatile and vengeful. Her family's safety was more important than winning. He told her she should just sell the business to Diorio for a dollar and walk away.

But true to her nature, Beth couldn't let it go. The Stavolas had already invested a million dollars in buying the land for the pot grow and building out the massive greenhouse, and she wasn't going to allow Diorio to get away with stealing from her and Jack, any more than she was ready to let him run the business—*her* business—into the ground. And when she talked it through with McDonald, they realized they had more than enough evidence to prove that Diorio was engaging in criminal activity that jeopardized the entire business venture. It would be an open-and-shut case. There were several eyewitnesses ready to testify, and even photographic evidence of Diorio shooting off the guns he wasn't supposed to have. They felt confident the good guys would prevail.

It was April when the court proceedings began, and the Stavolas' school-age children were on spring vacation, so Beth and Jack decided to bring the entire brood to sunny Scottsdale with a nanny in tow. The kids splashed and played in the pool of the well-appointed Phoenician Resort and Spa, located at the foot of Camelback Mountain, while their parents ventured two hours north for their court date with Diorio. Beth was terrified to leave them alone after all of Diorio's threats, so she hired a bodyguard to stay with them under the guise that the hired muscle was actually the nanny's new boyfriend. But her eldest daughter, Frankie, a savvy middle schooler, wasn't buying it. She figured out this well-built stranger was there to watch over them while her parents took care of some mysterious business, "just like Brad Pitt and Angelina Jolie" in the box-office blockbuster *Mr. & Mrs. Smith.*

Beth and Jack may not have been characters in a movie, but there certainly was high drama in the courtroom. When Diorio arrived sporting a brand-new expensive-looking Italian suit and shiny snakeskin shoes, Beth's first thought was that "someone was definitely funding this guy." At six-two, 250 pounds, with slicked-back dark hair, the fifty-three-year-old tough talker cut an intimidating figure. If Diorio wasn't connected to the Mafia, he certainly played the part well.

McDonald presented a number of solid witnesses, including a young man from Colorado who testified that Diorio had paid him a thousand dollars to traffic $5,000 worth of illicit, sought-after strains of marijuana plants to Arizona in an attempt to give the grow operation an illegal jump on the competition. The plan, he said, had been to cultivate the plants in a warehouse, but Diorio had decided that was too risky and decided to store them in his apartment. This testimony implicated Diorio in a host of federal and state crimes, and if it wasn't enough to prove he was threatening the legitimacy of the business venture, McDonald displayed photos of the defendant brandishing the automatic weapons he had purchased illegally and shooting them in the desert.

Diorio insisted on taking the witness stand to defend himself. When McDonald questioned him about the illegal gun purchases, the judge advised him of his Fifth Amendment rights: "Mr. Diorio, you have the right to remain silent. You don't have to answer these questions."

Diorio replied with an arrogant snarl, "I want to answer them." He wasn't about to be the guy who wussed out by pleading the Fifth.

In the end, the showdown lasted less than three days. In addition to the compelling evidence presented by McDonald, it turned out that Diorio still had two pending cases against him for DUI and driving with a suspended license. The judge found in favor of Beth, and Diorio was banned from ever setting foot in the Chino Valley grow ever again.

"We won on every count. We drove him out," recalled McDonald proudly, sounding a bit like an Old West marshal. The last he'd heard, the crook had scurried off to somewhere in California's Emerald Triangle, the northern corner of the state known for supplying, by some estimates, 60 percent of America's illegal marijuana.

The victory in court marked a critical turning point for the Stavolas in more ways than one. On the scenic drive back to Phoenix, McDonald offered them some advice that would prove prophetic. Now that she had succeeded in standing up to this thug, it was time to put some real muscle into oversight, cleaning house, and protecting the venture from the unsavory characters lurking around the cannabis industry. The former prosecutor was connected to a strong network of law enforcement officials across the state. What if Beth recruited some of them to go on the board of her company? McDonald thought it would lend credibility to the business while sending an unwavering message that she represented a new kind of operator in the marijuana trade.

Just as the conniving drug cartels would stop at nothing to preserve their illegal business, Beth would have to be equally ruthless about following the letter of the law, he argued. Why not prove she was running a tight ship by lining the board of directors with ex-cops and respected, upstanding members of the community? Not only could this help forge trusting relationships with the cities and towns where parts of the business resided, McDonald reasoned, it could potentially insulate her from becoming a target of federal raids. Despite Colorado, California, Washington, and Oregon permitting legal marijuana sales at the time, the DEA continued to crack down on state-sanctioned dispensaries and grows, seizing on any missteps. McDonald told her she needed to do whatever she could to prove she was committed to keeping every aspect of her enterprise unquestionably spotless.

And her new mentor had the perfect candidate in mind to help her do it.

Seventy-four-year-old Donald W. Tucker was a former agent of the U.S. Secret Service who'd spent twenty-five years protecting presidents, all the way from Lyndon B. Johnson through George H. W. Bush. It was exciting and dangerous work; once, he'd even been tasked with trying to infiltrate the Black Panthers to stop a potential assassination attempt on Richard Nixon just hours before the president was due to give a speech.

Tucker had served his country through some of the most politically turbulent and socially divisive times in recent history. And he had done it as one of the few agents of color, one whose tendency to call out systemic racism and injustice had earned him the nickname "Tucker the Troublemaker" among his colleagues. He also had firsthand experience with America's drug war and understood its complicated history. In fact, Tucker's very first law enforcement job had been chasing down heroin, cocaine, and marijuana dealers as a young narcotics agent on the front lines of covert operations on Chicago's South Side.

Although he was only five-ten and skinny, Tucker had long dreamed of playing in the NFL. He had even received a football scholarship to the University of Iowa but had never managed to beef up enough to make it to the pros. So, after graduating in 1961, the talented running back soon found himself returning to the rough-and-tumble neighborhood from which his mother desperately wanted him and his three younger brothers to escape.

With his Fu Manchu mustache, grown-out Afro, bell-bottoms, and platform boots, the twenty-two-year-old Don Tucker had held court at seedy dives posing as a tricked-out dope dealer. Tucker recalled spending many nights camped out in smoky bars from dusk until dawn in his very first undercover assignment for the Federal Bureau of Narcotics (FBN), the forerunner of today's Drug Enforcement Administration. He'd been hired as one of the few black detectives serving under the direction of the FBN's infamous commissioner Harry J. Anslinger, America's first "drug czar" and the bureaucrat credited with laying the punitive and racialized foundations that would underlie America's drug policies for generations to come.

Anslinger, who began his career enforcing the ban on alcohol during Prohibition, had led America's war on cannabis beginning with the passing of the Marihuana Tax Act of 1937. He'd served under four U.S. presidents over more than three decades, and was known for calling marijuana "one of the most dangerous and depraving narcotics known" and for the racist overtones in his dire warnings of "hot tamale vendors" selling the evil weed. Through his writings and speeches, he painted an ominous picture of cannabis as the scourge of white America that would drive people to violent crime and "reefer madness." It was his poisonous rhetoric and biased research that ultimately fueled congressional passage of the Boggs Act of 1951, which instituted federal mandatory-minimum sentences for drug offenses. Even after his retirement, Anslinger's bombast gave ammunition to the Nixon administration's 1970 inclusion of cannabis on its list of the most harmful and addictive illegal substances, along with heroin, opium, and cocaine.

Tucker says that even as he pursued pot dealers and users in the early 1960s, he never believed weed to be as dangerous as other illicit substances. But at the time, he was a young man with a good government job and the first in his family with a college degree. Working for the FBN provided an opportunity for a better life, although from the moment he took the position, he often struggled with the racism inherent in the law. Of course, those were different times. The Freedom Rides challenging segregation had only just begun in the summer of 1961, and Congress would not pass the Civil Rights and Voting Rights acts for several more years.

He quickly realized that he had been hired because of the color of his skin. The agency was targeting black neighborhoods, and who better to go undercover than a black agent? Armed with neither a badge nor a weapon—nor any training, for that matter—he was dispatched on his very first night on the job with two hundred dollars in his pocket to make a heroin buy via a sketchy informant high on coke. In his self-published memoir, Tucker would later recall of this era in his career that it was always the black agents who were charged with the fieldwork of grooming informants, posing as users or dealers, and setting up sting operations in the field, putting themselves in potentially deadly situations, often with little or no backup, while their white colleagues managed operations from their desks. And what's worse, he says, the dragnets often nabbed small-time, nonviolent black and brown offenders rather than the high-level "corporate" drug kingpins in suits and ties.

"I have a memory of all the people that I put in jail, that I locked up. There was a situation where a lot of people who were involved in narcotics were not your true criminals," he said with regret. The hypocrisy of it all still haunted him so many decades later.

Disillusioned by the FBN, he ultimately transferred to the Secret

Service when a post came up. He would go on to build a storied career protecting presidents and taking down counterfeiters and check forgers. But by the time McDonald met Tucker in Phoenix in the mid-1980s, it felt like déjà vu all over again; it was the height of the crack cocaine epidemic and President Ronald Reagan had picked up the War on Drugs where Nixon left off. At the time, McDonald was serving as a U.S. Attorney, putting away drug conspirators and crime bosses, while Tucker was running the Secret Service in Arizona. The two had struck up a professional friendship that evolved into a personal one over the years, as McDonald eventually went on to a flourishing practice as a criminal defense attorney and Tucker launched a new career as a private eye and crime novelist in Phoenix. But when McDonald dialed his old pal to tell him about Beth's venture and invite him to get involved as an adviser on security, Tucker was stunned. He couldn't believe his friend was getting into the marijuana business—legal or not. It seemed unbelievable that a onetime federal prosecutor who had spent his career putting away drug dealers was now playing for the other team. Plus, he didn't want to have anything to do with protecting some kooky rich lady from New Jersey trying to build a legal marijuana empire in the backyard of some of America's most notorious drug runners. He paused and shook his head and told his friend in the most respectful way possible, "I can't do this."

FOUR HOURS SOUTHEAST of Phoenix, in a pitch-black Arizona motel room, Beth rolled over and consulted the clock on the nightstand: 2:00 A.M. She had no shortage of things to worry about as she lay wide awake in the king-sized bed in a Holiday Inn less than a mile from the Mexican border. She had insisted to her family she would take this trip alone to Douglas, Arizona, and now wondered if it was really such a bright idea after all. This sleepy city of seventeen thousand ranchers, farmers, and U.S. Customs officials and border agents was a world away from her gated waterfront enclave on the Jersey Shore.

It seemed like an ominous sign that her hotel was just a few blocks from the site of El Chapo's first "James Bond tunnel." It was here, in 1989, that the elusive kingpin had directed lackeys loyal to his vicious Sinaloa gang to dig a subterranean passageway the length of a football field, from a cartel-owned house in Agua Prieta, Sonora, to a nondescript warehouse on the other side of the U.S. border. The entrance to the hidden passageway on the Mexican side was reportedly covered by a billiards table inside the home and could only be accessed through a sophisticated hydraulic system of pulleys activated by turning on a water spigot in the yard.

It was the first of El Chapo's underground systems for smuggling cocaine and other drugs into the United States and, later, for making his brazen getaways from prison. More than two decades after this tunnel was discovered and shut down by the DEA, locals who lived along this stretch of barren desert a hundred miles south of Tucson were still warned to lock their doors at night. Drug and human trafficking continued, despite the U.S. Border Patrol's latest attempt at cracking down on illegal activity by chasing the smugglers on horseback. It was top of mind for Beth as she pulled the thin motel blanket up to her chin. She was staying across the street from the stables.

What the fuck am I doing here? she thought to herself.

As she tossed and turned in the dark, the reality of opening a dispensary in this godforsaken place hit her hard. With its roots in copper smelting, an industry long gone, Douglas was one of the most remote, most desolate places in the entire state of Arizona. To make matters even more challenging, there were only *eleven* registered medical marijuana cardholders in the region at the time—the only patients who could legally purchase pot products for miles and miles.

It would be daybreak soon, and by lunchtime she would find

out if the trip down to the border had been worth it. Just a few months had passed since Vince Diorio assured her that the forty acres she had purchased in the cool, dry hills of central Arizona were the perfect place to build out a sophisticated and expensive indoor marijuana farm. In addition to the real estate, she had already sunk more than $200,000 in specialized lights to grow the plants in a 12,000-square-foot greenhouse—only to find out that the grow would most likely never turn a crop she could sell.

Now she had disentangled herself from Diorio, but when McDonald took a closer look at the cultivation Beth was building, alarm bells went off: turns out, it was uncomfortably close to a local playground. As McDonald—along with another Phoenix lawyer, Charles Houghton, who specialized in government relations—pointed out, while the local zoning technically allowed the grow to exist at that location, its proximity to kids would make it a prime target for federal raids like the ones happening less than five hundred miles away in California. This property would be "ripe for the picking" by the Feds, her legal experts told her. She would have to find another location to set up a whole new farm, or maybe give up on growing altogether and forge a new partnership so she could buy cannabis wholesale.

Once again, her mettle would be put to the test. The good news was that Beth already had some potential new partners in mind. A few months earlier, in the midst of her legal troubles with Diorio, she had been introduced to an earnest mother-daughter team who had run into similar obstacles with bad actors when they tried to get their own medical marijuana business off the ground. The three women met amid the glowing fire pits at the poolside lounge of the Fairmont Scottsdale Princess hotel and immediately hit it off.

What struck Beth at first was that the duo hardly fit the stoner stereotype, what with their corporate pantsuits and down-to-earth Midwestern accents. Michelle Magers, the daughter, was a husky-voiced, green-eyed millennial who worked for the information technology company Qwest. In 2001, a job transfer had brought her and her husband to the booming outskirts of Scottsdale, a world away from the tree-lined suburbs of Columbus, Ohio, where the family had been rooted for generations. Her parents, Sandy and Jim Clifford, were high school sweethearts who a decade before had also made their way to Arizona when Sandy, a longtime insurance executive, jumped at the chance to trade the harsh Ohio winters for sunshine and palm trees. Mom and daughter ended up settling just a few blocks from each other, and soon there were grandkids to raise, too. Over iced tea on many a spring afternoon, they often finished each other's sentences, bubbling with enthusiasm as they sketched out the plans for their nascent business.

The night they met Beth for the very first time, Michelle said she did a double take; she even recalls asking her mom if the actress Cameron Diaz was staying at the Princess. But after some initial small talk, the intimidation wore off and she and Beth started to bond over the fact that they both had been diagnosed with scoliosis as kids. Michelle explained that she had been using tinctures made of CBD to help manage her back pain, while Beth, who received two massages a week as part of her physical therapy, lamented her own discomfort from living with a curved spine and was thinking about trying a CBD skin rub herself.

The three women also found lots of common ground in the hurdles they faced trying to break into the male-dominated world of weed. They talked about the sexism they'd been confronted with throughout their careers and the challenges they navigated as working mothers; Michelle had just given birth to her first child, and Beth's youngest was barely two years old. When Beth confided that a tummy tuck helped her retain her slim figure after having six kids, their friendship was sealed. There was a level of candor none of them had ever felt from other business dealings in the space.

"It's kind of like a best friend that you haven't seen for ten years and then all of a sudden you're back with them and it's like you never were gone. That's the way we felt with Beth," Sandy said with a smile.

Beth felt the same way. Finally, she had fallen in with the "good guys." The night of their first meeting, after a few glasses of wine and lots of laughs, they even came up with a name for their future alliance and maybe even a marijuana strain they might one day be known for: the BSM, for Beth, Sandy, Michelle—or, in badass girl code, Bitches Selling Marijuana.

By August 2013, the BSM partnership was already becoming a reality. With the Diorio nightmare behind her, Beth's plan was to get the approval to open in Douglas and then, eventually, move the store to an area of the state with more customers. In the meantime, she would continue helping Sandy and Michelle scope out locations for growing their products and for their two stores in Mesa, a booming suburb southeast of Phoenix.

It wasn't easy to find a place to set up this kind of business. The zoning was strict and severely limited where they could operate. Landlords who were willing to lease space to marijuana businesses often jacked up the rents tenfold. Even if you were willing to pay the sky-high rent, there was a chance you could find yourself out on the street again, because if a bank discovered a landlord was renting to a cannabis company, the landlord could potentially lose his or her mortgage if the building wasn't owned outright. Beth decided to buy an entire commercial building so they would have the real estate to get started.

With a launching pad in place, the three started brainstorming about the kind of store that people like them would want to patronize. What would a modern-day marijuana shopping experience look and feel like? It needed to be light, inviting, and, well, respectable. They ultimately agreed on a Southwestern-themed décor with buttery, coffee-hued leather chairs, elegant hammered-copper light fixtures and accessories, and a royal blue and bright green logo in the shape of a sun. Having decided to focus on cannabis products targeting customers' overall wellness, they branded the dispensaries "Health For Life" and set out to hire a knowledgeable and professional-looking team of sales associates. When Mel and Cindy McDonald agreed to join the new board of directors, Beth and her new partners were thrilled. Mel and Cindy's profile as upstanding Mormons and unlikely medical marijuana supporters, and Mel's past as a Reagan-appointed federal prosecutor, lent instant credibility to Health For Life.

All they needed now was that critical expertise in security. This was a cash business, after all. It required sophisticated protocols and equipment to protect employees handling thousands of dollars in cash, not to mention a sought-after product that was still competing against a thriving illegal market. Mel McDonald hadn't given up on convincing his old friend Don Tucker to come around. And finally he did, thanks to a little help from an unexpected source: the telegenic Indian American physician and regular CNN commentator Dr. Sanjay Gupta.

Tucker was flipping around on cable news one evening when the unbelievable story of six-year-old Charlotte Figi, an adorable little girl suffering from a rare seizure disorder, caught his attention. Her parents had tried every experimental treatment they could find for Charlotte's condition before finally turning to oil extracted from a high-CBD strain of cannabis. Amazingly, her seizures dissipated almost immediately. Over time, Charlotte began to speak, walk, and even learn to ride her bike. Like millions of Americans watching CNN on that August 2013 night when Dr. Sanjay Gupta's *Weed* documentary aired, Tucker was deeply moved by the story of how the federally illegal plant had helped save young Charlotte, the youngest medical marijuana cardholder in the state of Colorado.

Following Charlotte's dramatic narrative, Gupta explained the growing science behind her turnaround, including the role of the body's endocannabinoid system, a network of neural pathways throughout humans that mirror the plant receptors found in cannabis. Further, Dr. Gupta prefaced the airing of the program with a striking apology. "We have been terribly and systematically misled for nearly seventy years in the United States, and I apologize for my own role in that," Gupta told his audience. He now believed there was therapeutic value in cannabis that warranted a second look.

"That was the shot heard around the world, media-wise," according to longtime cannabis rights activist and investor Troy Dayton. "I mean here is America's most trusted doctor getting on there and saying I am wrong and really explaining how cannabis works in positive ways . . . If this thing is safe enough to give to somebody who is struggling with a debilitating illness, then it's not going to be the end of the world."

The Charlotte Figi story spurred Tucker to rethink his views on medical marijuana, and this potential opportunity to work with Beth. He had known Mel and Cindy for years and, like many Arizonans, knew that they themselves had done an about-face on the issue when they saw how cannabis had improved the life of their son. The more he thought about it, the more he decided this odd gig might be a way to help people and put his undercover narcotics experience to some good use. By the end of the summer, Don Tucker had signed on to Team Stavola.

As the business got up and running, he started reaching out to longtime colleagues, including Mesa's chief of police, to discuss ideas for guarding against crime in the neighborhood where the new dispensaries were located, and keeping employees and customers safe. He reached out to the top brass he knew at most of the major police departments across the valley, offering to educate them on the burgeoning industry and advising them on how they could work together with entrepreneurs to protect communities from infiltration by the illegal drug trade. Mel and Don teamed up to train the staff and even made videos and PowerPoint presentations to document all of their strict security policies. If the Feds were ever to question the integrity of Health For Life, they would be armed with evidence to show how far they were going to follow the law.

By the fall of 2013, exactly a year since Beth Stavola had first decided to make a risky million-dollar bet on the future of medical marijuana, the doors at Health For Life were finally open. The harvests in the grow were bountiful. And the cash was already rolling in. At capacity, the indoor farming operation in Mesa could produce thirty pounds of dried flower per week. At between $2,000 and $3,000 a pound for forty-seven weeks of the year, this one facility could generate between $2.8 and $4.2 million annually. And that didn't even include the money they would make from the new types of cannabis products, like oils and concentrates, that they were in the process of creating and that would soon line the shelves of the dispensaries.

All of which prompted Beth, ever the ambitious businesswoman, to wonder: Could she launch similar cash machines in other cities across America?

11
420 GOURMET

New York, New York

January 2013

WITH HIS FORMER life behind him, Jeff Danzer had big dreams of launching a new career as a professional cannabis chef. He didn't go to a famous culinary school, didn't have any formal training, and had never worked in a kitchen. But he loved to experiment with new and creative dishes, and share them with his family and friends. And he was good at it; everyone who knew Jeff raved about his food.

Meanwhile, Colorado and Washington had just legalized recreational pot and, much like Ted Chung, Jeff felt confident that bans on cannabis would continue to be lifted around the country. Moreover, cooking with weed was no longer just the domain of stoners with a brownie recipe; a handful of gourmands, like chefs Andrea Drummer and Holden Jagger, were beginning to make names for themselves with their cannabis cookbooks and private tastings, lending the pursuit a previously unthinkable level of culinary legitimacy. Plus, having built a successful career as a branding maven for nearly three decades, Jeff knew how to tell a compelling story that connected with people.

Still, as a relative unknown in the culinary world—let alone this emerging niche that involved cooking with weed—he knew that in order to make a name for himself, he would need a strong personal brand. After staying up all night brainstorming with his best friend and next-door neighbor, Lilly Rivera-Steinberg, he came up with the moniker "420 chef." To his surprise, the URL The420chef.com was available. But for some reason, he didn't procure it right away. He was having a little bout of cold feet and decided to sleep on it.

Two weeks later, Jeff says he remembers waking up in the middle of the night panicked. He jumped out of bed, ran to his computer, raced to the domain marketplace GoDaddy, and saw that The420chef.com was taken! At first, Jeff thought this was the universe telling him something. Maybe this wasn't meant to be.

Unable to sleep, he stewed in his dark New York City apartment, which at that hour was illuminated only by the glow from his laptop screen. Suddenly *Jeff the 420 Chef* popped into his head. He searched for "JeffThe420Chef.com" and found that the domain was available. He quickly typed in his credit card number and snapped it up on the spot. Now he had a name, a brand, and a digital destination for people to find him. That was something. But he knew in the pit of his stomach that the branding wasn't the real challenge standing in the way of his success. The cannabis-infused cookies, cakes, and brownies he had been baking still tasted terrible. He needed to put all of his energy into perfecting his techniques. So he turned his kitchen into a makeshift lab, where he intended to figure out how to take the pungent and overpowering taste out of the plant that was to be the centerpiece of his dishes.

In the days following, he raced to Williams Sonoma and Bed Bath & Beyond in search of kitchen gadgets that he thought might help him hack a way to lighten the weedy taste in the emulsifiers he used in his cookies and cakes.

"He was always in the kitchen, like a mad scientist. All he needed was his goggles and the gloves, I swear," giggles Lilly, a neat freak, who recalls the many times she helped him clean up the growing array of funnels, bowls, strainers, pots, and pans piling up on the narrow counter of his tiny apartment kitchen.

He knew from his research that the trichomes, those tiny glands containing the resinous cannabinoids, are "hydrophobic"—meaning they don't mix with water, and therefore their potency can be retained even if they come in contact with water. So at first Jeff tried rinsing the ground-up cannabis buds in the sink with cold water. The idea was to clean off pesticides, mold, or any other contaminants that might be contributing to the earthy taste. But that didn't work. Then he tried washing the buds in hot water. That didn't work, either.

Soon, Jeff discovered that the strong taste comes from the terpenes: aromatic compounds that are also found in a variety of familiar vegetation like mint, rosemary, hops, and pine needles. He learned about flavonoids, plant matter that contributes to the odor—nature's way of warding off predators. He read that even the green chlorophyll found in the cells of the plant affects the way our senses perk up when we interact with cannabis.

What could he do to dull all of these sensory components? He tried soaking the cannabis in distilled water and then blanching it, using an easy cooking technique that entails quickly boiling vegetables like broccoli or sugar snap peas or carrots and then submerging them into an ice bath for one minute to stop the cooking, which keeps the veggies brightly colored and helps them retain their crispness. The boiling water, he reasoned, would open up the plant walls and remove some of the most volatile terpenes and flavonoids from the cannabis, while leaving the plant fiber and the trichomes intact. Blanching definitely lightened the taste, especially once he tried infusing the cannabis into butter or olive oil, but he thought it would be possible to make it even milder.

Then there was the issue of figuring out how to properly dose the CBD and THC, and how to release the psychoactive chemicals without damaging them. The problem with the pot brownies many people remember from college was not only that they tasted like weed, it was that the amount of marijuana in the butter or oil wasn't precise and it wasn't clear exactly how much to use—or how much brownie to eat—to get the intended effect. You could end up with a heavily potent batch that would knock you off your feet, or one that didn't have enough THC to make you feel anything; there was no way of knowing without actually consuming them. If Jeff could figure out the dosage to make a more potent oil or butter, he figured, he could use less of it, making the chocolate, vanilla, or other sweet flavorings of his treats the stars of the show.

He would need a laboratory far more spacious than his tiny apartment kitchen for the necessary trial and error ahead.

Jeff had grown up in Los Angeles and knew that if he really wanted to make a go of this, there were many reasons to relocate back home. Not only had medical marijuana been legal in the Golden State since 1996, when legendary marijuana and gay rights advocate Dennis Peron led the fight for compassionate care—inspired by AIDS patients who were being denied access to the plant to ease their suffering—legalization's roots in the gay community resonated deeply with Jeff. And he deeply admired Peron and Mary Jane Rathbun, aka Brownie Mary, another San Francisco activist, who fought alongside Peron for the landmark passage of California's Proposition 215. California had been the nerve center for marijuana counterculture since the free-love 1960s, when hippies moved to the hills for a back-to-the-land life off the grid. They settled in the Emerald Triangle. Just as the rolling hills of Napa and Sonoma that make up California's wine country are fertile ground for so many of the most popular grape varieties, Humboldt, Mendocino, and Trinity counties, which sit just north of that region, possess the perfect microclimate and soil for producing some of the most sought-after varietals of sun-grown cannabis in the world.

On the West Coast, Jeff could easily—and legally—procure the wide variety of cannabis strains he needed. He could get his hands on high-CBD varieties like Cannatonic and Harlequin, which were thought to help with inflammation, pain, and muscle spasms, among other ailments. And he could walk into numerous medical dispensaries and ask questions about any type of flower, its origins, composition, and ratio of CBD to THC. He could even grow his own plants.

Jeff started making more frequent trips to visit his parents, who still lived in his childhood home in L.A.'s Fairfax neighborhood: a crowded hub of kosher markets and Orthodox synagogues abutting the stylish restaurants and bars of West Hollywood. It was there, in his mother's kosher kitchen, with its late-1970s-style center island and original cabinetry, that he would ultimately crack the code on taste-free weed. As a kid, he had spent countless hours cooking and baking in this very spot, helping his mom, aka the Kosher Maven, prepare special dishes for Shabbat and Jewish holidays. Sylvia still fondly remembers Jeff and his three younger brothers appearing at the counter with their round cheeks and sweet faces, clamoring for a chance to lick the cookie batter off the mixer beaters.

Jeff was feeling a bit nostalgic as he got to work in the place where he had so many warm childhood memories. Then one day, among a jumble of his mom's well-worn kitchen appliances, gadgets, and tools, he spied a French press coffeemaker. He had already figured out that washing the cannabis first in distilled water and blanching it could make it taste less danky. Now, after carefully sprinkling it onto a baking sheet and curing it in the oven at a precise temperature to release its potency (a delicate process called decarboxylation, or "decarbing"), he reached for the coffeemaker.

First, he put a stick of grass-fed butter into the base of the contraption and melted it by standing the coffeemaker in a saucepan of simmering water. Then he mixed the cannabis into the viscous liquid and let it steep on the stove for several hours. Finally, using the plunger of the French press, he strained it and poured off the now infused clarified butter. He tasted it. It did *seem* lighter. But, of course, the proof would be in the pudding. He measured out a serving of the new canna butter and used it to bake a dense German pound cake with raisins for a friend's mom. Once she tasted it, it became clear he was onto something.

It was a big step in the right direction. But the process still left a hint of earthiness, and Jeff wanted to take out the taste of the cannabis altogether.

"So I'm like, 'Well, what if I could just take out the terpenes? What if I could just take out the flavonoids? What if I could just make it a blank slate?'"

He would go on to spend a year and a half trying, immersing himself in the scientific research on every cannabis compound that existed and relentlessly testing every nuance of the plant and its composition. Finally, after many late nights and countless hours of experimentation, he perfected his very own trade secret: an elaborate natural process consisting of eleven steps that rendered the plant flavorless and yet still very potent. The by-product could be infused into butters and oils, or it could be rolled into a joint and smoked.

But even though all the science checked out, Jeff didn't fully believe he had actually succeeded until he tested it on himself. Jeff remembers emerging from a mad-scientist haze wandering the snack aisle of the twenty-four-hour Duane Reade across the street from his New York apartment in his pajamas at one in the morning. He had no idea how he got there. Then he recalled that he had baked yet another batch of cupcakes using the latest version of his tasteless, odorless oil—and that he had eaten one of those cupcakes about two and half hours earlier. It tasted just like a regular old chocolate cupcake, but now he was realizing that the little cupcake packed a punch. That's when it dawned on him. He had finally achieved what he had set out to do. He wanted to shout it from the rooftops. Instead, he started dialing all of his friends.

The discovery was in many ways the culmination of a spiritual journey. Jeff's mom says she remembers her son telling her he had prayed about his new endeavor, asking God if it was a good thing. As a boy, he had aspired to go to medical school, and Sylvia marveled at how he seemed to have found a vehicle all his own to live his purpose. Once Jeff saw that he could help people through medical marijuana, she says, it really was as if he had found his calling. He and his family even gave a biblical nickname to his work, calling it "medical manna," in homage to the Old Testament story.

"When the Jews were in the desert they were given manna to eat, and anything they wanted it to taste like it tasted like. We basically said, 'Hey, you know, this seems to be that kind of thing for certain patients.' They couldn't taste the cannabis in it because he managed to get rid of the cannabis flavor," Sylvia explained.

By this point he had started to expand his repertoire beyond desserts and was testing out flavoring his infused olive oil with rosemary or thyme to make savory entrées. Lilly, who was often a taster back in New York when he was concocting new recipes in the kitchen next door, bugged her friend to write everything down. She thought he might even wish to do a cookbook someday, and wanted him to keep track of all of his ideas and hard work.

Jeff soon started catering private dinners, jetting off to states where marijuana was legal to prepare meals for celebrities and wealthy patrons (whose names he wasn't permitted to share). The business was indeed starting to take off. But it wasn't until he got some serendipitous national publicity that he became convinced he could finally quit his day job and turn his hobby into a bona fide career.

The day after his heady Duane Reade revelation, a friend connected him to a reporter at *The Daily Beast* who was covering new trends in cannabis and looking for an interesting angle. Jeff jumped at the opportunity and set up a brunch with the writer, Justin Jones, for the following day. Naturally, he came bearing one of his chocolate cupcakes made with his special tasteless canna oil. Justin told Jeff he would try it over the weekend.

Five days later, when the story went live, was when Jeff learned that Justin Jones had in fact eaten the cupcake—and loved it.

"I'm already a lightweight—so when it hit, I could only stay vertical for a short time before I had to call it a night. Would I eat it again? Hell yes. The taste was that good," Jones wrote in the online piece he published on November 13, 2014.

The headline at the top of the story said it all: "Meet the Julia Child of Weed."

12

CANNABIS CULTURE FOR ALL

San Francisco, California

September 2015

On an unusually warm autumn day, Silicon Valley insiders escaped the heat inside Pier 70, once the hub of the region's shipbuilding industry. The long-abandoned steel and iron mills on the sprawling site had at one time churned out the nation's warships, steamboats, and ferries at a dizzying clip, and had employed tens of thousands of workers when factories ran full tilt. Now, as the rest of San Francisco was bursting at the seams thanks to the latest batch of newly minted dot-com millionaires, the stretch of vacant waterfront along the Bay was undergoing a $100 million facelift to make way for more shiny office spaces, high-priced apartments, and trendy boutiques. And it was here, inside one of the cavernous spaces, with its run-down façade and exposed steel beams, that the latest generation of American industrialists, the "minds and the money" behind the Internet revolution, convened to anoint the next Dropbox, Airbnb, or Mint.

It was TechCrunch Disrupt SF 2015, and anyone who was anyone in tech (or aspired to be) made it a point to swing by to see the six-minute pitches in the epic "battlefield" where startups competed for $100,000 in funding and, of course, for the opportunity to see and be seen by important industry players .

Among the hackers in hoodies, baby-faced tech execs, and billionaire venture capitalists strolled a bespectacled Calvin Cordozar

Broadus, Jr., aka Snoop Dogg, in a navy Ralph Lauren sweater vest and royal blue bow tie, accompanied by his stoic business partner, Ted Chung. Of course, the sight of the iconic rapper known for his West Coast gangsta rap roots and his weed-smoking antics turned some heads in this geeky crowd. But the truth was, Snoop was no stranger to this scene. He and his business development team had been flying up to the Bay Area more and more over the last couple of years, as big tech players like Instagram approached him and his advisers for deals and endorsements of their platforms. This led the star—much like many celebs of his stature and means—to begin betting his own cash on a growing number of early-stage startups, many of which had paid off big-time, including the freewheeling online forum Reddit (valued at $3 billion in 2019). By October 2014, *Fast Company* had dubbed the rapper "a serious celebrity VC," joining the ranks of Bono, Ashton Kutcher, and Ellen DeGeneres. And it was smart money. His backing of cutting-edge tech companies did as much for his own net worth as it did for the fortunes of these nascent ventures.

Snoop and Ted's fireside chat with TechCrunch editors was scheduled for noon, just a few minutes after luminary investors—including Cowboy Ventures founder Aileen Lee and TPG Growth's founder Bill McGlashan (later of Varsity Blues notoriety)—wrapped up a panel called "Money Talks." As Snoop and Ted strode onstage, the singer-songwriter appeared downright studious. No visible jewelry. No dark designer shades. Wearing loose dreadlocks around his face, he looked earnest and even professorial in his angular navy glasses. As the applause died down, TechCrunch managing editor Jordan Crook dove right in, probing the star about his approach to investing.

"If I invest, it's gotta be fun," Snoop replied in his soft trademark drawl. "It's gotta be something that I feel that is different and amazing, you know? 'Cause that's what I like to associate myself with first and foremost. That's what I'm looking for when I do invest."

But he and Ted weren't really here just to talk about Snoop's growing tech startup portfolio. They were here to unveil something they believed to be far more "disruptive": their ambitious plans to help destigmatize legal cannabis across America.

The reality was that Silicon Valley was already bullish on monetizing marijuana, and had been watching the industry blossom for some time. But most venture investment funds had stayed on the sidelines, due largely to the "vice clauses" that kept their partners from formally backing federally illegal businesses. However, attitudes began to change in January 2015, when one of the most controversial tech titans in their midst announced his firm had taken the plunge. Peter Thiel, the legendary founder of PayPal and Facebook's first outside investor, gave his Founders Fund the green light to become the very first institutional investor in cannabis, contributing an undisclosed portion of a $75 million raise by Seattle-based Privateer Holdings, a private equity firm helmed by a squeaky-clean Yale MBA named Brendan Kennedy that was quietly building a family of cannabis brands.

The prescient wager would pay off handsomely just three years later, when one of Privateer's companies, the Canadian medical marijuana manufacturer Tilray, became the first "plant-touching" cannabis company to debut on a U.S. stock exchange, with one of the most celebrated IPOs of 2018. Tilray, based in a remote town on Vancouver Island called Nanaimo, was also one of the first pot businesses to get in bed with both Big Alcohol and Big Pharma, striking up pioneering partnerships with InBev, a division of beer maker Anheuser-Busch, to make THC-infused beverages; and also with Sandoz, an arm of the Swiss pharmaceutical company Novartis, to produce cannabis pills and oils to treat everything from epilepsy to PTSD. If the markets were any indication, these bets were paying off, earning Tilray an estimated valuation of $4.1 billion by early 2019. (The stock price would ultimately tumble as Canadian pot producers grappled with persistent competition from the underground market and less than expected retail distribution.)

Given his track record as a contrarian, it was not too surprising that it was Thiel's group that made this pioneering foray into weed. Thiel is a maverick who famously awards aspiring entrepreneurs under the age of twenty-two a $100,000 fellowship to forgo college and instead spend two years building their own startups. Known for his strong libertarian views—a rarity in these parts where progressive values reign supreme—he also contributed heavily to California's 2016 Proposition 64 campaign to legalize recreational marijuana. Even for those who strongly disagreed with his politics, no one could deny that Thiel's imprimatur signaled that cannabis was going to be, as they say in the Valley, "the next big thing."

But unlike Thiel's gamble with Privateer, Ted and Snoop's venture fund would *only* back startups that didn't directly handle the plant. It was the Gold Rush model, in which the tools needed to build this new industry were the investment targets, not the commodity itself. They named the firm Casa Verde Capital (*casa verde* means "greenhouse" in Spanish), and planned to make seed investments of a quarter million to half a million dollars in the most innovative canna-tech startups that were beginning to pop up. By focusing on investments like software, agricultural tech, packaging, and product testing, Snoop and Ted reasoned they wouldn't risk going to prison, having their assets seized by the government, or being tripped up by the onerous local licensing application process and ever-changing regulations. Plant-touching entrepreneurs like Beth Stavola were under constant scrutiny by the government, while also fending off fierce competition from old-school drug dealers and burning through millions just to comply with local laws and stay afloat. Based on research that emerged from the cannabis think tank they had formed in 2013, Ted and Snoop reasoned that Casa Verde Capital could circumvent all of these challenges and set itself apart by becoming one of the very first funds to embrace the safer upside of businesses on the industry's fringes—and one that could scale fast.

But there was a hitch. Despite Ted's enthusiasm and entrepreneurial talents, he didn't know the first thing about running a VC fund. He would have to take a step back and start learning the ins and outs from scratch.

"Oftentimes, we are instinctively hesitant to be in rooms where we may not know all the knowledge or have all of the experience. But over time, I've learned to want to be in those rooms, more than ever," Ted would say, looking back.

This was the attitude he brought to Palo Alto when he and his team set out to penetrate the insular world of venture capital, where the rooms were especially rarefied. And white.

The hierarchy of tech wasn't made up of the usual East Coast legacy power brokers. It was an exclusive club of self-made new money, boy geniuses, engineering savants, and serial entrepreneurs worth billions, all with their own insider lingo about "moving fast and breaking things" (translation: creating something revolutionary), "failing fast" (translation: learning from mistakes), and hockey sticks (translation: the steep growth curve VCs want to see year over year). Ted began to learn this language, and, over the course of a year, he put in the time knocking on doors and meeting with anyone who would agree to see him—over drinks, dinners, any opportunity to sit down with anyone who had ever done a VC investment in technology. He asked all of them basic questions, like: How do you raise money for a VC fund? Who are the people you need involved? What are the tax and legal issues? What kinds of people can you raise money from?

"And over time, I started to learn the process. And running a business, whether it's a marketing company or a fund, it's not easy. You have to really be completely focused and constantly search and hunt for the opportunity," he said.

While Ted was getting schooled in VC, a handful of techies had begun to dream ways to apply their engineering expertise to the world of weed. One of those entrepreneurs envisioned a new software platform that, with a swipe of a finger or click of a mouse, could help patients easily and discreetly receive medical cannabis deliveries—legally—to their door in under twenty minutes. It was called Eaze, and, similar to food delivery services like Seamless or Grubhub that are now commonplace, it was an app that enabled customers to quickly buy what they wanted from a glossy online marketplace while also making it easy for dispensaries to coordinate deliveries using their own fleet of drivers. Eaze's coders, data analysts, marketers, and other employees would never physically handle marijuana, insulating the business from conflicts with the Feds. With its on-demand model following in the footsteps of other popular new services cropping up at the time, the startup would quickly become known as "the Uber of weed" and go on to make history as one of the highest venture capital–backed cannabis tech companies ever, raising upward of $166 million by 2019. (In late 2019, faced with missed revenue projections and a capital crunch, Eaze laid off 20 percent of its workforce.)

Although he was just twenty-eight years old, Eaze founder Keith McCarty was a veteran by Silicon Valley standards. He had been employee number four and a founding member of the enterprise social networking system Yammer, which was snapped up by Microsoft for $1.2 billion in 2012. The acquisition made him insanely rich overnight, and suddenly he was faced with an existential question. *What was he going to do next?* The blue-eyed, boyish sales executive had been raised in a conservative Christian home in Orange County and was not a cannabis user. But he was intrigued by anecdotes and news stories about the healing powers of the plant. At the same time, in his own backyard in the Bay Area, the rise of on-demand technologies like Lyft and Uber were all the rage, prompting him to ask himself, "'What other sectors can we apply on-demand to?' So he did a bunch of research and there's laundry, there's food, and through his research, cannabis kept coming up," recalled Sheena Shiravi, an early Eaze employee.

The more the serial entrepreneur examined the marijuana market in California, the more he identified inefficiencies he thought software could fix. Medical marijuana had been legal in California since 1996, when voters passed Proposition 215, the Compassionate Use Act. Yet the lack of government oversight and messy conflict with federal law meant that the experience of buying pot legally was neither easy nor consumer-friendly. Getting a medical "recommendation" from a doctor was confusing and inconvenient, and dispensaries either were out of the way or located in seedy areas of town.

But by 2012, with political momentum growing for California to follow in Colorado's footsteps and eventually transition to a highly regulated commercial regime that would both tax and closely monitor cannabis commerce, McCarty saw an opportunity for technology to streamline the system for consumers, purveyors, and even government monitors—and, in the process, to capture a gold mine of data that could be analyzed to reveal key insights like, *What kind of people are buying cannabis? Why? What products do they buy most? Where do they live?* This kind of information had never surfaced before in the state, given that illicit drug dealers and cartels certainly didn't track customer behavior and trends with sophisticated algorithms, and California didn't even have an agency overseeing the sale of marijuana at the time.

"Nearly two decades after California legalized medical cannabis, there is still little statewide standard," wrote journalists Alyson Martin and Nushin Rashidian in *A New Leaf,* their comprehensive history of cannabis law published in 2014. "There could be hundreds of dispensaries or there could be thousands. There could be tens of thousands of patients or hundreds of thousands; a patient's cannabis could be moldy from a closet in Los Angeles or pesticide-free from a farm in Humboldt County; one patient could be on hospice care and another a high schooler with headaches," they wrote.

Eaze brought transparency, as well as legitimacy, to this messy and opaque market. No more driving ninety minutes to the nearest dispensary, and no more feeling limited by any one store's selection. The Eaze interface, where you could buy everything from drops to balms to gummies to a gram of flower, was clean and easy to use, and pulled inspiration from sites like Amazon and Netflix. Design-wise, the site avoided anything that even hinted at the stoner stereotype.

"We wanted to really subtly educate, subliminally educate through familiarity. It looks like any other e-commerce platform. You don't feel weird looking at it, scrolling through it," explained Shiravi, pointing out that the team deliberately stayed away from using the color green. Instead, the Eaze logo is light blue and white, and looks like an innocuous cloud.

Its user base grew fast—by 4,000 percent in the first year. After launching in eighty cities across California in 2014, the platform was servicing 100,000 patients by 2015. And this volume of customers, combined with the company's data analytic capabilities, offered a new line of sight into rapidly evolving habits and preferences. For example, Eaze found that most customers in Northern California liked to order marijuana at night, whereas in SoCal, deliveries went out throughout the day. The data showed that 50 percent more orders came in on Saturdays at 10:00 A.M. compared to the rest of the week, and that chronic pain was the biggest reason patients said they medicated.

And over time, as its user base grew, Eaze was able to dive even deeper into demographic changes. Conventional wisdom, based on foot traffic to California dispensaries, was that millennial males were making up the bulk of legal marijuana sales. But when Eaze came onto the scene with its ability to track transactions and demographics in real time, new types of customers began to surface.

"There are a lot of other people who had been interested in this [cannabis]. They just didn't know about it. And they certainly didn't want to go into the dispensary that was kind of in the back alley with security guards out front. It was more about the experience that they didn't want, not the cannabis itself that they weren't interested in trying or open-minded enough to try," McCarty explained.

To everyone's surprise, including his, it wasn't just millennial bros shopping for flower and edibles. In fact, he said, Chardonnay moms—those affluent suburban women who looked forward to sipping a chilled glass of white wine at the end of the day to take the edge off—were buying weed, too. Eaze's 2017 "Modern Marijuana Consumer" report surveyed ten thousand of its users and found that 63 percent of those consuming cannabis daily were parents, and 87 percent of them reported reducing their drinking because they had replaced it with cannabis use. Their survey also confirmed anecdotal evidence that women and baby boomers were two of the fastest-growing consumer segments, driven by interest in self-care and wellness.

Insights like these would end up driving innovation across the industry for years to come, spawning entire product lines, retail experiences, and female-focused marketing campaigns. From the outset, this granular information caught the attention of Ted and Snoop, whose think tank had hypothesized that women would be influencers in the new age of legal marijuana. In April 2015, Eaze became the very first investment of Casa Verde Capital, and one they did not regret. In four years, the platform had 450,000 users across California and Oregon.

"I think it was an investment for them that was not only in the core business but it was also in whatever we could share with them, like how consumers are ordering and the frequency," says McCarty, who eventually stepped down as CEO to turn his attention to a new startup called WAYV. "You know a think tank can get you moving in the right direction. But I think that having real-time [information] across both a saturated or advanced network, as well as a broad network, could accelerate their understanding of what was really happening out there," he said.

SIX MONTHS AFTER investing in Eaze, with Casa Verde Capital up and running and Snoop's new weed brand good to go, the business partners were ready to unveil the last piece of the battle plan conceived by their think tank. Here on the TechCrunch Disrupt stage, Snoop and Ted announced how exactly they planned to demystify and normalize marijuana for the masses. They would do it through Merry Jane, an entertainment company that would serve as a production house and broad umbrella for a range of TV and digital projects, plus collaborations with major brands looking for innovative ways to tap into the growing acceptance of cannabis use while traditional advertising was still banned (other companies' fears would give them a first-mover advantage).

Ted and Snoop gave the packed hall a sneak peek of a new Merry Jane docu-series called *Deflowered,* in which veterans talked about their first time smoking marijuana, and how it was an alternative to opioids. They told of enlisting the star power of singer Miley Cyrus and teased new content with comedian Seth Rogen. Behind the scenes, the *Pineapple Express* star and avid pot smoker, along with rapper Wiz Khalifa, a collaborator with Snoop and Bruno Mars on the 2011 "Young and Wild and Free," had signed on as partners in the company and were already working with Ted and his team on new content ideas. Ted pointed to the Merry Jane logo, its tagline "Cannabis. Culture. For All," and landing page designed by an all-female team geared to welcome all kinds of people, especially women and the canna-curious.

But the one juicy tidbit they kept to themselves was that Snoop and Ted were also in top secret talks to develop a wild new project with another A-lister, whom most fans would never suspect to be involved in a pot-related enterprise. It would be an announcement in the late summer of 2016 that would truly signify the mainstreaming of marijuana. But that big news would have to wait until just the right time. For now, they wanted the world and this Silicon Valley audience to know that the Merry Jane site was ready to launch.

"It gives me proud honor to say that Merry Jane will be the door to bring people out of the closet. 'Cause there's so many people in the closet right now that do what we do and they really want to come out," Snoop told the crowd with a broad smile. "I just feel like we're a better world when everybody comes out the closet and just admits that they like to smoke . . . Just admit it, baby. I'm a smoker. My name is Snoop Dogg and I'm a stoner."

13 IN BUBBE'S KITCHEN

Los Angeles, California

April 2015

As the sun set on Friday evenings, the mouthwatering aroma of Sylvia Danzer's home-baked Shabbat challah would fill her Los Angeles home. Each week, she woke up early to mix the flour, eggs, sugar, salt, and yeast into the stretchy dough that needed to be left to rise not once, but twice. When it was time, she would punch down the sticky mound, covering it in a bowl for a few more hours until it was ready to be dusted with flour, rolled out, and carefully braided into its traditional shape. Two loaves would be brushed with egg and baked in the oven until the crust grew shiny and golden, and the dense bread inside turned chewy and soft.

As an adult, Jeff always swore he'd never be able to bake a challah as delicious as his mom's. But he sure did try. Now he was back in her kitchen full-time at age fifty-two and the memories flooded back. He had uprooted from his New York City apartment for good, packed up his life and returned to his childhood home to make a real go of his new profession as a cannabis chef. He didn't have a new gig waiting for him in L.A., even though he had tirelessly interviewed for jobs. But the newly dubbed "Julia Child of Weed" *did* land in his hometown in the spring of 2015 with a newly inked deal from famed New York publisher HarperCollins to pen a cannabis cookbook. The recipes would feature his pioneering methods for mellowing the strong taste of marijuana. However, his patent-pending technique for completely removing the taste would remain a secret. The book deadline was eight months away, and Jeff took the fact that he'd arrived in L.A. unemployed as a sign that the cookbook was what he was meant to focus on.

"This is the universe telling me something. The universe is telling me, 'We gave you a blessing. We gave you something special,'" he remembered reassuring himself.

So it seemed. After the *Daily Beast* article about his THC-infused cupcake came out, his email inbox had suddenly become crammed with inquiries from reporters, socialites who wanted to hire him to cook for their private dinner parties in Denver and Seattle, and even luminaries from the culinary world who wanted lessons on how to cook delicious "elevated" food. Before he moved full-time to the West Coast, a few notable chefs had even invited him into their Michelin-starred kitchens so he could show them the way he infused butters and oils with cannabis. In exchange, they schooled Jeff on culinary skills that would help him up his game from home cook to polished professional.

"I taught them how to make the light-tasting [butter and oil] and in return, instead of getting paid cash, they taught me how to do some of the things they did. Some skills and tricks and stuff like that. I learned a lot of really cool things along the way," he said.

Many of these lessons proved indispensable as he expanded his repertoire, like how to tell the difference between farmed salmon and wild salmon by the distinct scent of the fish. But perhaps more important, the one-on-one training also boosted his confidence. Even though he was gaining more recognition for his dishes, he still had a long way to go before he could think of himself as anything more than an amateur cook. He didn't even refer to himself as a chef until one of the celebrity gastronomists who invited him into his kitchen called out to him, "Chef!" Jeff recalled asking him, "Did you say 'Jeff' or 'Chef'? I'm not a chef." And the famous restaurateur replied, "But you are. Don't you realize that you are a chef?" Jeff was taken aback. His mentor went on to tell him, "Own it. Because if you don't own it, nobody else will own it with you." That was it. Jeff vowed he would fully embrace being "JeffThe420Chef" and, from then on, began wearing an official chef's jacket embroidered with a bright green marijuana leaf over the pocket.

Although they had raised their boys in laid-back Southern California, where marijuana culture was as ubiquitous as surfing and stardom, Jeff's parents were decidedly not hippies. They hadn't smoked pot in the '60s, or ever. And they had always expected their four sons to stay away from drugs as well. So when their eldest son first shared his vision for launching his own business creating tasty THC- and CBD-infused food for cancer patients and others suffering from pain and illness, his parents weren't quite sure what to make of it. Was it legal? Would he get in trouble? And now he was turning their home into his 24/7 test kitchen! But they listened as he patiently explained his work was with marijuana for therapeutic purposes, and for people who could legally obtain it. His parents stood by him, just as they had when he'd made the wrenching decision to divorce his wife more than a decade before—to part from his strict Jewish customs and community, and emerge from the closet as a gay man. After all, Sylvia said, Jeff had always been a trailblazer and she expected nothing less.

Even so, she and her husband struggled at first to reconsider their long-held negative views of cannabis. But when Jeff started baking some of his infused brownies and cookies—using the high-CBD strain Harlequin—to help relieve his dad's back pain and ease his mom's recovery after her knee replacement surgery, they began to change their minds. Eventually, Jeff says, they couldn't get enough of his toffee-laden Heath Bar Canna-Cookie Butter Brownies, his Wake and Bake berry muffins, and his signature Canna Apple Roses, the delicate mini apple desserts that encase thin slices of cinnamon-sugary apples inside buttery, flaky pastry. And when he told them about the "entourage effect," the theory that CBD can be even more effective when it's paired with a full spectrum of cannabis phytochemicals, Sylvia and Manny even began to try some of the elevated desserts that contained small doses of THC. After all, they didn't want to get high. But they did appreciate the pain relief. At the very least, the treats seemed to take the edge off.

Now that his parents were on board, Jeff felt inspired to start experimenting with some of the traditional Jewish dishes he loved from his childhood. He renamed Friday night dinners "Pot Shabbats" and reimagined all kinds of family recipes, passed down through the generations, as his own "uplifted" dishes. Comforting chicken broth with his mom's fluffy matzoh balls transformed into "potzo ball" soup. The slightly sweet whitefish appetizer paired with bitter horseradish that would start many Passover seders became "infused" gefilte fish. And his mom's challah recipe was remade into a decadent cinnamon-and-chocolate–filled "Canna Challah." Talk about a spiritual high! Served with an entrée like roast chicken or brisket, his was a spread so authentic, it would meet the approval of even the most discerning "Bubbe." And by the end of the meal, the hope was that Bubbe would feel like she had enjoyed a couple of glasses of wine—but not so stoned she couldn't get up from the table.

Jeff took great care to measure the potency of the cannabis-infused oils and canna butter, and used a medicine dropper so he could ensure precise dosing. Timing was also essential, since THC in edible form can take as long as two hours to kick in after a person first eats it, and the high can last for about an hour. Jeff found that if he limited the amount of the high-inducing compound to under 10 milligrams spread over the course of one entire meal, his guests would come away two hours later buzzed and happy instead of dazed, lethargic, or, even worse, paranoid and sick. He decided he would also consult with guests about their tolerance levels and tailor the dosage in each dish to his or her preference, an approach he had down to a science and could apply whether he was catering an intimate dinner party for ten or, someday, a feast for two hundred.

• • •

THE POT SHABBAT dishes eventually made it into his cookbook, *The 420 Gourmet: The Elevated Art of Cannabis Cuisine,* along with Jeff's other favorites, which ran the gamut of flavors, including tangy Hazy Thai Wings, spicy "Green" Guacamole, and hearty Fire-Infused Roasted Vegetable Lasagna (which featured fresh peppery cannabis leaves along with the infused olive oil). By the time *The 420 Gourmet* came out in June 2016, Jeff's business was thriving. He'd appeared on a show for the Vice network, in which he cooked for comedian Margaret Cho, and was juggling bookings for his private cooking classes and invitations to whip up his dishes in the private homes of Hollywood stars and other high-profile clients.

But for Jeff, all this success—the media appearances, the class bookings, the A-list clients—was secondary to the joy of highlighting the recipes from his culture and heritage.

"I think part of that was bringing back who I was and saying, 'This is who I am,'" said Jeff. He and his mom eventually brainstormed about one day opening a kosher cannabis restaurant or writing a kosher cookbook together.

It turned out that Jeff's parents were far from the only people of their generation with more than just a passing interest in marijuana and its potential health benefits. Along with the Chardonnay moms, seniors would turn out to be one of the fastest-growing groups of cannabis consumers in the wake of legalization. A 2017 AARP/University of Michigan survey of Americans ages fifty to eighty found that a majority of them believed cannabis to be effective for pain relief, appetite loss, and anxiety. And 80 percent of those polled said they strongly or somewhat supported cannabis use when a doctor prescribed it.

So it's no surprise that startups serving the gray-haired market were beginning to pop up in California and other states where pot bans had been relaxed. A two-hour flight north of Jeff's home laboratory in L.A., residents of the Rossmoor over-55 retirement community in Walnut Creek, an affluent enclave outside San Francisco, took a break from playing bridge or water aerobics to gather in their clubhouse for standing-room-only meetings about marijuana.

What was once taboo was becoming a hot topic among this lively crowd frustrated by age-related ailments like chronic pain, sleeplessness, and anxiety. Like the elderly characters in the classic 1985 movie *Cocoon,* who stumble into a secret fountain of youth, they were yearning for a magical solution to turn back the hands of time. They wanted relief. But they were also suspicious of Big Pharma and wary of habit-forming drugs—and were loath to fill prescriptions for pills. Instead, these baby boomers (those between 55 and 75 years of age) and seniors (75 years of age and older) were clamoring for a natural alternative to deal with the aches and pains of aging.

The market was more than happy to oblige. At Rossmoor, a spry resident, eighty-something-year-old Jeannine Faull, handed out cannabis sprays and balms for the crowd to try on stiff necks, arthritic knees, and gnarled fingers. Faull was a consultant for a company called Octavia Wellness, which the media would later call "the Mary Kay for marijuana," due to a business model that involved selling cannabis products directly to seniors in home gatherings in the Bay Area. Among Octavia's offerings were an assortment of white-label "oral drops," formulated specifically for aging adults who preferred low levels of THC and higher levels of CBD and CBN (cannabinol), two non-intoxicating compounds of the cannabis plant that can aid in relaxation and sleep; infused bath salts to calm inflamed joints; and body cream made with with cannabis oil, turmeric, and arnica to soothe pain.

The company was the brainchild of tech executive Carrie Tice, whose eighty-year-old mother had just been diagnosed with Alzheimer's disease and was struggling with agitation and sleeplessness in the facility where she was living. When one of the caregivers whispered after a rough night that perhaps her mom might benefit from "pot drops" to calm her down, an odyssey into medical marijuana began and a business idea was born. Carrie saw firsthand the challenges of obtaining a medical card for older people who either felt uncomfortable applying for one or who no longer drove, or both. And on top of it, the whole experience of visiting a dispensary to pick out products didn't feel right to her—and certainly not to her mom. But her mother did seem to find relief from oral drops and gummies containing low levels of THC. And witnessing the effect gave Carrie the courage to quit her job of twenty years with videogame software maker Ubisoft to focus full-time on developing a new way for seniors to access cannabis products and services.

"It's unbelievable. The things they can live with 'til [age] ninety-eight. So, we're really working with people to try to just make their lives better and make them feel better," Carrie explained in August 2017.

Of course, Carrie was far from the only entrepreneur to recognize that they needed to meet this growing canna-curious market where they lived—in nursing facilities, assisted living or retirement communities. After merging with Viva, a home-sales-based cannabis marketing and tech company, in 2016, Carrie began hiring and training an army of "wellness consultants" like Jeannine to introduce retirees to the range of new options for treating their most common complaints in the comfort of their own home. Others were also looking for ways to reach the elderly and the canna-curious. Serial entrepreneurs Pamela and Mark Hadfield came up with the idea for HelloMD, a telemedicine portal that made it easier for people to receive medical recommendations from doctors, while also offering access to a crowdsourced platform of information about the therapeutic applications of cannabis. The company soon evolved into an online marketplace and delivery service—just like Sava, a boutique delivery service with a clean, Amazon-like online interface that opened in 2015 with the goal of offering discretion and education to put the modern marijuana customer at ease.

"What I created is something that feels comfortable and safe . . .

I wanted [to build] something where someone who knows nothing about cannabis can come and start learning without feeling overwhelmed," says Sava founder and CEO Andrea Brooks, whose company services the Bay Area with a curated menu of everything from transdermal patches for pain relief to THC-infused marshmallows and popcorn, to CBD intimacy products.

Like Jeff's parents, the seniors Carrie encountered when she first started running focus groups were not familiar with the new ways to consume marijuana. It was a brave new world of tinctures, sublingual strips, lotions, elixirs, balms, and sprays to choose from—not to mention vapes and edibles like infused candies, cookies, and beverages. They needed to be introduced to new concepts like dosing, going "low and slow," and the range of effects and sensations different products might offer. Instead of the old-school stoner distinction of sativa versus indica strains, these new cannabis customers learned about the nuanced effects of dozens of different cannabinoids that might make them feel sleepy, less anxious, more energetic, and so on.

"If you've never been into cannabis or have like blocked it out and have no reason to explore it—why would you know that there's tinctures and topicals and patches and juices and coffees and gummies? . . . You just wouldn't. I think the number one misconception is that just everything is about getting high, and that everything is just like literally a joint," says Kimberly Dillon, former CMO of Papa & Barkley, a startup that launched in 2015 with a cannabis pain relief balm aimed at seniors.

While companies like Octavia and Sava allow seniors to peruse their wares from the comfort of their own living rooms, Papa & Barkley garnered headlines in 2018 for sponsoring a free monthly shuttle from one of the largest retirement communities in the country, Laguna Woods Village, to a marijuana dispensary twenty minutes north, off the traffic-clogged 405 Freeway in Santa Ana, California. The program offers an air-conditioned bus, deli sandwiches, and a seminar to keep the seniors up to speed on all the latest products. On a sunny afternoon in the fall of 2018, the elderly visitors to the Bud and Bloom dispensary were both curious and eager to stock up on hundreds of dollars' worth of merchandise for themselves and their friends.

"I'm a person who never thought I would seek out cannabis. I was so much against it. I thought it was really terrible. Now I have been on opioids for years and years which have done nothing for me . . . and I just want to feel better," explained Elaine Perez, a seventy-three-year-old woman pushing a walker who suffers from neuropathy, migraine headaches, and back and knee issues, and whose son encouraged her to try cannabis to ease her pain and help her sleep.

"My kids think it is hysterical," sixty-seven-year-old Sandy McPheron, a perky blonde in dark sunglasses, said with a smile as she stood in line for lunch outside the dispensary. "They think it is good if I am controlling my moods and I am happier. They don't see anything wrong with that." The mom of three has been vaping THC every day to manage her anxiety and restlessness for the last two years. She says some of her neighbors in the retirement community don't like the smell of pot smoke, so vaping keeps them out of her business.

"I use medical cannabis for pain and for sleeping. But I enjoy the whole package," admitted seventy-two-year-old Richard Levy. He smoked pot in the '70s but quit as a young man after a friend was thrown in jail for possession. In his straw sun hat, camo shorts, and a plaid flannel button-down shirt, Levy equates the balms he uses every day on his arthritic knees to popping an Advil or Tylenol.

As she waited in a long checkout line, sixty-four-year-old cancer survivor Donna Nowakowski reviewed a handwritten three-page shopping list for herself and for friends who didn't feel comfortable visiting a pot store.

"My friends will take me aside and ask me on the sly to buy it for them. You just have to be out about it. More people need to be out about it to show that it is normal," she said.

According to Linda Gilbert, who studies consumer attitudes about cannabis for BDS Analytics, as retirees across the country have become more accepting of cannabis and open to trying it, word of mouth has been essential to changing hearts and minds.

"You might have an eighty-five-year-old woman with back pain who is prescribed some kind of drug but it upsets her stomach. So she tries a topical cannabis lotion and it works and so she tells her eighty-six-year-old friend about it," Gilbert explained. Her own parents live in a full-care facility, and she predicts the growing trend toward acceptance of marijuana in the United States hinges on the conversation about cannabis as a healthcare tool. "It's going to defeat the arguments against it," she said.

This was certainly the case for Jeff's mother, who, once she started to understand the potential benefits of her son's work, began spreading the word to her friends, too.

"He's trying to take the boogeyman effect out of the cannabis so people understand that it's not a boogeyman at all," Sylvia said, adding that she still gets stopped in the supermarket by friends whom most people would never suspect of being interested in cannabis.

"I kind of opened up the doors to him, for certain people. Someone would say, 'I'm looking for this or I'm looking for that.' I would say, 'Talk to Jeff, my son Jeff. Talk to him and he'll tell you what's what,'" Sylvia recounted with pride.

Far beyond California, attitudes were shifting fast as Jeff put the finishing touches on his cookbook, *The 420 Gourmet*. And he was just getting started. He saw even bigger opportunities ahead that would open doors to introducing his mellow muffins, brownies, and pastries to new fans. But the trial and error in his mom's kitchen wouldn't get him there. He needed an even bigger stage. The chef's next move would take fine dining and entertaining to even greater heights.

14
DOUBLE OR NOTHING

Las Vegas, Nevada
Fall 2013

BETH STAVOLA HAD survived a rocky initiation into the emerging rough-and-tumble world of medical marijuana in Arizona, and now the money was finally rolling in. Keeping the business going was far from easy, though. There were fires to put out nearly every day. From ferreting out double-dealing employees, to figuring out creative ways to safely handle all of the profits from the cash-only business, to lab testing the harvest to make sure it was high quality and free of mold, she was on call 24/7 even as she continued to fly back and forth to her six children and husband in New Jersey.

Of course, she had her new posse behind her: her trusted attorney Mel McDonald and ex–Secret Service agent Don Tucker advising her on security and helping her deepen ties with local police and politicians, as well as Jason Gully, a well-connected former dispensary owner from Montana who wanted to do things her way—strictly by the book. Through Jason, she gained the trust and loyalty of a handful of cannabis experts who had spent years working on the fringes. Beth paid these mentors handsomely, sometimes even bought out their businesses just to bring them into the fold. For example, she recruited Aubrey Bradley—whose hydroponic lighting company had supplied Beth with equipment for her very first grow house in Mesa—onto her team to tutor her on everything there was to know about cultivating and manufacturing pot products. This was how she learned about the surging popularity of those potent oils extracted from the plant, and the delicate chemical processes used to isolate the most active cannabinoids.

In June 2013, a whole new Green Rush was in motion just a short plane ride away on the other side of the Grand Canyon. Nevada's legislature, controlled by the Democrats, had just approved a controversial bill to allow medical marijuana dispensaries to open in the state. When she heard the news, Beth couldn't resist the challenge.

"I was, like, 'Wow, you know what? Vegas is this big shiny city, and, you know, I want to go in, and see what I can get,'" she recalled.

What was particularly tantalizing to Beth, and to other power players who decided to make a run at Nevada's medical market, was the unusual prospect of tapping into the more than forty-two million tourists who flock every year to Sin City's glittering casinos, trendy nightclubs, and star-studded shows. Unlike anywhere else in the United States, if you had a medical card issued out of state, you would still be able to legally buy weed in Nevada. This meant the potential customer base—and potential profit margin—was staggering, according to Jay Matos, an early cannabis lobbyist who helped pass the medical law. Moreover, unlike states that only allowed the sale of smokable bud, the sale of concentrates would be allowed in Nevada, too. And making those increasingly in-demand products like vape cartridges, waxy cartridges for dabbing, and edibles, would require hundreds of thousands of pounds of marijuana. He estimated that a pound of flower could be grown for $700 and sold for between $2,800 and $3,000 wholesale, and that the retail and wholesale markets would eventually be worth tens of millions.

"When you take those numbers and the number of people you can sell it to, heavy hitters start turning up," explains Matos, a scrappy Democratic lobbyist who previously made his living helping business owners negotiate Nevada's tightly controlled gaming and liquor regime. Basically, Jay was the hired gun your lawyer called if you needed a zoning variance, or if your liquor license was going to be pulled because one of your employees sold to a minor. He would quietly go down to the county commission or city hall to "fix" the problem, and the client would be none the wiser. The goateed operator, born in Spanish Harlem and raised in tough North Las Vegas, knew all the power brokers that ran Sin City and would go on to help many of the early cannabis prospectors get a foothold in this new market. Including, for a time, Beth Stavola.

For all of her moxie, Beth was still an outsider trying to break into what amounted to a good old boys' club run by Nevada's powerful families and major political donors. Early on, the Nevada Gaming Commission had ruled that casinos couldn't do business with the medical marijuana industry, for fear that inviting a federally illegal substance into their highly regulated industry might set off unwanted scrutiny from Washington. But with the casino moguls forced to sit on the sidelines, all kinds of other wealthy investors jumped in to bet on this burgeoning industry in their backyard: everyone from the Findlay family, who owned a profitable chain of car dealerships, to the well-heeled boosters for the University of Nevada at Las Vegas, to high-powered (and highly paid) attorneys for the local professional sports teams. Even advertising mogul and Bush family friend Sig Rogich had skin in the game. They all wanted in on licenses to grow, manufacture, and sell cannabis, setting off a frenzied race to ingratiate themselves with local officials, and a nasty turf battle to snap up the few desirable locations.

From the moment she began to scout out real estate in the fall of 2013, Beth's carpetbagger status was made crystal clear. She still remembers the time when a smug Clark County commissioner corrected her pronunciation of the state in front of a standing-room-only meeting hall after she mistakenly uttered, "Ne-VAH-duh" instead of the local version, which is pronounced "Nev-AD-uh," with a short *a* like the word "bad." "We know you're not from here, Miss Stavola," the imposing official scoffed. Titters broke out but Beth just brushed it off. She was never one to try to blend in or make apologies. Perhaps that is what attracted her to another tough-as-nails female entrepreneur, a maverick like herself, who just happened to be one of the most polarizing Republican figures in the state. Against the will of her caucus, Assemblywoman Michele Fiore had switched sides and cast the lone GOP vote for medical marijuana in the 2013 legislative session that led Nevada to this very moment. She and Beth would become thick as thieves.

Fiore, a fiery Brooklyn-born, card-carrying NRA member and grandmother of five, turned heads even in a party town teeming with flashy high rollers and sparkling showgirls. This was a woman who once sold a pinup calendar of herself for a campaign fundraiser, who (to the chagrin of her Republican caucus) supported same-sex marriage, and whose family holiday card once featured her kids and grandkids posing in red Christmas sweaters while gripping a variety of firearms. More than once, she had injected herself into a standoff against federal law enforcement agents on behalf of an anti-government militia group. As Michele liked to say of the two pistols she always carried on her person, "Two is one and one is none."

"If you have two guns and one malfunctions, you only have one. If you only carry one gun and it malfunctions, you have none. So two is one and one is none, okay?" she explained matter-of-factly one afternoon in an interview at the Caesars Palace convention center.

The well-manicured politician liked Beth from the first moment they met. But they weren't introduced while knocking off at a glamorous cocktail lounge or getting facials at a luxury spa on the Strip. Instead, they set eyes on each other for the first time at a Macaroni Grill in a suburban shopping center during a dinner with local elected officials and prospective marijuana investors organized by lobbyist Jay Matos. They were the only two women at the large round table for ten, and were seated next to each other. Once they started talking, it was like the rest of the room no longer existed. They quickly learned they were both transplants from the East Coast with large, tight-knit families. Michele, like Beth, had been married more than once. The two women nodded their heads knowingly as they traded stories about their tough divorces and ex-husbands to whom they were ordered to pay alimony. It went without saying they were both all too familiar with the challenges of standing out as strong women in a man's world; they were used to being underestimated by powerful men, and relished stealthily turning it to their advantage.

"I mean, it was like looking in a mirror," marveled Michele, now serving on the Las Vegas City Council, as she reflected on how her tight friendship with Beth had begun.

The assemblywoman's populist appeal drew from her deep suspicion of the federal government and her "live and let live" attitude. A *Politico* profile in the summer of 2016 likened her theatrical style and popularity with fringe groups to those of the forty-fifth president of the United States with a headline that read: "The Lady Is a Trump." She would go on to serve on Donald Trump's campaign advisory board, and arranged for Beth's mother, Kathie, to visit the White House.

Like Beth, Michele was very close to her own mother, a lesbian single mom with whom she had arrived in Las Vegas from the Big Apple in the early '90s. Michele found work as an actor for a time, and ultimately decided to try her hand at politics. In the spring of 2013, she began serving her freshman term in the statehouse representing Las Vegas. An outspoken gun and LGBTQ advocate who had lost neither her Brooklyn accent nor what she called her "hot New York Italian temper," Fiore quickly earned the ire of her party when she first considered voting with Democrats to commercialize medical marijuana. The pressure to oppose the measure was immense: not only from members of her own party, whose conservative constituents held strong anti-pot views, but also from the private prison industry, which aggressively tried to strong-arm the freshman to help kill the bill.

"They felt they could intimidate her because she was a woman.

They were very distraught on her voting against the party line and they didn't understand. They were bashing her and threatening her," recalls Matos, who helped the bill's author, Senator Richard "Tick" Segerblom, get the two-thirds majority the Democrats needed in both chambers.

But Michele refused to be bullied—especially not by the corporate lobbyists who assumed they could lord their longtime experience in state politics over a first-term representative. Further, she says she was troubled by what she knew about the profit motives of private prisons when it came to the jailing of marijuana offenders.

"Marijuana in a state isn't about smoking marijuana. In my viewpoint, as an elected official, I don't smoke it. Never have, never will," she says. "What is my thing, is criminal justice reform. And we have a lot of people in jail because of this industry, of them using it . . . You threaten that industry and you go, 'You know what, we're not arresting folks for marijuana.' They're like, 'Whoa, whoa, whoa. We've gotta keep that illegal.'"

One day, a burly lobbyist representing a private prison corporation with big financial interests in the state showed up at her office and tried to convince her to vote against the legalization measure. She listened politely but wouldn't commit to how she would vote, even after he threatened that she could easily lose in the next election if she wasn't careful. After he called her office a dozen times to set up a follow-up meeting, the assemblywoman had finally had it. She told her personal assistant to summon the man to her Carson City office at the capitol. On her desk lay her Glock 17 and 19 in plain sight. She recalls him commenting, "Those are nice," to which she retorted, "Yeah. It's an equalizer for a big guy like you and a woman like me."

"I understand you are going to vote against us," she remembers him saying, before vowing to make sure she faced a tough opponent in the next primary.

"And I said, 'Good luck with your threats . . . but my guns are bigger than yours,'" she recounted years later. Her political enemies easily outspent her in the primaries the following year. But she won a second term anyway.

By then, Beth was in the process of learning all the new players and navigating the opaque, fiercely competitive—and costly—application process. Unlike Arizona's lottery to win a license to operate dispensaries in the state, which anyone could enter, Nevada's sixty medical licenses would be won only by people with pockets deep enough to play.

The contest stretched on for two years. During that time, contenders shelled out hundreds of thousands of dollars in billable hours for well-connected attorneys and consultants in hopes of gaining an advantage over rivals in the application scoring process.

The red tape didn't stop there. One of the most expensive and risky requirements for applicants like Beth was the rule forcing them to secure the real estate for their future businesses even before they knew whether they had won. Beth had decided she would go after nine licenses—which meant procuring nine different locations. Jay Matos began advising her on the strategy as she sought out properties where she could house her cultivation, manufacturing, and retail businesses. But cannabis ventures could only occupy certain areas of town, which gave all the leverage to the property owners. Massive markups were common, and it wasn't unheard of for landlords to charge $150 to $200 per square foot for 10,000 square feet—more than $1.5 million annually to lease property to build out a small grow.

The bills kept adding up. Beth says she spent more than a million dollars in Nevada before she even knew if she had secured one license. On more than one occasion, she was forced to reluctantly phone her husband, Jack, in New Jersey and ask him to wire her another $200,000 to secure a new lease for a grow, or to pay fees to her fixers, or make some political contributions. Years later she could laugh about how Jack, her typically even-keeled husband, would yell, "Beth, you've lost your shit!" They would quarrel, but he always sent the money anyway. At this point, she was in too deep to jump ship. Forking over the money turned out to be the only choice they had.

Back home, Beth and Jack were dealing with financial troubles of a different sort. In November 2013, they learned they had been swindled by a former Wall Street stockbroker and fast-talking Casanova who was being investigated by the FBI for running one of the largest Ponzi schemes in U.S. history. Louis J. Spina had been a friend of the family ever since a longtime friend of Beth's had married him, becoming his fourth wife. Beth and Jack had even attended the couple's lavish, intimate wedding.

When Spina was indicted on federal wire fraud charges in the fall of 2014, it came to light that he had run an elaborate shell game promising huge returns on investments while bilking more than $20 million from forty-two people—including the Stavolas, other Monmouth County families, and even his own wife and her elderly parents. Beth and Jack, the largest investors in Spina's company, LJS Trading, lost more than $6 million. Spina, who went on to rob a Florida bank in May of 2014 while he was out on pretrial release, was ultimately sentenced to ten years in prison after pleading guilty to one count of wire fraud and the bank heist.

Not only did the entire fiasco rock Beth to her core, it also wiped out the Stavolas' liquid assets, forcing her and Jack to unload some of their marijuana interests in Arizona. She fell into a deep depression after learning of the scam and how much of their savings had been squandered. The typically sharp-dressed executive could barely bring herself to get out of bed—let alone choose an outfit from her massive closet of designer duds. Finally, after a few weeks, a friend of the family and business mentor picked her up off the floor. Tom Ruane and his wife, Anne, had been living in Beth and Jack's guesthouse while their luxury home was being rebuilt after Hurricane Sandy. They, too, had lost money in the Spina scheme.

Beth remembers that it was kindhearted Tom who finally shook her out of her funk.

"He practically pulled me out of the fetal position and he said, 'You have to get up. You have to get up and fight and make this marijuana thing work,'" she said.

Beth realized he was right. She wasn't going to let herself be derailed by the actions of a fraudster. In a ballsy move, the Stavolas decided to put it all on the line. They took out a multimillion-dollar mortgage on their luxury estate in Red Bank and doubled down on cannabis.

"This situation was either going to make or break my marriage," she recalled soberly, looking back on the go-for-broke moment. Like everyone else in Vegas, they had rolled the dice. And they needed a win.

The high stakes pushed Beth and her team to work even harder.

"We weren't playing with other people's money. We were playing with the house's money. With the house's money, we had to make sure that everything we did was a winner move," remembers Jason Gully of the tense conversations he had with Jack at the time. He was on the ground helping Beth navigate the competition. Holding fast to her mantra, "Losing is not an option," she pressed onward, ingratiating herself with politicians both blue and red, hiring multiple lobbyists, and forming key alliances to claw her way to the finish line. Finally, after all the frantic late-night calls, the countless cross-country flights, all the sharp elbows, backbiting, and financial uncertainty, her tenacity paid off. To the surprise of the slick Nevada businessmen who had once dismissed her, the firecracker from Jersey had played her cards right, and now she had three highly valuable medical licenses to show for it: two cultivation and one manufacturing permissions. She quickly sold off one of the cultivation licenses for a million dollars and recouped all she and Jack had invested in Nevada. Even better than money, she had earned crucial respect from her rivals.

"You've got some heavy businessmen coming at you, other people are trying to take whatever you got away, people are talking about you—and she just kept on going on the path and she would not relinquish her vision, her dream, or her goals. She would not. She is very fierce; she's probably the fiercest woman I've ever met. Once she gets her mind set to something, she's going to continue and continue even if she has to drag herself there to continue," reflected Matos, who said that even though they went their separate ways, he still considered Beth a friend.

With some new partners, Beth began to build a brand presence in North Las Vegas under the name GreenMart. The plan was to build a massive pharmaceutical-grade cultivation site and state-of-the-art lab with top-of-the-line hydrocarbon extractors to mass-produce powerful THC oil for the various dabbing, vaping, and edible products in demand. She would look to bring all she had learned about cannabis oil to Nevada, including the brand she had started with partner Jason Gully: Melting Point Extracts. Known by consumers by its acronym, MPX, it was named after her company's new proprietary method for producing THC oil for vape cartridges for pipes and disposable vape e-cigarettes, and also a range of waxy, smokable products called shatter, resin, and rosin, which appealed to both medical patients in need of high dosages of THC and stoners looking for a fast-acting and hard-hitting high. (By 2019, MPX wax was the top-selling non-vape concentrate in Nevada.)

Beth's windfall would soon get even bigger once Nevada's voters approved a ballot initiative for recreational sales in the fall of 2016, giving medical license holders like Beth first crack at the new over-21 market. Unlike Colorado, which maintained separate medical and recreational programs, in Nevada the state simply "flipped a switch" and told the medical companies they could now sell to anyone over twenty-one, according to former state senator Segerblom, who went on to become a Clark County commissioner. Now the licenses Beth and Jack bet the farm on would be worth as much as

$20 million apiece by the beginning of 2019. And perhaps even more satisfying was knowing that she had a seat at the table with the big boys who didn't see her coming.

And Beth sure wasn't stopping now. She had her eyes on opportunities to expand to the East Coast, where new medical and recreational programs were starting to come online. She would need more cash than ever to gain a foothold in places like Maryland, Massachusetts, and New Jersey. Even with Nevada in play and Arizona running full tilt, she and Jack could only finance the massive startup costs for so long. Scaling up and moving into more states demanded much more money.

Luckily, this former equities broker had been keeping a close watch on the public markets in Canada, which had started allowing cannabis producers to trade on stock exchanges, where they could easily raise millions of dollars to keep their expensive operations going. Bruce Linton's behemoth, Canopy Growth—previously named Tweed—was the first to go public and now there were more Canadian companies following suit. The stock market in the United States was closed to plant-touching companies like Beth's, which were high risk and tended to burn through cash. But Beth had an idea. What if she found a way to merge with a Canadian company that was already trading on the Canadian Securities Exchange?

Fate would intervene in 2016 when a middle-aged blue-eyed gentleman strolled up to the MPX booth at the Marijuana Business Conference in Las Vegas with a proposition Beth couldn't turn down. Scott Boyes was a Toronto investor who had applied to Health Canada to become a federally approved licensed producer (LP) of medical marijuana, just like Bruce Linton. Since Canopy went public in April 2014, the government had been inundated with hundreds of such applications from aspiring LPs, and the approval process dragged on for years. Rather than simply sit back and await news from Ottawa, Boyes and his partners decided to start investigating the possibility of buying assets in the United States. Beth remembers that she had been standing all day at the expo and her high heels were killing her when Boyes asked her to name her price for the Arizona properties. At first she was taken aback. Then she took a breath and coolly threw out the first number that popped into her head: $25 million for the two dispensaries and the cultivation and MPX concentrate-manufacturing operations in Arizona. Boyes didn't blink. He would go on to raise the funds to buy Health For Life and MPX and fold them into a company that was already primed to begin trading on the Canadian Securities Exchange. A year later, when the deal closed, Beth would receive the first $15 million payout and a $10 million promissory note that would come due in 2020. Sandy Clifford and Michelle Magers, the mother-daughter team who helped start Health For Life, would get a cut as well, and she would hand out generous bonuses to all of her veteran staffers. Beth would stay on as head of U.S. operations for the new public company they would rename MPX Bioceutical Corporation, and would use the much-needed capital infusion to begin applying for even more weed licenses in other parts of the United States. Soon after, MPX would buy the Nevada assets, too, and fold them into the new company.

Now Beth was suiting up for the land grab that was shaping up in the emerging East Coast markets like Maryland, where the medical program was just beginning, and Massachusetts, where voters had approved recreational use. She knew that only the most cunning, well-connected, and well-financed cannabis companies would triumph in these tightly controlled East Coast locales, where only a handful of business licenses would be handed out by states. The cash from Canada would help, but she knew the competition would be cutthroat and, to boot, she would remain one of the only women on the front lines. Even with Jack by her side, it was increasingly lonely work. She craved a female confidante with whom she could brainstorm any time she wanted. Naturally, she needed someone who would always have her back, and who had the background to understand the financial and legal complexities of the business. It was time to circle the wagons and bring on someone she could always count on in a pinch.

And she knew just the woman for the job . . . someone cut from the same Jersey cloth . . . a person who could read her mind and practically finish her sentences . . . her youngest sister, Julie.

15 POT ON PRIME TIME

Los Angeles, California

August 2016

UNDER DREAMY HOLLYWOOD lighting, a glowing Martha Stewart delicately sprinkled fresh spinach and mint on a three-cheese pizza while soothing music played in the background. It seemed like a promo for another new show starring the celebrity homemaker. But then the music shifted to a hip-hop-beat. It turned out Snoop Dogg would be in the kitchen, too.

"Just to clarify, I'm not high right now. But whoever gave us this show must have been." Snoop laughed while cuddling up with Martha in pj's under a blanket in the slick commercial promoting the duo's unexpected new show on VH-1.

The big reveal at the end of the summer of 2016 was the culmination of years of development and creative collaboration driven by none other than Merry Jane, the cannabis media company Ted Chung and his marijuana think tank had conceived back in 2013. For Ted, the matchup of Martha and Snoop presented an opportunity to take the normalization of pot consumption to a completely new level. Perhaps it would be a *Will & Grace* moment, just as that hit show had helped move the needle toward acceptance of marriage equality in the late '90s. There was no doubt about the power of entertainment and media to change public perceptions and help erase long-held stigmas. Interestingly enough, pollsters had compared favorable attitudes of marijuana legalization to the trajectory of same-sex marriage. Would this celebrity pairing resonate with the Middle American moms and grandmoms who admired Martha's sensibilities and taste, and pique their interest in Snoop's favorite pastime, which would be prominently featured?

They wouldn't know what the response would be until the show premiered in a few months. But what wasn't lost on Ted, as they geared up for the first episode, was that the first seed of an idea for a show of this type had been sown out of tragedy. It began on a dreary wet morning in St. Louis when thousands of mourners gathered to grieve yet another senseless death of an unarmed black teenager at the hands of a white policeman.

Baby-faced Michael Brown was just eighteen years old and a few weeks away from starting college, when he was shot six times in broad daylight in the nearby city of Ferguson while merely walking to his grandmother's home one afternoon with a friend. The tragedy ignited a firestorm of outrage in his hometown and across the nation, and set off nights of violent riots, quelled only by a fervent call for calm from the young man's father and community leaders just hours before Brown's funeral.

Among the tearstained throngs of mourners who packed the church and overflowed into the street sat a somber Snoop Dogg, who was there to pay his respects to Brown and his family. He didn't know them personally, but Brown's untimely death and the anger it sparked moved him deeply. The service also drew America's most recognized civil rights activists; the families of Trayvon Martin and Sean Bell, two other black young men lost to racially charged violence in scuffles with law enforcement; and a host of other celebrities, including Spike Lee and Sean "P. Diddy" Combs. They stood in solidarity with the hundreds of friends and neighbors who turned out at the Friendly Temple Missionary Baptist Church for the emotional closed-casket service wearing red ribbons on their lapels and buttons bearing the innocent face of young Brown.

"All of us are required to respond to this. We can't have a fit. We have to have a movement," preached the Reverend Al Sharpton at the pulpit in his fiery eulogy, telling the packed pews, "We are required to leave here today to change things."

It was a message Snoop took home with him to Los Angeles. It was true that his early gangsta persona and hit lyrics had once glorified violence and lawlessness. Now a father, grandfather, and his son's youth football coach, the rap icon was determined to take action against gun violence. He and Ted quickly began planning a "No Guns Allowed" summit in Atlanta to coincide with the BET Hip Hop Awards the following month; they welcomed Michael Brown's father along with youth activists to discuss solutions to gangs, racial strife, and police brutality.

Always hustling and multitasking, the two were also simultaneously deep into developing their entertainment company, Merry Jane. They kicked around all kinds of ideas and wondered if there was a way to somehow use the megaphone of a media company to spur some much-needed goodwill and understanding among black and white America.

"Snoop and I were trying to figure out a show that we could do that would sort of be something reflective that Americans could see onscreen and hopefully placate and just bring some positive energy into the ethos of entertainment," recalled Ted several years later.

Over time, Ted and Snoop brainstormed about different possibilities for a new TV show that could offer America a taste of cannabis culture in a fun and familiar format. The big idea would be to pair Snoop with an unlikely pal, someone with whom the audience would never guess he shared a common bond. Why not take the star and team him up with someone who represented the polar opposite of his hip-hop image? They could show viewers how it was possible for two people from completely different Americas to not only get along but to enjoy each other's company—along with some pot-infused humor. They needed to nail the chemistry for it to really work.

Luckily, serendipity had reunited Snoop onscreen with an old friend who would end up making the perfect counterpart. Eight months after attending the Brown funeral, Snoop was invited to Comedy Central's roast of Justin Bieber and was seated next to the one and only Martha Stewart. The celebs had actually known each other personally for more than six years, and Martha had just taken part in an AMA, or "Ask Me Anything," chat on the popular platform Reddit (Snoop is an investor), in which she told users she wished she was better friends with the rapper. Later, on Instagram, she posted playful photos of herself in red platform heels lounging next to Snoop in his red massage chair at his "Mothership" studio in L.A. The caption hinted at a potential partnership in the making as she shared with her 470,000 IG followers that her friend was in "high spirits" and "in an ultra-creative mood, if you know what I mean" during their "long planning meeting." At the roast, the famous homemaking mogul, dressed in a black top with sparkly pink and red flowers, and with her trademark blond bob, seemed to be having a ball palling around with the cornrowed hip-hop legend.

The two first met in 2008, when Snoop made a memorable appearance on her TV talk show, *Martha Stewart Living*. Stewart taught him how to mix up her signature creamy mashed potatoes while Snoop gave her and her studio audience an earnest tutorial on his unique L.A. street lingo. In his gentle voice, he patiently translated phrases like "fo shizzle," which he told her means *for sure,* and "What's crack 'alackin?" defined as *What's cracking?* or *What's happening?* The episode went on to become one of Stewart's highest-rated shows ever, prompting the producers to bring Snoop back for a much-anticipated encore: the Christmas cookie episode the following December, in which they baked what else but green brownies. During the segment, the "Drop It Like It's Hot" singer, in a playful wink to tokers in the audience, suggests to his gracious host that the treats should go into the oven at 420 degrees. Stewart, in her Christmas sweater, deadpans that at that temperature the brownies will surely be overdone. After all, as she admonishes her guest, "baking is an exact science."

When it was her turn to launch zingers at Bieber and the other celebrity guests at the roast six years later, Stewart began by telling the crowd that she loved to make Snoop's special brownie recipe so much that she'd eaten three of them that evening. She grinned mischievously and went on to joke about decorating Shaq's enormous house, offered Ludacris a bawdy tip on his sex life, and gamely made light of her prison time. The crowd roared. Reviewers lauded Martha for "killing it" and heralded "a new phase of her career." She later told *Late Night* host Seth Meyers that during the roast, she couldn't help but feel the effects of the secondhand smoke drifting from his direction throughout the four-hour taping of the show. "I was totally high by the time I got to that microphone," she said with a laugh, adding that she is not a weed smoker herself.

Her irreverent performance during the roast and the breezy rapport she shared onscreen with Snoop looked like ratings gold to veteran *Jersey Shore* producer SallyAnn Salsano, who had been thinking about pitching a new cooking show to VH-1. And from her vantage point that evening, as she later told *The Hollywood Reporter*, she could tell this odd couple just clicked.

The concept of *Martha & Snoop's Potluck Dinner Party* was as simple as it was brilliant. The lifestyle guru and her pot-loving cohost would invite the audience along for a friendly cooking competition, with the two stars sharing recipe tips as they whipped up everything from Martha's signature Perfect Roast Turkey and Seventeen-Lemon Mint Juleps, to Snoop's Honey-Blazed Ham and Pepperoni Pizza for Playas—which they would then serve to a parade of celebrity friends from their respective orbits. As Ted and Snoop had envisioned, all of it would be peppered with not-so-subtle references to getting high, casual mentions of munchies, and Snoop's favorite time of day, 4:20. The pot-themed set would feature artfully displayed bongs and pipes and all kinds of lush greenery, and Stewart—the doyenne of domestic life, who made millions upon millions showing the world how to set a proper table, fold a fitted sheet, and make the perfect holiday centerpiece—would comfortably let her hair down and casually chat about blunts and spliffs while joking and flirting with rappers Rick Ross and Reverend Run. It was an unusual pitch, to be sure. But the network execs apparently thought it was just crazy enough to work.

"The underlying message behind the show, even down to the set design, is the feeling of, 'This is how I roll, this is how you roll, and now we roll together,'" executive producer Salsano told reporters.

On November 7, 2016, at 10:00 P.M., 2.3 million people tuned in to VH-1 to watch the debut of *Martha & Snoop's Potluck Dinner Party*. It was the night before Donald Trump shocked the world by edging out a victory against front-runner Hillary Clinton in the same historic election in which California, Nevada, Massachusetts, and Maine voters would usher in a momentous tipping point in U.S. marijuana legalization efforts, giving the thumbs-up to expanding pot use in those states to anyone over twenty-one years old.

In a brief respite from the political partisanship roiling America, the very first episode featured an epic fried chicken throwdown, with Snoop and Martha trash-talking each other's recipes while their sous chefs, Seth Rogen and Wiz Khalifa, egged them on. Rogen and Khalifa were already working with Snoop and Ted as partners in Merry Jane, so it made sense for the two to kick off the first episode. In one memorable moment, Wiz greets Martha with a bag of "herb" and gets a laugh as Martha goes along with the joke and compares the gift to rosemary and thyme, prompting comedian Rogen to blurt out what everyone watching was surely thinking: "This is the weirdest group of people ever onstage together!"

But that was exactly the point, according to Ted, who was deeply proud of the production and what it stood for.

"We're utilizing icons who represent two different groups [to present] a social justice message. Bringing them together, bringing their friends together around a table, breaking bread and just showing that different people all at the end of the day have a common bond," he recalled earnestly as he looked back on how it was born out of the tragedy in Ferguson.

"The melding of cultures is really what I want to see happen in the United States, and so does Snoop," Stewart told the press. "There shouldn't be any divides. There shouldn't be any question that we can all get together and get along."

And when it came to normalizing marijuana, who could argue that seeing seventy-six-year-old Martha Stewart, the arbiter of good taste, endorse cannabis as a perfectly acceptable lifestyle choice wasn't a key moment? After all, it doesn't get more mainstream than Martha Stewart, and even with her 2004 felony conviction for lying to federal investigators in a stock trade case and her five-month prison stint, the savvy businesswoman had by this point redeemed herself and reclaimed her sterling image, along with her perch as one of America's foremost influencers of aspirational living. Her endorsement mattered and was in line with shifting attitudes, particularly in white, suburban America. Indeed, a few weeks before the first show aired, a Gallup poll revealed that 60 percent of Americans supported legal marijuana, the highest percentage ever recorded in a forty-seven-year trend.

"So someone smokes marijuana? Big deal! People smoke cigarettes and die from cancer. I haven't heard of anybody dying from cannabis. I'm quite egalitarian and liberal when it comes to stuff like that," Stewart told *The Hollywood Reporter*.

Martha & Snoop's Potluck Dinner Party went on to become the top-rated unscripted premiere of 2016 and even earned an Emmy nomination. It also led to Snoop's first cookbook, which bore the ingenious title *From Crook to Cook: Platinum Recipes from Tha Boss Dogg's Kitchen*.

With their "high-class dinner party" a certified hit and company Merry Jane recognized as a legitimate force, Ted and Snoop already had plans to take their cannabis empire to the next level. They had launched a cannabis entertainment company, established their own venture capital fund, and successfully put Snoop's name on a premium brand of weed in Colorado. The table was set. And now it was time to get the party underway. They weren't going to wait on Washington, D.C., to catch up with America's growing acceptance of marijuana—and neither was the rest of the world. As they eyed potential new partners in California, they believed that for the moment the big money could be made via Canada, where companies like Canopy Growth had plans to expand across the globe. Prescient as ever, Ted and Tiffany Chin had already broken out their snow boots and down parkas and journeyed to Ontario, to conquer the next big frontier in cannabis.

16

SNOOP'S STAR POWER

Niagara-on-the-Lake, Ontario

October 2016

As a prolific dealmaker for one of the most recognized entertainers in the world, Ted Chung had earned a reputation for being as exacting in his business dealings as he was in his personal style. He might race into a meeting late with his Louis Vuitton backpack hanging off one shoulder, sporting red suede Adidas sneakers with tiny jade rings dangling from the laces and a black waistcoat with a cheeky gorilla logo emblazoned on the breast pocket—the hallmark of trendy Japanese designer A Bathing Ape. But once the cerebral entrepreneur sat down, he was all business. He and his team never made a move on behalf of Snoop Dogg until they painstakingly vetted all the angles. Ted once said in an interview with E! that, after his dad, his greatest business idols included the perfectionist visionary Steve Jobs and the ruthless mob accountant Meyer Lansky. Like his role models, he was deliberate and detail-oriented down to the molecular level. And despite his chill demeanor, he always managed to extract precision from everyone involved.

But long before deal terms could be hammered out—or even entertained—there was one condition that trumped all others. Your vibe. If you didn't have a vibe that gelled with Ted and his tight-knit group of close advisers, you weren't getting a seat at the table. And you certainly weren't getting anywhere near Snoop. They needed to feel like you were the sort of person who could fit in and hang with them, whether it was late at night over a vape and a Scotch at a hotel bar in Toronto, digging into chicken and waffles at Sylvia's in Harlem around the corner from the historic Apollo Theater, or kicking back at the velvet-roped Light nightclub on the top floor of the Mandalay Bay Resort and Casino in Vegas, where DJ Snoopadelic spun a nostalgic set that didn't start until 1:00 A.M.

By necessity, it didn't take Ted much time to size you up. He put in marathon hours and was often on a plane, crisscrossing the country to and from investment meetings, sound checks, recording sessions, film shoots, and everything else that went along with the responsibility of representing Snoop Dogg's business interests. His schedule was so jam-packed that he often answered email at 2:00 or 3:00 A.M. and sometimes forgot to feed himself until he finally sat down at the end of his fourteen-hour day. Driving with him in his white Escalade, one could experience his hustle ethos firsthand as he juggled three calls on speakerphone while chatting with a reporter in the passenger seat as he navigated his way to a premiere party in Culver City, twenty minutes from his office in Playa Vista.

On one such evening, Frank Sinatra was playing on satellite radio in the background as he cruised through the usual snarled traffic that's just part of life in L.A. After quick handshakes and air kisses with the principals of a new HBO show his agency, Cashmere, was marketing, the rest of Chung's night unfolded at a garden cocktail party where he schmoozed with a cocky tech investor who was a potential funder for Casa Verde Capital, the cannabis-adjacent VC fund he'd started with Snoop. By 9:30 P.M., he'd be back in his SUV, making his way to a bar across town to hear a pitch from an eager screenwriter with a new movie idea for Snoop. And if the meeting ended before midnight, he'd hopefully be pulling in to his home on the Westside in time to catch up with the love of his life, his wife, Shvona Lavette, an actress, singer, and devoted vegan, before hopping back on his iPhone to wrap up any lingering calls or emails.

If you were lucky enough to gain his trust and be welcomed into the inner circle, you were treated like family. The bar was high, as Tiffany Chin, the business development chief for Snoop's marijuana brand Leafs By Snoop, knew all too well. She had gone through her own initiation when she first started with Ted's entertainment management company, Stampede, as an intern. Now she had been elevated to one of Ted's key cannabis consiglieri, entrusted with all the on-the-ground intelligence gathering for their enterprise. As a soft-spoken Asian American woman with a degree from Wharton, she enjoyed the looks of barely concealed surprise she elicited from the legions of male cannabis growers around the world when she showed up at their doors asking pointed questions about fertigation, automated lighting, and trimming systems. The bros would learn soon enough that whip-smart Tiffany wasn't *just* on a fact-finding mission; she was also Snoop's gatekeeper for all of these deals. She would field as many as five to ten incoming calls a day from ganja-preneurs or investors looking to get involved with Snoop's expanding cannabis portfolio, and her antennae for who would and wouldn't blend with their team was finely tuned. Some would even try to curry favor with her, like the guy who offered her the cool painting of Prince that she admired on a tour of his facility. It still hangs in her office. She said thank you to the artwork but not the deal.

With Canada's medical marijuana market growing by thousands of patients a month, Tiffany, Ted, and their colleagues had been carefully sizing up potential partners. When they first saw the opportunity, they were preparing to go live with Snoop's line of flower and edibles in the Rocky Mountain State. But with the way things worked in the United States, where cannabis couldn't legally cross state lines, there was no way yet to build a national brand or supply chain. What they were doing in Colorado was limited to, well, just Colorado. Like always, Ted had much-grander plans in mind. Canada's population was seven times the size of Colorado's. Expanding north of the border would give them access to an entire nation of potential customers while they waited for more states back home to lift their bans. And support for recreational legalization was continuing to grow in Canada as it looked ahead to a possible change of its governing party in Parliament. If adult-use legalization came to pass, the consulting firm Deloitte predicted, the Canadian market alone could top $5 billion to start, on a par with Canadian sales of whiskey, rum, and vodka. But even more important, the opportunity wouldn't be limited to what they could sell within Canadian borders. The bigger play was the export business—seizing Canada's early-mover advantage to sell cannabis across the world. But to get in on any of this action, they would need a Canadian partner.

Ted and Tiffany closely scrutinized all the obvious players—licensed producers like Tilray, Aurora, and of course Canopy Growth—that had been granted some of the first permissions to grow and sell as the country commercialized and regulated the sale of cannabis to medical patients. The team looked at the nuts and bolts—market position, capitalization, profits and losses, etc. But what really mattered in the end was that gut instinct about whether the folks running the company held the same values and could hang with the tribe. Ted wasn't just about making money; he cared about doing something with purpose, something that challenged conventional wisdom, something that underscored his belief in "unlocking the potential that cannabis had for the world," meaning the social, financial, and health benefits he thought marijuana could have, especially for those on the margins of society. So the story of the abandoned Hershey's factory and the town saved by cannabis intrigued him immediately.

In late 2014, Tiffany didn't have many contacts yet in Canada and had to resort to cold-emailing various startups through the generic email addresses on their websites. As the story goes, when the Canopy team received her email, they couldn't quite believe that someone representing Snoop would be reaching out to them. But after an email exchange and a phone call convinced them it was a legit inquiry, they agreed that Tiffany would fly out to Ottawa to sit down with Mark Zekulin, the studious attorney and employee number five who had risen from the post of general counsel to become Bruce Linton's trusted deputy. He and Tiffany hit it off immediately, and she remembers telling Ted, "He's got a vibe like us. He seems like a good guy and he understands what we're looking for."

Ted and Snoop would finally meet Mark face-to-face after a few months of calls back and forth. As usual, that spring, the duo's schedule was frenetic. The artist, who had dropped his Snoop Lion moniker by now and was back to going by Snoop Dogg, had just released his thirteenth studio album, *Bush,* in May 2015. Produced by Pharrell Williams, it was a party-themed series of laid-back tracks celebrating the "high life" of Los Angeles, and even featured a memorable collaboration with Stevie Wonder singing, "Get yourself a medical card, yeah." A few weeks later, the rapper and his crew were touching down in Toronto for one of the many children's charity events Snoop attended, when Ted invited Mark at the last minute to drop by his hotel.

The meeting went well, but not for the reasons one might think. Unlike what Ted half expected, Mark didn't roll up to the hotel decked out in a flashy suit with an entourage in tow. He presented as the math major he was: authentic, smart, and a policy wonk who had come on board to help the Canopy founders navigate the confusing regulations that were being written and rewritten in the early days of the business. He had experience as a policy adviser to Ontario finance minister Dwight Duncan, and had also worked on Prime Minister Dalton McGuinty's successful reelection campaign in 2011, before joining a prestigious firm in Toronto to specialize in international trade law.

Mark had no idea that this would be the night he would meet the global superstar. But a few minutes into his chat with Ted, in the lounge of the luxurious Shangri-La Hotel, the stylish young entertainment exec surprised him by offering to bring him upstairs to

Snoop's hotel room to say hello. Mark quickly dialed his wife to say he was most likely missing his flight home. He wasn't going to rush through this momentous meeting just to get to the airport. This was one of the biggest things that had ever happened to the fledgling startup he had helped build.

He genuinely tried not to be starstruck when he shook Snoop's hand. But as soon as he looked Snoop in the eye and started speaking, Ted remembered, Mark endeared himself to Snoop with his earnestness. At the time, Ted and Tiffany were fending off a lot of "canna-climbers," arrogant opportunists only in the business to make a quick buck. It was hard to cut through all the puffery. There was so much hype around marijuana in Canada, and so much froth in the market, that even a couple of thin press releases could send a stock soaring. Mark wanted to convey to Snoop that he and CEO Bruce Linton were the real deal: genuinely serious about their mission to serve patients, and in it for the long haul. Canopy's purpose, he told Snoop and Ted, was about much more than simply being the biggest or the best. It was about promoting the wellness and medicinal benefits of cannabis.

That was music to Snoop's ears. After all, he was not only the world's most discerning cannabis connoisseur. He was also a proud medical cardholder in California and a champion of the economic, social, and literal healing powers of cannabis. The partnership just felt right.

"There was just a different level of vision and professionalism and care in what the brand in Canopy and Tweed was going to stand for [compared to other licensed producers we assessed], and what sort of principles and tent poles there were going to be," said Ted in announcing the first global partnership whereby Snoop would lend his influence and valuable intellectual property to a marijuana company.

With Snoop's blessing, Ted and Mark headed back downstairs to get down to business, as the quick meet-and-greet stretched into a two-hour brainstorming session in the lobby bar of the hotel. Over drinks and dim sum, Ted and Mark crafted a road map for a three-year potential licensing deal.

"And we were off to the races," Ted said, smiling.

Back in Smiths Falls at headquarters, Bruce was humbled when he first opened the email from Mark saying that Snoop and Ted wanted to work with the company.

"I don't know about you, but . . . often I like people because they like me, you know? Like my threshold is reasonably low, and so when they approached us and said, 'We think what you're doing is interesting,' we were flattered, right? Because *everybody* knows Snoop," Bruce would recall years later.

In this, he was absolutely right. Over the course of his two-decade career, Snoop had gone from being a West Coast hip-hop/gangsta rap legend to a celebrity with mass appeal across demographics. You couldn't really pin him down. Yes, he was synonymous with weed and, of course, with hip-hop. Who could forget "Drop It Like It's Hot"? But the "new" Snoop was also a successful TV personality—as comfortable running the show on *The Joker's Wild* as he was dishing Hollywood gossip on Ellen's couch or rolling pizza dough in Martha's kitchen, and as magnetic in concert as he was on social media. He was also a Silicon Valley investor, a youth football coach, a married dad of four, and on and on. There was texture to his celebrity. And Snoop seemed to be everywhere, admired by everyone—exactly the kind of diverse customer pool Bruce had in mind. Plus, an alliance this big would bring on a massive media blitz, making it an especially brilliant way around Canada's prohibition on advertising. It was the best kind of publicity—the free kind.

Then an even more fortuitous chain of events in Canadian politics took the potential payoff from the deal to the next level. Within six months of Ted and Mark's first rough term sheet, Canada's new prime minister, Justin Trudeau, announced that the ban on recreational marijuana would be lifted by 2018. What was initially an agreement structured around medical marijuana was about to explode into an even bigger opportunity for them all.

On the heels of this big news—and after months of flirtation between Hollywood, Smiths Falls, and Toronto—the players were finally ready to unveil their newly formed cross-border cannabis alliance. They timed the announcement for a night when lots of reporters would be in Toronto covering the 2016 NBA All-Star Game. Snoop would be there, too, for festivities that included a celebrity basketball game with rapper 2 Chainz to raise money for the local schools. They announced a three-year collaboration in which Canopy would sell three Leafs By Snoop products through its Tweed online shop. All went according to plan. The news made instant headlines and generated breathless media coverage, including the money shot: Snoop in a Tweed T-shirt, on a jumbotron two stories high, looking down on New York City's bustling Times Square.

But the even more perfectly orchestrated photo op came the following fall, in 2016, when the Doggfather and the Willy Wonka of Weed would meet in person for the first time to announce—on camera—that the first LBS flower would be available for purchase in a few short weeks. Their respective staffs prepared for a summit like none other: the two weed-industry giants would be hailed like heads of state at a sort of cannabis Camp David, discussing not a trade deal between their two countries, but how they could partner to take on the rest of the world. Naturally, the setting would be Tweed Farms, the site of the biggest greenhouse on the planet at the time.

Situated two hours from Toronto in picturesque Niagara-on-the-Lake, a quaint Ontario town with a charming clock tower, Tweed Farms was the pot farm of the future. Under 350,000 square feet of shimmering glass and buzzing fans, the thousands of encased plants were carefully tended around the clock by dozens of horticulturists wearing dark sunglasses, hairnets, and white lab coats. The scene was like nothing Snoop and his entourage had ever seen—or maybe ever imagined. Donning his Leafs By Snoop lab coat with its gold logo emblazoned on the back, and sporting a Tweed hat, the lanky star toured the rows and rows of potted cannabis flowers, team in tow, and with Tweed's master grower on hand to take questions. Later, off camera, Snoop sampled some of the products.

One week later, Snoop Dogg and Martha Stewart would debut their pot-infused cooking show, *Martha & Snoop's Potluck Dinner Party,* on VH-1, marking a new milestone in marijuana's journey into the cultural mainstream. The very next evening, as Ted and Snoop celebrated the sky-high ratings and Donald Trump's White House victory shocked the pundits, California and eight other states gave the thumbs-up to ballot initiatives legalizing marijuana in some form.

California would be the largest market in America when retail sales commenced on January 1, 2018. But recreational legalization hadn't happened overnight in the Golden State. Although California was the first state in the United States to allow medical cannabis when it passed the 1996 Compassionate Use Act, a 2010 ballot initiative for an over-21 market stalled out when Republican governor Arnold Schwarzenegger, along with top state Democrats, raised questions about the confusing way it was written. And so, Colorado had beaten California to the punch. But by 2016, Californians were primed to catch up after seeing the rollout in the Rockies and more states opening the door to medical use. Moreover, the new proposal sought to address social justice head-on. It would provide for resentencing of marijuana offenses for those who were serving time, and also create a system to wipe clean old criminal records. Thanks to lobbying from celebrities (including Snoop Dogg) as well as campaign contributions from tech titans Sean Parker and Peter Thiel, and support from hedge fund billionaire George Soros, Proposition 64 passed with 57.1 percent of the vote.

The measure rang in a new commercial regime for cannabis that would require existing businesses in California's sprawling gray market to come under state authority. They would have to apply for licenses from the new Bureau of Cannabis Control in Sacramento, as well as from local communities. Their products would be subject to new rigorous tracking from seed to sale: testing for pesticides, mold, and potency. There were complex rules on labeling, dosing instructions, childproof packaging, and more. The inaugural system would present costly and confusing new challenges for operators trying to bring their businesses into the light, while testing the flourishing underground industry that had managed to flout federal enforcement for decades.

Not every entrepreneur would reap the benefits. No one knew which towns and cities would allow dispensaries to open or delivery services to operate, or how many consumers would continue to source their weed from unlicensed dealers and growers. Even Tiffany and Ted would have lots to figure out before they could entertain alliances to introduce the Leafs By Snoop products in their home state.

But back in Toronto, their Canadian wager looked more promising than ever. A week after the 2016 U.S. elections, Canada's Canopy Growth Corporation, trading under the TSX ticker WEED, would be named by stock traders as the world's first marijuana "unicorn."

17
DRINKING SALAD DRESSING

Smiths Falls, Ontario

December 2016

THE FACT THAT his company was housed inside a former chocolate factory made it impossible for Bruce Linton, the consummate pitchman, to resist playing up his image as the Willy Wonka of Weed. Sporting his standard uniform, a black tee with the Tweed logo, tweed sport coat (wink-wink), and a playful gold lapel pin that read HI, he was a talented talker with a down-home charm—both behind the scenes and in public. Whenever Bruce presented Canopy Growth's genesis story to conference rooms full of investors in suits and ties, or to any of the countless TV anchors whom he had happily granted an interview, the talking points almost always included a joke about how he had "figured out why the Oompa Loompas were really so happy" when he started a weed company inside the defunct Hershey's plant in Smiths Falls.

The narrative stuck. It didn't hurt that the factory still bore many reminders of its storied past: the CHOCOLATE SHOPPE sign that had once marked the entrance to the old Hershey's visitor center was repurposed in the front offices, while a poster of Johnny Depp playing the 2005 version of the eccentric chocolatier hung above the call center where operators took thousands of orders from around the country. And tucked into the corner of the interior window that looked into the CEO's modest office strung with marijuana leaf Christmas lights was a white scrap of paper that read *Mr. Wonka.*

As it turns out, the parallels to the famous children's story by British author Roald Dahl were real. In December 2016, for example, Canopy announced that it had secured its golden ticket—namely, a highly sought-after dealer's license from the Canadian government that allowed its brain trust to formally begin developing the cannabinoid-infused confections of the future. Ideas had been bubbling in the pipeline for years, but now they could publicly announce that Canopy's Tweed division had gotten the federal stamp of approval to launch a top secret operation testing controlled substances they were not permitted to sell just yet.

From the beginning, Canada's newly legal pot producers had only been allowed to sell their cannabis in a single and simple form: dried flower. Which meant that by 2016, the illicit market was already light-years ahead in its product innovation. Underground hawkers had long trafficked in extracts, the by-products of the plant made from the sticky resin—the fatty substance that contains the potent THC and CBD inside the delicate sacs that cover the folds of marijuana flowers and leaves. Once pressed and refined via a host of homegrown heating techniques to release the compounds, the oil can be used in chocolates, gummies, cookies, fizzy beverages, and every possible treat you could think of. It can be sealed inside oral gel capsules or cartridges filled with amber oil for vaping; formulated into oral drops or skin lotions and balms; or hardened into an array of waxy or gooey solids known as concentrates, used to achieve an intense high by heating the oil over a hot surface and inhaling the smoke (otherwise known as dabbing).

As someone who didn't like to fall behind, Bruce worried that if Tweed didn't start innovating—and fast—this precious crude material and the plethora of products created from it would continue to give the pot dealers thriving in the shadows an edge over law-abiding companies like his own.

"If we don't match up to the illicit market offerings, then they have a very substantial opportunity. Day one, if we don't sell any concentrated products or vaporizable products, that is good news for the bad guys until we get to," he explained.

Just as in any other business, it all came down to demand. Medical patients and recreational consumers alike increasingly wanted more diverse options. Specifically, they wanted legal access to a menu of smoke-free alternatives created from extracts, and ultimately argued it was their right to possess them in a case that made it all the way to the nation's highest court. In June 2015, a landmark Supreme Court of Canada ruling known as the "*Smith* decision" forced the government to amend Canada's Constitution to expand lawful pot products to include "cannabis derivatives." The action paved the way for Canada's corporate producers to finally begin R&D on extracts. By the first quarter of 2017, just a year after cannabis oil was first introduced to the market, it already accounted for half of all legal marijuana purchases in Canada, reported *Marijuana Business Daily*.

Production started first on medical oil gelcaps with the hope that by 2019, the government would allow edibles, skin creams, and other topicals and vapes to be sold across Canada in retail stores, once new local regulations were hammered out. The newly elected pro-pot prime minister, Justin Trudeau, had upped the ante in the fall of 2015, vowing to stamp out the illicit dealers and open up a domestic recreational market potentially worth between US$2.3 and $4.5 billion according to estimates by *Marijuana Business Daily*. One year later, with Prime Minister Trudeau in office, Snoop Dogg as a new partner, a massive war chest from investors, and the new license, Bruce's team finally had everything in place that they would need to create the next generation of pot products.

The stealthy experiments led by scientists would take place under strict lock and key in a high-tech incubator deep inside the Smiths Falls facility, where researchers had to possess top-level security clearance from the government in order to enter. It was a CIA-reminiscent operation so airtight, only a rival as slick as Wonka's nemesis, Slugworth, could finesse a way in to steal the precious formulas inside.

Past the sterile cultivation rooms, down the hall from the dented two-story water storage tank once filled with corn syrup to make batches of Almond Joy and Take 5 chocolate bars, around the corner from the shiny machines measuring out precise-to-the-milliliter doses of cannabis oil for thousands of tiny blue and red capsules, and beyond the 70,000-square-foot steel vault storing purchases ready to ship was a windowless room staffed by PhDs in pale blue lab coats and goggles. Amid the bubbling beakers and whiteboards, this top secret lab was one of the first and only places in all of Canada where top pharmacologists and food scientists were assiduously working to invent new ways for people to consume cannabis and other controlled substances.

It was here that Bruce's dream would come to life. His version of Wonka's "Everlasting Gobstopper" was the ultimate cannabis-infused beverage—a nonalcoholic drink that was so enjoyable and guilt-free, it would attract even the most hesitant cannabis customer to trade a nightly cocktail or glass of Chardonnay for it. After college, Bruce had spent a summer driving across Canada promoting the Molson Brewery. Now he wanted to create a portfolio of beverage products that would appeal to everyone from hard-partying millennial bros to old-timers with diabetes and heart disease to Chardonnay moms. His drinks would be zero-calorie and hangover-free—and without a trace of marijuana's notorious herbaceous taste. Best of all, Bruce hoped they would bring on a consistent, predictable buzz soon after imbibing.

If done right, he imagined, these beverages could one day satisfy the thirst of the world's spirits, wine, or beer drinkers. Once the scientists perfected the formula and tested its shelf stability, he envisioned these alcohol-free drinks being mass-produced on a fast-moving, high-tech assembly line, and shipped to stores. And in theory, they would offer the taste, experience, and price point that the underground edibles market could never match. With millennials drinking less booze than their parents, he reasoned that one day they just might give Big Alcohol a run for its money—not only in Canada, of course, but across the world.

That was the vision. The reality was that it wasn't going to be so easy to create this beverage of the future, nor to convert casual drinkers into customers. Plus, the first generation of cannabis-infused drinks were already being sold in pockets of the United States, and let's just say they weren't a hit. The 2012 Green Rush in Colorado had inspired a handful of entrepreneurs to give beverages a shot. But by 2016, the fruity soft drinks, root beers, and colas in Colorado, Washington, California, and Oregon were not exactly flying off the shelves. Not even close. BDS Analytics, one of the first companies to track retail sales in newly legal markets, found that beverages made up only 1 percent of the entire cannabis market (a number that had barely inched up by the fall of 2019).

The reason for these lackluster sales wasn't too hard to figure out. First was the simple fact that the drinks didn't taste very good, according to Wanda James, owner of Simply Pure, one of the first dispensaries to open in Colorado and an early edibles company. She didn't mince words, describing the drinks as overly sweet due to the loads of sugar needed to mask the weed taste. And they often *looked* unappetizing when the oil-based THC ingredients separated from the water in the products and settled like sediment at the bottom of the bottle. Some industry insiders, like Rick Gillis, president of California's Tinley Beverage Company, described the first versions on the market as "a little like drinking salad dressing."

Further, the early serving sizes were geared toward someone who really wanted to get exceptionally stoned—or who had a very high tolerance. A bottle might contain 100 milligrams of THC—or ten healthy servings. Worse, and this is a common problem with most edibles (or in this case drinkables), the timing and nature of the buzz were completely unpredictable. It wasn't like having a glass of wine or a vodka tonic, where most drinkers knew how long it would take for the alcohol's intoxicating effects to settle over them and what they would feel like. The dosing for cannabis could be imprecise and varied widely depending on so many factors, like whether the extracts came from trim—the leftover plant material after the valuable cannabis flowers were harvested (similar to the meat scraps often used to make sausages)—and if so, whether that trim was a random mix of strains or just one kind, and which one. Further complicating the equation was the fact that in its oil form, cannabis is metabolized through the liver, so there are lots of individual and biological variables that determine how the body responds to THC, and when. A person's size, their past pot usage, and even what they have eaten that day could all affect the type of high, its duration, and precisely when it will hit, making a good high hard to replicate. Plus, as with run-of-the-mill infused chocolates or gummies, it could be as long as two hours after cracking open a bottle that one might start to feel a buzz, by which point a person could easily be tempted to sip a little bit too much in frustrated anticipation.

In 2016, most consumers of legal weed in the United States preferred to smoke their cannabis anyway, with edibles, including candy and beverages, accounting for only 15 percent of the entire legal market, according to BDS Analytics cofounder Roy Bingham. But while some in the industry looked at those numbers and saw low demand, others saw vast opportunity. Fruit gelées and chocolate bars were the fastest-growing and most-sought-after products by newbies, and everyone from the manufacturers to the retail shop owners knew there was a huge market waiting to be tapped if they could break through to the canna-curious with the right messaging, packaging, and consumer education. Edibles were a product category ripe for disruption; it would be challenging to figure it out, but the first company to succeed at perfecting the science would soon be raking in the profits.

Bruce knew he wasn't there yet with his cannabis-infused beverages. Not even close. So he started quietly looking for allies. He needed a partner who understood the ins and outs of the beverage business, had plenty of capital to invest, and could bring their expertise in bottling and distributing to his new project. So in November 2016, when the CEO of a major U.S. alcohol company, Constellation Brands' Rob Sands, revealed in an interview with Bloomberg News that his company was getting into the cannabis business, it got Bruce's attention immediately.

This was the first time Big Alcohol had signaled it would dip a toe into cannabis, even as the $25 billion industry sensed a growing threat to its core profits. In September 2016, the investment management firm Cowen & Company had released a report showing that alcohol consumption had steadily slipped among men in the United States over the previous five years, just as cannabis use had ticked up. "Why wouldn't big business, so to speak, be acutely interested in a category of that magnitude?" Sands said, in reference to financial analysts' forecasts showing that the legal cannabis industry could grow 800 percent over a decade and be worth as much as $50 billion by 2026.

Not surprisingly, wine, spirits, and beer makers had historically opposed legalization, and had even reportedly spent tens of thousands of dollars to lobby against pro-pot referenda. So when the story about Constellation Brands—the company that distributes Corona beer and Svedka vodka—doing a one-eighty on weed made it to the top of the news feeds, Bruce Linton made his move, asking colleague Mark Zekulin to make a discreet overture through LinkedIn to a Constellation contact. And so began a covert and delicate dance between the liquor maker's upstate New York campus and Canopy HQ in Smiths Falls. It was a long courtship; the two companies kept their due diligence under wraps for over a year while they decided whether or not it was a match. When they were finally ready to wed, the big announcement stunned major players in Canada and the United States alike. No one saw it coming. Constellation Brands would invest CA$245 million in Canopy Growth and take a 9.9 percent ownership stake. CEO Rob Sands told *The Wall Street Journal* at the time that the deal was made in anticipation of the United States legalizing marijuana nationwide.

"We think that it's highly likely, given what's happened at the state level," predicted Sands.

It was a heady moment. But back in that lab, it was heads down. Fueled with a new injection of capital and loads of PR, the scientists worked feverishly on perfecting a cannabinoid-infused beverage that was both clear and devoid of an off-putting skunky smell or flavor.

The absence of color or odor, in Bruce's mind, was key in signaling the purity and quality of the product while avoiding the "salad dressing" effect. "When you can make a clear beverage, you have done your shit," Bruce explained. "That is not the way it naturally comes out, and the reason a lot of [manufacturers] like dark stuff. Chocolate's a great place to throw crappy dark opaque oils. No one can see."

By November 2017, just a month after the Constellation deal was announced at the Canadian Cannabis Awards in Toronto, Bruce was already talking up "Tweed and Tonic," a ready-to-drink product concept in a can that was fizzy and lemony and would offer a subtle earthiness that reminded the consumer it was weed. The scientists also mixed up recipes for a line of teas, tentatively called Loose Leaf, that might come in a green tea or a black tea variety with a 2-milligram microdose of cannabis meant for those who preferred a light buzz to being all-out blazed. Of course, for the millennial crowd, there would be a party product, too. One with images of outer space on a dark can offered a more "elevated" experience, if you will.

But Bruce and his new partner knew that none of these drinks would catch on if consumers didn't trust the consistency of the product, including the onset of its euphoric, mellowing effects. People wanted a reliable experience. They wanted to know how it would make them feel, how it would make them act, when it would kick in, and most important, when it would wear off. So the researchers worked tirelessly, trying to figure out how to dissolve lipid-based THC into water to quicken its onset and make the experience more predictable and consistent.

As its researchers toiled away, in October 2018 Canopy purchased the IP for a cutting-edge water-soluble delivery method with the $19.2 million acquisition of a Colorado company called Ebbu. The clinically tested technology allowed for rapid onset, meaning that a consumer would reportedly feel the effects of the cannabis within fifteen minutes—much closer to a glass of wine or can of beer. The technology was already fueling sales of a new alcohol-free, cannabis-infused line of California Sauvignon Blanc launched by Rebel Coast Winery. The company was also pioneering genetic mapping of cannabinoids and hemp research, all part of Canopy's master growth plan.

In just five short years, Canopy had grown into a technologically sophisticated enterprise with an ever-growing staff of highly trained botanists and top organic chemists who used high-tech data gathering and analysis in the grow operation to measure and optimize progress. Bruce estimated they were on their fifth iteration of their indoor cultivation system and still tweaking it, using monitors powered by artificial intelligence to help calibrate humidity, water temperature, and oxygen levels. They had created their own in-house breeding program where scientists were "phenotyping" new combinations of cannabis strains to address evolving consumer tastes and uses.

It was the spring of 2018, and by this time the brightly lit rooms represented a fraction of the company's million-plus square feet of cannabis farming across Canada's five provinces. In recent months, Tweed had been on a shopping spree, acquiring cultivation operations around Canada and snapping up intellectual property and emerging brands.

Bruce had always believed the cannabis game would be won with science and technology. No fancy packaging or branding alone would sell a product that was mediocre. To him, dominating the new global marijuana market was really about taking an existing product and making it better through rigorous and methodical research and innovation. He would often draw a comparison between his startup and Google, telling reporters that the biggest search engine in the world wasn't the first to index information on the World Wide Web. But it blew past Yahoo!, AOL, and Bing because Google founders Sergey Brin and Larry Page had crushed the competition with the best algorithms. The best science.

"If you use science, engineering, technology and create something so much better than anybody else, you can have incumbent brands that have been around for ten years before you, and you kill them," Bruce underlined. This was how he planned to take on the booming market for marijuana still being sold on the street.

At the heart of his strategy was rigor—formulating hypotheses and testing them over and over in the lab—and then trying them out on real consumers in focus groups.

As he knew all too well, experimentation was expensive, but it was also essential. "We have made and poured more cannabis beverages down the drain than you could possibly want to know," he remarked dryly as he looked back on the exhaustive process.

Less than a year after they struck up their partnership, Constellation was bullish on Canopy's progress. In the summer of 2018, the alcohol giant doubled down on the cannabis corporation, which had just become the first plant-touching marijuana business to trade on the New York Stock Exchange. On August 15, the beer distributor increased its stake in the Canadian company to 38 percent, bringing its total investment to an eye-popping US$4 billion. That's "billion" with a *b*. Constellation was playing to win. And its wager spurred other big alcohol and tobacco companies to make their own moves in the Canadian cannabis market.

"When Constellation dipped their toe into the water, Diageo and everybody else sat back. You never heard a word from them. Never heard a word from Molson Coors or any of those people. Once Constellation made their double-down bet, everybody said, 'Okay, no unintended consequences here, now we can start doing it,'" observed Chuck Smith, cofounder and CEO of the THC-infused beverage maker Dixie Elixirs, a month before Dixie would go public in Canada and would eventually announce a landmark licensing deal with AriZona Iced Tea.

Constellation's giant bet on Bruce and Canopy Growth set off a wave of cross-border alliances between alcohol and cannabis businesses. By the end of 2018, the Canadian unit of Molson Coors would strike up a $100 million joint venture with Canada's Hydropothecary Corporation, and Anheuser-Busch's InBev unveiled a $100 million deal with Tilray to develop THC and CBD beverages. Big Tobacco waded into the Canadian market, too. Philip Morris's parent company, Altria, invested $1.8 billion in the Toronto-based global cannabis giant Cronos Group.

It was still unclear, however, exactly when all these newfangled beverages, edibles, skin lotions, and vapes they had worked so hard to develop would be permitted for sale. The federal and provincial officials were still working through timelines. But Bruce would be ready; he had already purchased the old Shorewood Packaging plant across the way from his headquarters. The company that had once manufactured the paper wrapping for cigarettes, vitamins, cosmetics, and candy had, like many others, decamped from Smiths Falls a decade before, laying off more than two hundred workers. The old building soon would be demolished to make way for a fancy new bottling operation spanning its nineteen-plus acres. Lots of new jobs were expected to follow.

In fact, to ensure they would be ready to go as soon as it was time to begin shipping cases of the new beverages, Canopy's Tweed division was already on a hiring spree. Nearly every Monday in the spring of 2018, thirty to forty wide-eyed new employees would arrive ready to put on a white lab coat and security card dangling from a lanyard, roll up their sleeves, and get to work inside one of the largest cannabis companies in the world.

Less than two weeks after Constellation announced its mega follow-up investment, and less than two months away from Canada's full legalization, the Willy Wonka of Weed realized his longtime dream of reopening the old Hershey's visitor center, where, decades ago, the beloved confectionery had given visiting candy lovers a peek into how they made their famous kisses and peanut butter cups. But while the aroma of delicious cocoa had faded, the site's tourist appeal had been restored, thanks to a gift shop where you could buy baseball hats and hoodies, a café with gray-tweed-upholstered furniture where baristas whipped up cappuccinos embellished with a marijuana leaf made of ground cinnamon atop the milky froth, and a colorful exhibit in English and French educating visitors about the anatomy of the plant, the long history of its use, and the science of its interaction with the human body. This new visitor center, with its giant Tweed signage, signified a new swelling pride. Bruce hoped tourists would one day arrive by the busload to hear his company's story and learn about the science of this incredible plant. Unlike the Hershey's visitors, who got to go home with candy, Tweed guests would have to wait to buy smokable souvenirs.

The opening of the Tweed Visitor Centre was capped off a few days later by an all-day music festival on the front lawn of Canopy Growth's headquarters. The annual shindig had always attracted thousands of people from the surrounding area. But this year, whispers of a major headliner taking the stage spurred a run on the first thousand free tickets. Yes, Snoop Doggy Dogg would be in the house. It was one of the biggest things to ever happen in a town that only a few years before was still reeling from a rash of layoffs that had sent the community into a downward spiral.

As the sun set on the warm summer night of the show, Bruce and the mayor of Smiths Falls, Shawn Pankow—a Tesla-driving fourth-generation financial planner who had lived through the downturn that had given way to the cannabis boom—were looking forward to welcoming Snoop and his business partner Ted Chung to their neighborhood. The plan was to take the A-lister and his manager to Chuckles Jack, a curiously named South Asian–inspired bistro run by a charismatic Sri Lankan immigrant, Chef Ram Mogandas, and one of the only nicer places in town to grab a meal. Chef Ram was a fixture over at Tweed, where he often catered spicy meals for the execs, and Bruce was particularly fond of his curries and naan. Despite new restaurants like Ram's and the prosperity that cannabis had brought to Smiths Falls, many storefronts on Market Street remained vacant and boarded up. It was a reminder of just how far Smiths Falls had fallen—and how much more room it still had to grow. Bruce had been passionate about bringing the town back to life from the start. He was a frequent patron of the local businesses, including the barbershop. Even the new lunchroom inside his company headquarters didn't serve food, so as not to compete with the local joints.

As the CEO and the mayor waited outside Chuckles Jack for Snoop's entourage to arrive for dinner, the Old Post Office across the street caught Bruce's eye. Built in 1893 by Thomas Fuller, the chief architect for the Canadian government in the late nineteenth century, the edifice's red sandstone was crowned by a stunning clock tower. To Bruce, it seemed like the most beautiful building in town, but it was crumbling. It hadn't been used as a post office for decades. Bruce pressed the mayor for intel about who owned the building and why it had become such a wreck. Within minutes, he had convinced the mayor to give him the owner's telephone number and was texting the landlord to make a serious offer to purchase the historic site, so he could personally restore it to its former glory.

With dinner out of the way, it was time for the big show. The crowd jumped to its feet and began screaming as soon as the global icon strode onstage, flanked by his backup dancers in their black-and-white Adidas track pants and crop tops, while he gave a shout-out and salute to Tweed and to the mayor.

After performing his legendary tracks "Gin and Juice" and "Drop It Like It's Hot," the Doggfather threw in a dramatic flourish, the kind that only he could pull off. As he swayed along to the beat, Snoop announced that he would now introduce Canada's "new national anthem," in a nod to the impending date of national legalization—October 18, 2018. Everyone went crazy once they heard the memorable first notes of—what else?—"Young and Wild and Free," the hit song with Wiz Khalifa and Bruno Mars.

So what we smoke weed?

. . .

That's how it's supposed to be
Living young and wild and free . . .

18
THE END OF PROHIBITION

Sonoma County, California
July 2017

DEEP IN THE rolling vineyards of southern Sonoma County, a group of epicurians gathered on a cool July evening. But they weren't there to talk about Pinot Noir or Chardonnay grapes. They had traveled to the heart of wine country for an evening of kinship celebrating the new frontier of weed. It was one of several events in the summer of 2017 at which cannabis entrepreneurs and winemakers could meet each other and find common ground in their biodynamic growing practices, respect for sustainable agriculture, and appreciation of the unique terrain that bore their fruits. Tonight, they would break bread at a glorious THC- and CBD-infused gourmet feast.

Chef Jeff Danzer was at the center of all the action, scurrying about in his black double-breasted chef's coat as he prepared to show off both his culinary chops and the trade secret he had worked long and hard to perfect—his method for erasing the grassy flavor of cannabis. His mise en place had to be particularly sharp this evening as he prepared a locally sourced meal for two hundred foodies. This was a private fête, in the birthplace of the farm-to-table movement, honoring longtime marijuana rights activist and serial entrepreneur Steve DeAngelo, who would be on hand to sample the meal. It would be Jeff's biggest and possibly most discerning audience yet.

Waitstaff in crisp white shirts and freshly pressed black ties kicked off the inaugural NorCal CannaCuisine Gala with a canna-cocktail hour, offering guests flutes brimming with alcohol-free hibiscus coolers and creamy mocha libations—mixed with an optional microdose of THC—as they mingled outdoors and enjoyed the stylings of a local band. On the dinner menu: pink watermelon gazpacho served in martini glasses garnished with a fresh green marijuana leaf, Cornish game hens (or stuffed portobello mushrooms for the vegans), and a gooey brownie dessert, each decadent course infused with tiny droplets of Jeff's tasteless THC tincture. Before they dug in, guests were quizzed by servers on individual preferences, THC tolerance levels, and whether or not they wanted their dinners spiked with weed at all. Every table was staffed with two waitpersons, each responsible for delivering dishes marked with discreet green and red stickers to ensure everyone received the correct meal—virgin or not.

Behind the scenes, Jeff wielded a medicine dropper to add the star ingredient to each artfully plated portion before it was whisked away to the white-tableclothed dining room. The THC would be layered into the three-hour meal in stages, so that by dessert, those who opted in would consume a maximum of 10 milligrams and, hopefully, feel as if they had indulged in a few glasses of wine while still retaining the presence of mind to meet their Uber or Lyft car when it was time to go home.

"Niney-nine percent of the other chefs out there . . . rely on the terpenes and the flavonoids to pair with their food. I don't know any other chef that does it the way I do it . . . Every other chef out there is pairing the taste or working with the taste to bring it into the meal as an ingredient," explained Jeff of his unique process.

He was right. The other pioneers at the forefront of the emerging cannabis culinary scene had completely different approaches. Some wanted to find ways to use the whole plant, while others wanted to make a virtue of its component parts and flavors. But the one thing all of these gourmands shared was a desire to dress up cannabis in a new, sophisticated way for those with expensive tastes and refined palates. One such attendee was an ambitious young woman named Erin Gore, the founder of the high-end cannabis lifestyle company Garden Society, and a sponsor of the event.

She hailed from the heart of wine country and was married to a second-generation grape grower, whose father had built the company that planted most of the grapes stretching across the hilly landscape of Sonoma, beginning in the 1970s. Her husband, Tom Gore, who had long worked for Constellation, now had his own wine brand backed by the Big Alcohol giant.

While she learned her husband's family business, Erin had started to dabble in cannabis. A onetime Division 1 basketball player with a degree in chemical engineering, Erin was using medical marijuana to manage the painful recovery from a grueling hip-reconstruction surgery. Just for fun, she and her husband started growing a few plants in a corner of their two-acre micro-farm, outside of Healdsburg, where the couple grew sixty varieties of fruits and vegetables and even pressed their own olive oil. Their private Eden was a short drive to the farm where Tom grew 1,600 acres of grapes for award-winning vintages of Constellation's Chardonnay, Sauvignon Blanc, and Cabernet, and the 165-acre vineyard where he harvested the grapes for the celebrated bottles bearing his own name.

She wasn't at home much to enjoy it, though. The tall, auburn-haired go-getter with a wickedly dry wit had a fast-paced, all-consuming day job managing a $100 million glue business for the mega consumer products company Henkel, and regularly flew back and forth between the Bay Area and her Shanghai office. As she climbed the corporate ladder, Erin and Tom were also trying to start a family. And when they struggled with heartbreaking fertility issues, Erin says she turned to cannabis once again, this time to help her sleep and manage the stress of it all. That was when she began to notice that pot products geared specifically toward women were nearly nonexistent, and the shopping experience at existing medical dispensaries was rather unappealing to the typical female consumer.

"Everything was a super high dose. Super gross, super bro," she pointed out.

Between business trips in 2014, she and a few girlfriends began experimenting with cookie and candy recipes using the finest dark chocolate, organic sugar, grass-fed butter, and choice strains of cannabis. Her friends were the sort of educated, professional millennial women who did yoga, ate well, and appreciated a glass of chilled Chardonnay at the end of the day to relax after putting in long hours at the office or chasing after kids. In the kitchen, they would laugh and chat about life as they mixed up chocolate bonbons and caramels. Erin, the chemical engineer, would concentrate on the "stoichiometry"—measuring out the precise dosing of the cannabinoids from indica and sativa strains, and testing the potency to ensure the sweets would give a slight buzz similar to a glass of wine, but without the hangover or headaches. It wasn't about getting wasted. This was about a new and possibly better way to shrug off the day.

"Life is fucking difficult. You can't just eat kale and be happy, or we'd all be skinny, happy people because we'd all fucking do it, right? It doesn't work. You need something," she says, underscoring her belief that cannabis could be a healthier tool than alcohol to help smooth over the sharp edges of life.

Over two years, the "high holiday" parties and cookie exchanges quickly grew from four friends to eight to a dozen, to eventually standing-room-only gatherings of forty women. Everyone wanted more. Erin started bringing her medicated treats to her mom's best friend, who was battling Stage 4 breast cancer—and who would end up giving Erin the gentle push she needed to pursue a new career in cannabis. It happened on a weekend before a big meeting, at a time when Erin was reeling from a second miscarriage and feeling burned-out from her job. She remembers her mom's friend grabbing her arm and telling her she was missing her calling.

"She was like, 'What are you doing?' Like, 'This is your passion and your purpose. You need to make a change,'" Erin remembered.

That conversation gave her the courage to ultimately quit the corporate track and launch her own artisanal edibles company aimed at women like her and her friends. In 2016, she began working with a Lehigh University researcher studying the endocannabinoid system to learn more about how the human body's receptors interact with the active chemicals in the plant, and the impact on its "bioavailability"—meaning how long it takes the body to process certain compounds before a person feels the effects. She was especially passionate about using all of the parts of the plant, the "full spectrum" of cannabinoids, terpenes, and flavonoids, in order to get the most therapeutic benefit, as opposed to distilling and isolating only the most psychoactive chemicals. In her view, it was analogous to the way her husband made a fine Chardonnay, in which the whole fruit, including the grape skins and seeds, contributed to the wine's full-bodied character. She decided that her startup would specialize in handcrafted batches of low-dose candies made from marijuana grown by small farmers, along with other premium locally sourced ingredients. Every aspect of her wine country life informed her take on the long-misunderstood plant.

At first, she was hesitant to talk about her business around her husband's Constellation wine colleagues. Not only did weed still carry a heavy stigma (and Constellation still drug-tested its employees at the time), but there was growing sensitivity around the potential rivalry between the two substances.

"I can tell you that the constant mantra within those types of [Big Alcohol] companies is what they call 'share of throat.' That means that any consumer has a given amount of space in their body for however it is that they want to let their hair down," explained Tracey Mason, CEO of House of Saka, who had a completely different way of approaching wine and cannabis. While there were still those in the wine business who viewed pot as a direct competitor, this twenty-five-year veteran of the wine industry saw it as a potential complement, and was on her way to figuring out how to take the alcohol out of wine and replace it with THC to create the first alcohol-removed, pot-infused sparkling rosé. The whole gourmet landscape was shaping up like a riff on those old "Hey, you got peanut butter on my chocolate" Reese's TV commercials where two strangers bump into each other and suddenly realize that chocolate and peanut butter are actually a delicious combo. Everyone was trying to create fresh mash-ups to entice a new group of people who already enjoyed wine to discover cannabis.

Wine and weed soon converged yet again for Erin when she decided to woo Karli Warner, the PR wiz who used to represent her husband's wine brand, to become her intrepid partner. Karli had worked in wine for most of her career and had long been a cannabis consumer. She had taken a break from her job at Constellation to focus on her family, but was now itching to get back to her professional life. When Erin approached her, she jumped at the opportunity. In 2016, Erin gave birth to Garden Society, and the following year, she also welcomed a son of her own. By then, the two moms had started holding their first Tupperware-like parties in private homes, selling signature chocolates and fruit gelées infused with pot grown in Mendocino County, and delivering the goodies to local events, including weddings and bridal showers. They were not alone. The bon vivant spin on marijuana was beginning to catch on among wine connoisseurs, inside chefs' kitchens, and at underground dinner parties across the Bay Area.

In fact, the emphasis on terroir—the climate, soil, and farming practices that are said to contribute to a wine's body, flavor, and aroma—was becoming a trendy way to educate new consumers and compare the methods of legacy farmers from Northern California against the new large-scale corporate growers buying up land in the south. All you had to do was look to Canada and its licensed producers, with their airplane-hangar-sized indoor cultivation facilities and towering greenhouses, to catch a glimpse of how cannabis might turn into Big Agriculture in the blink of an eye. Thousands of California marijuana farmers who had made a living covertly for generations in the Emerald Triangle, and in the counties that make up wine country, had started growing their heirloom strains out in the open on small parcels of land. With full legalization coming soon, and estimates that the market could be worth as much as $4.72 billion by 2025, they were watching well-funded outside players come in and snap up tens of thousands of acres in traditional farming areas like Salinas, the "Salad Bowl of the World," and farther south in the Santa Ynez Valley near Santa Barbara. These were big-money companies with an eye on mass-producing cannabis as a commodity like lettuce or soybeans. The new lawful era would come with stiff new regulations, including extensive tracking and lab testing for pesticides and quality control, not to mention taxes and a slew of licensing fees. Small farmers worried they wouldn't be able to compete or even afford to transition into legitimate businesses. And then there was the question of whether consumers would really care or know enough to ask where and how their bud was grown.

California legislators hoped so. After the passage of Proposition 64, which created the state's new commercialized market, lawmakers tasked the state's Department of Food and Agriculture with taking a page from the wine industry to award "appellations" to certain types of cannabis from specific geographic regions by 2021. Just like Napa Cabernet Sauvignon or Sonoma Chardonnay, weed grown in Humboldt or other distinguished regions would one day be validated by its own stamp of approval certifying its prestige to the world. The practice underscored an optimism that eventually California cannabis would be legally exported across the globe. Industry estimates projected a weed market worth $11 billion (once the illicit market was absorbed into the lawful one), bigger even than the state's almond or grape exports. Appellations for growing regions was one avenue toward ensuring California remained the leader in this market.

"The reason why appellations are so important with cannabis, just like they are with wine, is because of microclimates, and terroir, and the effect of being on the sunny side of the hill versus the shady side of the hill," explains Van Solkov, founder of Happy Travelers Tours, a cannabis-tasting tour company based in Sonoma that teaches its guests about clean, regenerative farming techniques. "When you talk about artisanal growers, you're talking about someone who understands the microclimate of that grow, the soil, the terroir of that grow. And they've experimented enough that they know which strain is the strain that they really want to produce there."

Like grapes, each of the thousands of cannabis strains presents a unique bouquet of fragrances, colors, and flavors. An hour drive's south of Sonoma, a wine expert who calls herself "the Herb Somm" regularly gathers well-heeled guests at private underground dinners and speakeasies around San Francisco to demonstrate how fine wine and high-quality cannabis can be appreciated through a similar lens. Her mission is to expose a completely new audience to the various botanical components that give each strain its character, by pairing vapes and pre-rolled joints with fancy food and wine. Whereas Chef Jeff sought to discard the earthy taste from his dishes, Jamie Evans (the Herb Somm's real name) and the Bay Area chefs with whom she collaborates put terpenes in the spotlight.

Before guests were served a four-course tasting menu featuring dishes like roasted fennel, CBD-infused fava beans, prosciutto, pecorino cheese, and Meyer lemon dressing prepared by cannabis chef Coreen Carroll, Jamie handed out pastel-colored cheat sheets. It was the 2019 Feast of Flowers, and the purpose of the cards was to inform diners of the olfactory qualities of the different terpenes that would be highlighted during the meal. For example, the terpene called "limonene" evokes notes of lemon, grapefruit, or blood orange. "Linalool" gives a more flowery palate like lavender, rose, or geranium. The first-course salad was meant to emphasize limonene, so guests were offered a chance to sniff Do-Si-Do buds grown by Bloom Farms and smoke pre-rolled joints containing Sour Diesel, as well as sip a glass of Correlation Wine's 2018 Sauvignon Blanc, which complements the citrusy flavors.

"There's actually this craft cannabis movement that's happening. I mean, we see craft wine, craft beer. People are just wanting to connect with the plant more. You're also seeing gourmet products, like infused olive oil, honey, gosh, there's like, butter . . . These are really high-end products. And once you establish that category, as well as beverages—we're seeing infused beverages now as well—I think eventually, it will spread throughout the country," enthuses Jamie, who spent more than a decade working as a certified wine specialist overseeing events for Jackson Family Wines, Folio Fine Wine Partners, and Napa Valley Grapegrowers, among others.

But would these gourmet items really catch on for the average Jane? Or would lower prices prevail over the gourmet experience?

"[What] I see in the dispensary is every day it's like, 'How much THC is in it, what's the cost?' Literally, they want the biggest bang for their buck," observes Dennis Hunter, founder of CannaCraft, one of the largest edibles and beverage manufacturers in California. Hunter grew up in Mendocino and made an illicit living off growing pot in Humboldt for decades. He was arrested in one of the biggest federal raids in state history in 1998, but managed to live on the lam for four years until he was finally captured, tried, and convicted on marijuana charges. After serving six and half years in federal prison, he was now cashing in on a range of new legal products, including the THC-infused sparkling water Hi-Fi Hops, Care By Design's CBD rubs and ointments, AbsoluteXtracts, and infused Satori Chocolates.

"I'm not sure the consumer cares whether it came from this

mountain over in Sonoma Valley or if it came out of Santa Barbara, or maybe they do . . ." he pondered.

Erin believed that preferences would run the gamut, just as with any other consumer product.

"There are going to be false, cheap products available that are from indoor grows or are very commoditized. And then there's going to be your sixty-dollar bottle of Pinot Noir that's very specific. It's artisanal. It's grown on a family farm in Humboldt or Mendocino. So you're going to have a consumer that demands both, and you're going to have a supply chain that provides both," predicted Erin, who joined the board of the International Cannabis Farmers Association to advocate for small farmers.

It was still too early to know for sure what consumers would care about or what types of products would be in demand, and when big brands would finally have the chance to expand nationally. At the time, the patchwork of state-by-state legal hurdles prevented companies from selling their wares all across America; on top of that, advertising was forbidden. But even so, the hope among the diners who gathered in southern Sonoma County on that July night was that as marijuana went mainstream, there would be room for everyone—from the potent "Two-Buck Chuck" varieties to the fanciest microdosed handcrafted pot products one could afford, and from Chef Jeff's tasteless infusions to alcohol-removed cannabis wine and more.

BACK AT THE NorCal CannaCuisine Gala, Erin handed out samples of her Garden Society sea-salt indica milk chocolates from a display table, as Jeff chopped and seared and seasoned in the makeshift kitchen next to the banquet hall. What he cared about most that night was showing people a good time—and showcasing how his cannabis-infused dishes could be at the center of a fine dining experience. Further, he knew this well-attended gathering portended the next frontier, a time in the not-so-distant future when cannabis would be consumed just like wine—out in the open in public social settings. There was speculation that new upscale cannabis bistros and cafés were on the horizon for California, but no one knew exactly what they might serve, or whether people would actually want to walk into a neighborhood restaurant and order pot to consume with their dinner or . . . in their dinner. Who would be first to open these new bistros? And an even bigger question: Which chefs would be backed by millions of dollars to create the first critically acclaimed dishes for these newfangled elevated eateries?

The feedback on Jeff's food was a good sign of what might lie ahead in his culinary career . . . or at least he hoped so. After the last brownie was served, several of the attendees spoke with local reporters and offered glowing reviews. The meal—and the event itself—was a decided hit. Honoree Steve DeAngelo thanked the organizers for "putting together something really classy for cannabis to emerge in a social space."

Jeff's ambition to become a preeminent cannabis chef had already gone from being just a pipe dream to something he could actually envision. This night in Sonoma, sharing his food on such a grand scale, was another leap forward. And it was only the beginning. As Chef Jeff declared, with a twinkle in his eye, in a TV interview, "This is the end of Prohibition."

19
CBD SISTER ACT

Monmouth County, New Jersey
January 2018

THE WINDOWED PARLOR just off the cathedral-like foyer of Beth Stavola's plush home had been overtaken by stacks of cardboard boxes piled five feet high and three feet deep. Inside the sealed cartons were hundreds of shiny black jars and tubes ready to be shipped around the country. This was Beth's new "side hustle"—a growing enterprise hawking the potential beauty and wellness applications of CBD. The whole thing had really taken off after she convinced her youngest sister, Julie, to step away from her respectable career in banking and eventually reeled her all the way in.

Back in 2014, temptation was calling, and Julie Winter couldn't resist. She always picked up the phone when she saw her older sister's number pop up—even though she knew every word of their conversations would be recorded by the Wall Street bank where she worked in credit derivatives. The twenty-seven-year-old was always on the edge of her seat when Beth shared her adventures in the world of marijuana, where she was a rising mogul. And every time Beth mentioned the word "marijuana" on these calls, Julie rushed to clarify—to whoever in Compliance was listening in—that this cannabis stuff had nothing to do with her. At the time, pot was legalized in some form in twenty states and the District of Columbia. But on Wall Street—and in banking in general—the federally illegal weed industry and any dealings with it were strictly off-limits. Bank loans for marijuana entrepreneurs were off-limits. And businesses like Beth's were mostly shut out of financial services altogether, and forced to deal entirely in cash—even paying taxes, contractors, and wages in stacks of big bills. Her Arizona retail shops had resorted to sometimes using private ATMs that the dispensary could fill with cash from pot sales in order to keep it safe. It was a big reason Beth always kept her two cellphones close.

But Beth was much too smart to tell any of her really crazy stories over the phone in any case. For those, Julie would have to wait until the weekend, when the extended family would often gather around the long kitchen table at the Stavolas' gracious estate after Sunday mass. The news was always juicy, to say the least. Every day, Beth seemed to be playing out scenes from some action movie; there were vaults packed with thousands of pounds of weed and millions in cash that needed to be secured, an ex–Secret Service agent keeping a watchful eye over the retail locations and ready to spring into action at the first sign of danger to employees and customers. There were the freewheeling young "street blasters," the slew of *Breaking Bad*–like characters on Beth's payroll with their homegrown methods to extract cannabis oil using all kinds of jerry-rigged contraptions and highly explosive chemicals. And that was just running the day-to-day operations of her marijuana empire. There were also the politicians and local police to charm, the community activists to appease, the shakedowns from landlords, the complaints from neighboring businesses who were typically less than thrilled about the dispensary moving in next door, and local bureaucrats seemingly always on the take. And, of course, always lurking in the background was the relentless competition from drug cartels and illegal growers, even as local police attempted to run them out of town.

The sisters, who shared identical matching highlighted blond tresses and blue-gray eyes, were close despite the sixteen-year age gap between them. Beth liked to say Julie, the second-youngest of the seven kids in their strict Irish Catholic family, was a younger, smarter version of herself. Julie and her siblings had grown up near the Jersey Shore, where their father, Joe Beggans, a successful Philip Morris accountant, and his wife, Kathie—a stay-at-home-mom with a bawdy sense of humor, whom all the grandkids and pretty much everyone else called "Big Nanny"—had opted to raise their sizable family. Five foot ten with flaming red hair, Big Nanny had towered over her own mother, a petite fireball known as "Little Nanny," who had survived the scars of an abusive, alcoholic father and raised six tall and outspoken daughters in the tough tenements of Jersey City. Big Nanny's hardscrabble upbringing—and her never-ending quest to overcome it—defined the family legacy. As a teen, she finished high school early and enrolled in a local Catholic college, and soon afterward wed Joe and started a family. But the young mother refused to drop out of school, even though the nuns weren't too thrilled when she brought baby Beth to class with her. In 1971, she was valedictorian and triumphantly rode on a commencement float with Beth on her hip, who sported Big Nanny's oversized graduation cap and tassel askew on her tiny head.

Julie, the fun-loving baby sister of the Beggans clan, had always looked up to Beth, the eldest of Big Nanny and Joe's large brood. As a young girl, Beth had played the role of mom's dependable helper, and could frequently be found lining up the baby bottles on the counter and filling them with milk or juice for her younger sisters and brothers, changing diapers, keeping an eye on the kids when her mom ran to the store, or hunched over the piles of pink, green, and blue cash she amassed playing her favorite board game, Monopoly. Beth was the first of the seven siblings to go off to college, and the first to move out and follow her dreams to Wall Street.

Their conservative brothers, who also worked in high finance, didn't approve of Beth's marijuana business at first, and their parents were still trying to decide what to make of it all. But to Julie, her sister's stories were fascinating. During the generous six months of maternity leave she took after giving birth to her first daughter in

April 2014, Julie began to learn much more about Beth's enterprises. The sisters could talk more freely now that she was home in her Hoboken apartment all day. Julie was admittedly going a little bit stir-crazy during the sleepless early weeks of new motherhood; and Beth, who had six children of her own, could tell her sister needed something more to occupy her mind beyond diapers and nursing. And to be honest, Beth really needed help from someone she could trust. That was the thing about selling a federally illegal product that was coming out from the shadows. But around her youngest sister, Beth felt she could bare it all. Julie was certainly intrigued when her older sister invited her into the business, and immediately read up on the potential medical benefits of marijuana, trying to learn all she could while the baby napped. She soon began regularly toting her infant along to meet with Beth at her home office, where a staff of loving nannies and housekeepers stood at the ready to assist.

Within a year, what began as a part-time gig turned into a full-time job for Julie. As luck would have it, Beth had recently turned her enterprising eye toward CBD, at the time a little-known cannabis compound outside of marijuana subculture. She first heard about CBD in early 2013, while petitioning Arizona authorities for clearance to open her first dispensary in Douglas. She says it was grower Jason Gully, who would go on to become a key partner in the business, who first told her that CBD might help ease her back pain. Beth, who had long suffered from scoliosis, needed biweekly massages and physical therapy to sustain her through the marathon days spent on her feet.

Beth didn't use marijuana herself. But she was certainly open to experimenting with the CBD-infused skin lotions and oils he passed along to her. The homespun CBD salves seemed to make her feel better, and when she applied them to her hands and feet, she noticed how well they seemed to soften her dry skin. Around the same time, CBD was suddenly thrust into Middle America's consciousness after CNN's Dr. Sanjay Gupta explained—in that pivotal 2013 medical marijuana documentary—that CBD, unlike its sister cannabinoid THC, did not induce a high and might offer significant therapeutic benefits still being investigated by scientists. Few of these benefits had been clinically proven in humans; nor, at the time, had CBD products been approved by the Food and Drug Administration. But just as Chef Jeff had learned when he first started delving into the cannabinoid research of Israeli chemist Dr. Raphael Mechoulam, early studies suggested CBD might be efficacious in treating a host of other ailments, including run-of-the-mill aches and pains, anxiety, and stress. Even Snoop Dogg, the star whose public image was synonymous with getting stoned, believed in the potential health benefits and included high-CBD flower and concentrates in his Leafs By Snoop offerings in Colorado (and later in Canada, when he launched his LBS products with Bruce Linton's company). According to LBS's Tiffany Chin, Snoop and Ted's team always thought CBD-rich strains of cannabis would be important to include in the "regular" line because of their "wider audience appeal." As it turned out, she was right. Soon after the CNN show aired, Beth and her sales associates noticed a significant uptick in Arizona patients looking for cannabis products to help with pain and overall well-being, without the buzz.

"Beth said . . . You wouldn't believe that people are coming in who have medical cards and asking, 'Hey, I have to drive my kid around today' or 'I have a soccer game' or 'I have a PTA meeting' or . . . for whatever reason, 'I don't want to be high,'" recalls Julie.

The sisters' wheels were turning. Beth began talking to Jason and his staff of "cannabis processors"—who were already spending hours on end in the lab working to distill THC to its essence for their popular MPX concentrates—about how CBD could be isolated from the plant in pure form. Could it be blended with scented essential oils, which were already gaining popularity in the beauty and wellness space, to create salves that could be rubbed onto the skin to relieve everyday aches and pain, as well as to moisturize and soften fine lines? Beth soon learned that in order to harvest enough CBD from her Arizona and Nevada cannabis crops, she would need to track down high-CBD strains to grow locally. The problem was, it wasn't easy to find those plant genetics, and it was illegal to import the seeds across state lines. The underground growers had historically bred CBD out of most of their marijuana plants in order to serve patients seeking increasingly stronger amounts of THC. But then Beth discovered that CBD molecules could also be extracted from another cannabis sativa species called hemp, which is rich in CBD but low in THC—less than 0.3 percent, depending on growing conditions.

The timing couldn't have been better. For years, high-fiber hemp and marijuana had been lumped together and outlawed by the federal government under the Controlled Substances Act. But in an unlikely twist, the future and fortune of hemp all began to change when yet another strange bedfellow—one of the staunchest Republicans around and a longtime drug warrior—inadvertently created a new opportunity. In 2013, Republican senator Mitch McConnell of Kentucky began to take a surprisingly strong interest in hemp. Persuaded by the libertarian junior Kentucky senator, Rand Paul, and the state agriculture commissioner, who argued that legalizing hemp might help struggling farmers, McConnell ultimately would go on to champion efforts on behalf of farmers to chip away at hemp's illicit status; and in 2014, when Congress authorized the federal Farm Bill, the soon-to-be majority leader led the charge to authorize farmers in Kentucky, Colorado, and Vermont to grow hemp through pilot research programs administered by state universities. The idea was to help demonstrate the potential for a new cash crop by reintroducing industrial hemp as a commodity whose use actually dated back to Colonial days. With its strong fibrous stalks, hemp could be manufactured into rope, fabrics, biodegradable plastics, and cosmetics; and its seeds, rich in protein, fiber, a bevy of vitamins and minerals, and essential fatty acids, were thought to be one of the most nutritionally complete food sources in the world. Moreover, as Beth soon discovered, it could also be harvested for valuable CBD.

The rules on where and how hemp-derived CBD products could be sold remained a bit murky back then, but the go-ahead from Capitol Hill on the agricultural production of the plant paved the way for Beth and other cannabis entrepreneurs to start using CBD in novel ways. Now that she could access the raw materials she needed, Beth quickly commenced product development at Suite-K, an FDA-regulated cosmetics lab near her home in New Jersey, run by longtime family friend Kathleen Croddick Molyneaux. Beth and Julie started brainstorming how the new line of CBD beauty treatments might be branded to evoke good health and well-being, and attract customers like themselves and their friends—affluent, image-conscious women and men with active lifestyles. They called it "CBD For Life"—a play on the name of Beth's sunny Arizona–based Southwestern-themed Health For Life dispensaries.

The ambitious entrepreneur knew that to turn CBD into the much-hyped sensation it would soon become, she needed to find a way to reach those consumers who, like the wealthy moms she and Julie knew in tony Monmouth County, New Jersey, thought nothing of spending $750 on their La Mer under-eye cream or $1,200 a month on spinning or barre fitness classes, and who wouldn't be caught dead walking into a pot shop. These women were the polar opposite of the Cheetos-eating stoners portrayed in movies and on TV. They enjoyed other vices, like a glass of white wine at lunch or a stiff skinny cocktail before dinner. But like most "one-percenters" in America, they were increasingly obsessed with "wellness" and were game to try everything from hot yoga to detox juice cleanses to cryotherapy to herbal supplements to achieve it. Wellness was on its way to becoming a global industry—worth $4.2 trillion by 2017, according to the Global Wellness Institute—that encompassed personal care, beauty, anti-aging, healthy eating, nutrition, fitness, mind-body science, and alternative medicine. Beth and Julie thought CBD just might be the next big thing and began developing an array of offerings aimed at customers willing to pay top dollar for high-end products promising everything from a toned body to better sleep to fewer wrinkles to more satisfying sex. But they knew, given its controversial cannabis roots, CBD had to be presented just right.

The opportunities seemed almost endless. Well-packaged CBD beauty products were hard to find in those early days, and the ones that did exist were not exactly what Beth had in mind. "It looked like it was made in people's basements or in people's garages. And it was very not-luxurious. It was very, very weedy. It was just nothing that we would want to put on shelves in our dispensaries or could break into the mainstream market," explains director of sales Mollie Twining.

Julie stepped in to oversee marketing and sales. But they had to operate gingerly, because CBD still remained in a legal gray area even as the hemp industry grew and individual states passed varying laws on its sale. As a result, they knew that if they wanted to get wide distribution, they would have to pound the pavement. Julie hired Mollie, one of Beth's longtime friends, to work on commission as their very first sales rep. Mollie, a stay-at-home mom of three whom Beth first met in their daughters' preschool class two decades before, and who had previously worked in finance at Merrill Lynch, soon began knocking on doors across the state of New Jersey, trying to woo locally owned spas, exercise studios, pharmacies, and smoke shops—anyone who would take a meeting—to consider carrying their lavender and lemongrass rubs and peppermint foot creams.

While this might have seemed like a diversion from her core business, Beth maintained that it was anything but. "I think people are focused on the current marijuana customer, and that's not who I'm focused on. I'm focused on the new marijuana customer and CBD is a way for people to try, to get in and experience, some of the wellness benefits," Beth would say, looking back on how CBD would ultimately fit into her grand plans.

Getting distribution for the products was slow and hard, slogging work. They were starting from scratch just to educate the marketplace on products that had never before existed. Working out of Beth's home office, which doubled as HQ for all of the cannabis operations as well as the makeshift shipping center for CBD For Life, they started selling online, too. With the help of a PR agency, Julie and Mollie started scoring desk-side meetings with beauty editors at major magazines in New York City, and the products earned kudos in the pages of *Allure, Elle,* and *New York* magazine.

"We really created this story, went out there hard, and started educating people on this. And at the time, maybe one or two brands were popping up. There wasn't really huge competition. Our hurdle was people would say, 'CB what? This is from marijuana?' " Julie says. "And they just had a lot of questions. How does it work? Does it get you high? Will people fail a drug test? Is this legal? How do you know? Where are you testing it? Do you have any science or is it more anecdotal?"

Julie and Mollie's ready answers were based on preclinical trials in Israel and anecdotes that suggested CBD interacts with the body's own endocannabinoid system to regulate inflammation and pain. No, they would patiently explain, it will not get you high. No, you won't fail a drug test because their products were just for the skin, not digested or smoked, and furthermore, they contained no THC because the CBD molecules in the hemp had been isolated and separated from the mind-altering compound. Yes, they conducted their own third-party quality testing for potency, pesticides, and toxic contaminants, even though at this point the FDA wasn't regulating it. It was complicated information to get across. But they found an insatiable curiosity about this "new" natural ingredient that had actually been around for thousands of years. As they predicted, the interest coincided with a rise in consumer spending on newfangled elixirs for stress, insomnia, and aging.

"I think the explosion of CBD and cannabis in general is happening at the same time as a bunch of other trends we're looking at that all end up tying-in in some way. So it's what people are calling the 'anxiety economy,' and then in general . . . wellness, moving from a focus just solely on physical, to emotional well-being, and mental wellness, and mental health. And obviously CBD and cannabis do both. So that's the perfect ingredient for this new focus. And then the whole self-care industry, which is also, again, physical and emotional well-being, it's a perfect product for that," observed Marian Berelowitz, the U.S. trends analyst for the British-based trend-forecasting company Stylus.

CBD For Life may have been one of the earliest cannabis beauty brands, but by 2015, Beth wasn't the only entrepreneur who saw the potential of CBD to appeal to trendsetters. Around the time Beth and Julie began to unveil their line at trade shows, artist Rob Rosenheck and his wife, PR guru Cindy Capobianco, were starting to sell their brand of luxury CBD-infused confections, Lord Jones, in California medical dispensaries. They quickly launched an online shop for hemp-derived varieties of their CBD treats—as well as tinctures and body lotions—and struck up partnerships with The Standard and other luxury boutique hotels to stock their non-high-inducing fruit gelées, which sell for $45 to $60 a box. The enterprising pair already had deep experience launching big brands for health and wellness enthusiasts. They were the marketing brains behind Lärabar, the gluten-free fruit and nut bar company bought by General Mills in 2009. Now, with Lord Jones, they drew inspiration from the California lifestyle they loved and the same instinct that Beth and Julie had about a whole new high-end market for cannabis.

"We had friends who used cannabis who were Whole Foods shoppers and Equinox members . . . They were artists and professionals and soccer moms, and there was nothing in the marketplace that spoke to them," said Rosenheck, who felt at the time that there was "an opportunity of a lifetime to build a best-in-class brand." Lord Jones would go on to attract a slew of Hollywood endorsements, including a notable shout-out from actress Olivia Wilde in a full-page *New York Times* Style section story and top billing at the goop summit.

By the close of 2018, the FDA and Congress had unwittingly turbocharged the CBD industry after the FDA bestowed new credibility on its medicinal properties by approving the first pharmaceutical containing cannabis-derived CBD—Epidiolex, produced by the United Kingdom's GW Pharmaceuticals—which could now be prescribed by doctors to treat two rare childhood seizure disorders. Then, less than six months later, the passage of the 2018 Farm Bill (otherwise known as the Agricultural Improvement Act) removed hemp from the federal government's banned substance list for good, legalizing its sale across all fifty states.

"For far too long, the federal government has prevented most farmers from growing hemp," Majority Leader McConnell pronounced in a self-congratulatory statement to the press after the bill was passed by the Senate. "Although it was a foundational part of Kentucky's heritage and today you can buy hemp products at stores across the country, most American farmers have been barred from planting it in their fields. I have heard from many Kentucky farmers who agree it's time to remove the federal hurdles and give our state the opportunity to seize its full potential and once again become the national leader for hemp production. That is why I strongly advocated for this measure to be included in the Farm Bill, which will finally and fully legalize industrial hemp."

Up until this point, hemp—and effectively, the hemp-CBD industry—had operated under the radar, and CBD tinctures, lotions, vapes, bath bombs, candies, and drinks had remained mostly behind the counter in cannabis dispensaries in states where marijuana was legal, according to BDS Analytics, which began tracking CBD purchases in 2016. But now that the floodgates had opened, everyday retailers—including Bed Bath & Beyond, CVS, and Walgreens—announced that a host of cannabidiol products (or at least products claiming to contain varying levels of CBD) would be sold on their shelves. From red-carpet swag bags to SoulCycle to health food stores to Barneys New York and Neiman Marcus, overnight CBD was seemingly everywhere, even as outgoing FDA commissioner Scott Gottlieb warned the public that regulators would crack down on companies making health claims that had not been approved by the FDA, underscoring that CBD was not legal as a food additive.

But the threat didn't seem to stem the tide. The craze continued to give way to a host of new profiteers, or what Mollie called "rogue cowboys," who were singing the praises of CBD as a panacea for just about everything—Alzheimer's, cancer, eczema, ADHD, Crohn's disease, anxiety, arthritis—anything you could think of.

"People will tell you CBD cures anything. It doesn't. But people are buying into this hype. And this happens in other areas. It's not unique to CBD or to cannabis. But it is a hype-driven industry that I think is going to eventually have a very difficult day with the federal government," cautioned Brookings Institution cannabis policy expert John Hudak.

CBD quickly became a hot commodity among everyone from well-off self-care acolytes to grandparents to stressed-out millennials to weekend warriors. And soon it was being added to anything you could possibly think of—from foot cream to bath salts to coffee and even to pet treats. By April 2019, Google searches for "CBD" would outpace queries for exercise, meditation, and yoga, according to a paper published by the *Journal of the American Medical Association*. A 2019 Gallup survey found that one in seven Americans was using CBD for therapeutic purposes. The compound would quickly go on to receive high-profile plugs from Kim Kardashian West, who threw herself a CBD-themed baby shower a few weeks before the birth of her fourth child; and from celebrity athletes, including soccer sensation Megan Rapinoe and former New England

Patriots tight end Rob "Gronk" Gronkowski, who inked deals to become spokespersons for CBD pain relief products.

And then there was the explosion of CBD-infused food—a whole other genie for federal overseers to try to put back in the bottle. You couldn't walk down the street of most major cities by 2018 without seeing signs for CBD smoothies, coffee, and even ice cream. The fact that CBD was not cleared as a food additive seemed to be completely overlooked by consumers and restaurateurs alike. Fast-food chains like Carl's Jr. and fresh&co blatantly promoted new CBD menu items. It got to the point where the New York City Department of Health began issuing citations to restaurants plugging new CBD offerings. But customers were clamoring for it.

Pet lovers joined the chorus, too. Intrigued by CBD's potential to quell anxiety and pain in dogs and cats, veterinarians found themselves on the receiving end of countless questions about the cannabinoid and not much research to draw from. The growth of the space for furry friends was explosive. A CNBC report announced that sales of CBD pet products quadrupled to $32 million in just one year from $8 million in 2017, citing research from the Brightfield Group, a cannabis research firm.

Even the one industry that perhaps carried as much taboo as marijuana was not immune. It wasn't long before intimacy products aimed at women were starting to pop up—like the "arousal oil" made from CBD mixed with other herbal aphrodisiacs that the California-based company Foria began shipping in discreet bottles to homes around the country. The company also introduced new CBD suppositories alleged to relieve period pain, and was partnering with a Harvard clinician to study the validity of its claims.

On an extraordinarily icy Friday night in February 2019, about forty canna-curious guests convened at The Alchemist's Kitchen, an airy herbalist shop in New York, for a panel discussion on sex and cannabis hosted by *Miss Grass*, a digital cannabis lifestyle magazine that had scored a high-profile seed investment from Snoop Dogg's Casa Verde Capital. But the frigid weather didn't stop the crowd from showing up to ask their most burning questions about weed and sexual satisfaction.

"There are so many dead ends for women's health, and I think cannabis is a great way to incorporate some alternative medicine for women," twenty-two-year-old NYU student Julia Rosenberg enthused in the moments before things got started.

Foria founder Mathew Gerson kicked off the frank discussion by encouraging the audience to "embrace sexual pleasure as a form of wellness," a sentiment echoed by Cyo Nystrom, cofounder of Quim, which markets its intimacy oils to "people with vaginas." As it turned out, the sexy side of CBD wasn't just for young folk, either.

"It helps with blood flow, vasodilation, it gets the blood moving. And when blood moves, sensation moves," explained Gerson as he discussed how applying cannabis-infused oils to genital tissue has helped his clients deal with discomfort from hormonal changes, like menopause. And according to Kimberly Dillon, former CMO of Papa & Barkley, the cannabis company that markets CBD pain relief and relaxation products to seniors, cannabis lube appears to be one of the most popular products for the over-65 crowd.

"There's so much about sex that's mental. About 'How do I look, how do I feel, do they like how my boobs are sagging?' These are the things that came up [with seniors]," she explained. "And so we found that . . . [the benefit of using cannabis] was to get yourself mentally right for embarking in unencumbered sex, in addition to lowering your inhibitions in a way," she explained. (Dillon moved on from Papa & Barkley to found Plant & Prosper, a cannabis brand consulting firm.)

All told, CBD would amount to a nearly $2 billion industry in 2019, according to BDS Analytics, which forecasted the CBD market would shoot to $20 billion by 2024. And yet, with the exception of Epidiolex, the epilepsy medication, none of these new CBD products had been approved by the FDA—a fact few consumers seemed to understand. Further, there were no federal rules on labeling, dosing, or testing, nor much oversight from Washington. A 2019 Leafly investigation found that of forty-seven products tested, only twenty-four actually contained the amount of CBD they claimed on the label. And since clinical evidence was only emerging, there were wildly different instructions for how much CBD a person (or pet) was supposed to take to get the intended effect. Scott Gottlieb of the FDA warned it would likely take years for the government to issue guidelines on CBD. On the other side of the world, Dr. Yossi Tam, who runs the Hebrew University Multidisciplinary Center for Cannabinoid Research founded by Dr. Mechoulam, expressed concerns that in the United States, business was outpacing the scientific discoveries at a feverish pace.

"It seems all the buzz around cannabis nowadays basically triggers the business development in this direction. However, the scientists do not make such an advancement at that pace. It takes a much longer time to make new discoveries in this field," cautioned Dr. Tam in the weeks running up to Congress reauthorizing the 2018 Farm Bill. Eventually, the FDA began cracking down on big companies making unsubstantiated medical claims. In one of the most dramatic shows of muscle, regulators sent a warning to Curaleaf, a "leading medical and wellness" cannabis operator, with whom CVS had signed a momentous deal agreeing to carry its transdermal patches and lotions in eight hundred stores. But the drugstore pulled Curaleaf's products from its shelves when federal overseers singled the company out for promoting its products as "cures" for chronic pain and anxiety, in violation of the Federal Food, Drug, and Cosmetic Act. The slap on the wrist sent a chill across the industry—and stock prices took a hit—but CBD companies were not to be stopped, and kept right on pushing out more and more products.

Still, Curaleaf and its scuttled CVS deal was a cautionary tale, one sufficiently frightening that Beth and Julie were constantly re-evaluating packaging for CBD For Life to make sure it didn't run afoul of the emerging rules. By 2017, revenues had skyrocketed from $750,000 to $3 million annually, despite the fact that the company was still small enough to be run out of Beth's first-floor sitting room. Even Big Nanny's conservative country club was carrying the products in its pro shop. But the sisters still considered CBD For Life a side project. Beth, for one, was much more focused on her bread and butter: expanding the footprint of the multistate cannabis growing, manufacturing, and retail operation that was now the core of MPX Bioceutical, the publicly traded Canadian company for which she now ran U.S. operations. It was no easy task, given the cutthroat competition in new East Coast markets, but at least the company now had the cash to propel Beth's plans forward. While Julie took the lead in going after new medical licenses in Baltimore and Bethesda, Maryland, Beth was already working behind the scenes in the hope that New Jersey's politicians and power brokers would soon be opening up new opportunities in her backyard. After all, the Garden State's newly installed Governor Phil Murphy had made passionate campaign promises to bring recreational-use cannabis to her home state within his administration's first one hundred days; naturally, she had been a donor, and it was no secret that Tammy, the First Lady, was a friend. And while it was still anybody's guess when New York would legalize recreational weed, Governor Andrew Cuomo was expected to reverse his stance against it, upping the ante for both states, which would be competing for potential cannabis tax revenue and new jobs if/when it came to pass.

But even with this prize on the horizon, for Beth the risks were just as daunting as ever. Her bank accounts continued to get shut down. Credit card companies were calling with suspicious questions about her business dealings. She still slept with one eye open and her two cellphones at her bedside, always waiting for that dreaded call in the middle of the night telling her a dispensary had been robbed or raided, or that a harvest had gone bad—or worse. So many things could still destroy this fragile operation she was building, one brick at a time. Would all the drama be worth it in the end?

20
GREEN GOLD

Las Vegas, Nevada

November 2018

LESS THAN A mile from the action on the glittering Vegas Strip, another set of high rollers touched down with dollar signs in their eyes. Armed with legal pads and briefcases, they had come by the thousands hoping to get a bigger piece of a new industry that had taken in more than $9 billion across twenty-nine U.S. states (plus the District of Columbia) in 2017—and yet was still against the law in the eyes of the federal government. But here in Sin City, the burgeoning business of marijuana flaunted itself out in the open under the bright lights of the Las Vegas Convention Center, where, only a few weeks before, legions of specialty-car-part salesmen had convened for their annual expo. With the hot rods long gone, the two-million-square-foot exhibition hall was crowded with thousands of vendors pitching wireless gadgets for measuring pesticides and mold; sophisticated AgTech like "smart" greenhouse lights, thermostats, and fertilizing systems; five-foot-tall commercial-grade kitchen mixers customized specifically for stirring up massive batches of (pot-infused) brownie and cookie batter; cutting-edge chemical engineering tools for distilling dynamic cannabis extracts and measuring potency and doses; and newfangled software for tracking the "supply chain" of plants from seed to sale.

The impressive canna-tech display was sandwiched between

booths occupied by buttoned-up CPAs and lawyers offering advice to marijuana business owners on one side, and a plethora of cannabinoid beauty and wellness products promising better sex, firmer skin, and shinier hair on the other. Then there was the mouthwatering selection of feel-good chocolate bars, fruity gummies, and other eye-catching edibles in virgin versions only, since the event barred cannabis consumption on-site.

This was the Marijuana Business Conference and Cannabis Expo, the largest legal pot convention in the world, attended by 27,600 marijuana professionals—and some wide-eyed newbies—sharing trade secrets in double time. Dealings that were once the realm of shady street corners and back alleyways were liberated from the darkness and put on proud display at a real industry trade show. Looking around, it was hard to disagree: legal weed was legit.

With their official "MJBizCon" lanyards and green tote bags full of swag, attendees were bursting with questions and brimming with business ideas. While throngs paced the exhibition floor, thousands of others with iPads and laptops conscientiously took notes as they soaked up the MJBizCon Crash Course, where veterans like Phoenix dispensary owner Lilach Mazor Power schooled the novices on plant science 101. In their sport coats and sweater vests, this crowd defied the stereotypical image of long-haired activists in tie-dye whose crusade successfully opened the door for medical marijuana beginning with California in 1996.

But while the healing properties—and growing availability—of the plant sought by patients struggling with a host of serious ailments gave way to the recent shift in public opinion of cannabis, the real gasoline that set the marijuana movement on fire was the prospect of big profits, says Troy Dayton, founder and chief strategy officer of The Arcview Group, one of the first angel investment firms devoted to cannabis. The business opportunity crystallized in 2014, he says, when Colorado launched the first legal cannabis sales to adults over twenty-one, and an America already obsessed with *Shark Tank* dreams began to witness upstanding people making lucrative, lawful livings off pot.

And here we were just four years later, and eleven states and the District of Columbia were allowing so-called adult use. In the short history of the commercialized cannabis industry, 2018 was a watershed year that began with California officially opening up its over-21 market, the largest in the world. Even the news that longtime pot foe Attorney General Jeff Sessions had rescinded a 2013 document called the Cole Memo—a letter to U.S. Attorneys that gave weed startups confidence they could operate without fear of federal intervention, as long as they abided by state laws—couldn't dampen the feverish optimism among investors. It was like the tech boom all over again, where sky-high valuations didn't match up with balance sheets but financiers didn't seem to care because the sector was so hot. Taking a page from Beth Stavola, U.S. companies were going public in Canada, in order to gain access to the millions of dollars needed to take on rivals in the land grab for new markets.

Money changed minds about cannabis. Even pot's staunchest opponents, like former Speaker of the House John Boehner, were not immune. Suddenly the man who once said he was "unalterably opposed" to weed had joined the board of Acreage Holdings, one of the largest U.S. pot companies, penning an op-ed in the *The Wall Street Journal* singing the praises of cannabis, and hosting web infomercials entreating everyday investors not to miss their shot at generating life-changing wealth.

It's not that there weren't voices chiming in to say the market was getting overheated. Even Cassandra Farrington, the founder of this mega-conference and its profitable media properties, compared the frenzy to the dot-com boom and had some sobering thoughts on where things were headed. But from the talk on the expo floor, it was clear that this was a point of view few enthusiastic prospectors were ready to hear just yet.

"There will be a bust for sure. Every single industry goes through cyclical ups and downs, right? We've seen booms and busts in oil, booms and busts in corn and everything. This is going to be another," Farrington predicted. She pointed to the lack of transparency and the outrageous valuations, explaining that companies were saying they were worth $15 million because they raised $1.5 million from investors so they could keep the lights on, but really didn't have the fundamentals to be self-sustaining. "The tech crash is not the only boom-and-bust that's happened there. We're gonna see that here, too. It's gonna be a normalized industry just like everything else, and be subject to those market forces," she said soberly.

Still, none of this seemed to matter to the entrepreneurs at MJBizCon, who were eager to come up with new ways to tap into the growing recreational market. To that end, there were weed-themed wedding planners; real estate developers sketching out marijuana-themed strip malls and office parks; "Tinder for tokers" dating apps; chefs following in the footsteps of Jeff, cooking up cannabis catering services; and animal lovers touting the benefits of pot for pets. All were here to network with investors and scope out the competition.

The giddiness in the air was palpable. These people smelled money. And as was fitting for the location, they knew they were playing a high-risk, high-stakes game. They came to roll the dice on a fragmented industry being built state by state—one that analysts predicted would swell to $21 billion by 2021, rivaling U.S. mainstays like healthcare, banking, and IT. Many of these modern-day prospectors admitted they had missed out on the tech boom and now, armed with their life savings, nothing was going to keep them from missing their shot at building a fortune.

In its seventh year, the conference and expo continued to draw a veritable who's who of the pot business. Attendance had grown 52 percent year over year, making it an event that industry veterans and newcomers alike couldn't afford to miss. Beth had flown in from Jersey for a packed schedule of closed-door meetings with investors and local politicians, and also to peek at her Vegas grow and dispensaries. Bruce Linton squeezed in as many face-to-face conversations as he could while on the ground for a mere thirty hours. Ted and Snoop made a quick stopover, too—just long enough for Snoop to headline a sold-out DJ Snoopadelic show at the Mandalay Bay Resort and Casino, where the legendary MC spun a late-night set at the resort's cavernous dance club packed with MJBizCon attendees. As he sang "Nuthin' but a 'G' Thang," VIPs from Merry Jane, Leafs By Snoop, and Casa Verde Capital—his trifecta of cannabis investment vehicles—settled in behind a velvet rope to unwind with a nightcap after a long day of glad-handing and dealmaking.

Jeff Danzer was also taking in the scene in Las Vegas that week, and he'd even brought along his twenty-six-year-old son, Jared: his "mini-me," as his grandma Sylvia called him. Father and son had recently become business partners after Jared and his girlfriend traded their cramped Bronx apartment for the chance to get in on California's Green Rush. And no place better to do it than in L.A., a brave new world where giant marijuana leaves were plastered on billboards over the freeways, pot was sold in glossy Apple Store–style shops with glass display cases and solicitous sales associates at the ready, and one could partake in "lit" yoga classes, sex and cannabis workshops, or CBD massage treatments. Even the posh department store Barneys, overlooking fancy Wilshire Boulevard in Beverly Hills, was about to open its own head shop. There, one could purchase a $10,000 solid gold smoking tray, rolling papers imported from Paris, and hand-blown, one-of-a-kind stained-glass bongs. It had been a wild ride for the businesses trying to navigate the host of ever-changing rules and regulations, never mind compete with the still thriving illegal market. And yet, new startups kept sprouting up.

Jared's girlfriend had landed a job at a law firm that focused on cannabis law, while he began working full-time to build up the JeffThe420Chef brand. A natural salesman with a firm handshake, Jared was now growing his dad's Instagram following, fielding media inquiries, finding commercial kitchen space for Jeff to create his dishes, and chasing and developing new leads. Though busy as ever, they still made time to gather at Sylvia and Manny's for the weekly Shabbat dinner as often as they could.

This pilgrimage from Los Angeles to Vegas and MJBizCon marked an important moment for the father and son. They were here to finally unveil Jeff's patent-pending process—which he'd named FreeLeaf—for eliminating both the taste *and* the odor from cannabis while still retaining its powerful punch, as much as 23 percent THC. Jeff had graduated beyond just oil for baking; in May 2019, in an unscientific test, this reporter stood by as Jeff and Jared lit up a pre-rolled blunt that contained the odorless flower inside mango-scented hemp rolling paper, and can corroborate that the smell was faintly fruity, with no hint of the typical funk most people associate with weed.

Jeff and Jared had come to the land of the high-stakes game hoping to persuade some of the investors attending MJBizCon to take a gamble on them—and on Jeff's inventions. They hoped to take the family business to the next level by raising millions to start licensing the intellectual property and making it available across the industry.

"Just imagine this: You live in New York. You want to smoke weed, but you don't want anyone to know you're smoking weed. You don't want to vape. You just want to go out for a smoke. Well, now you can, because you'll be able to take FreeLeaf, smoke it, and people won't know what you're smoking. It doesn't smell like cigarettes. It doesn't smell like weed," explained Jeff, by now effortlessly rattling off his talking points. But no matter how convincing he was, it was hard for most people to wrap their heads around how it was scientifically possible.

"I'm more excited about odorless cannabis than anything else, because it's never existed in the world as far as I know. When was the last time you heard of anyone smoking weed that didn't smell?" asked Jeff.

Well, never. But if he and Jared were going to garner real money from serious investors, they would have to prove to them on the spot that FreeLeaf actually fulfilled that promise. They got their shot at an after-party one night when a curious investor who had heard about their odorless weed struck up a conversation. He wanted to learn more, so he invited the father-and-son team for a drink at one of the Strip's most opulent hotel and casinos, along with two of his attorneys. Although the establishment, like the rest of the casinos in Las Vegas, had a strict no-cannabis policy, Jeff shocked the group by lighting up one of his faint-smelling pre-rolls on the spot. Over the incessant dinging and bleeping of slot machines, the investor (whom Jeff declines to name) warned in a concerned voice, "You can't smoke that in here. We're going to get kicked out." But Jeff was confident. The group watched in disbelief as a few minutes passed and the casino floor security didn't bat an eye.

"After four pre-rolls between all five of us and the hostess coming over and asking if we wanted a new ashtray, and the security guards rolling around and not bothering us, [the investor] was like 'Let's go to dinner,'" recalled Jeff. The evening culminated in a sumptuous meal at the Bellagio's five-star Picasso restaurant, followed by a handshake deal.

But this particular deal was not meant to be. The timing was off. A month after their trip to the largest marijuana trade show in the world, Jeff and Jared learned they had scored another opportunity—one that any professional chef would find challenging to resist. The new business prospect would keep Jeff in L.A., doing what he loved most—spending more hours in the kitchen composing exciting new recipes. Only instead of catering fancy private parties, now he would be creating "high-concept" (in both senses of the term) dishes for the patrons of a brand-new restaurant opening in West Hollywood. The man who was once too humble to even call himself a real chef was about to make history as a partner and the executive chef of the first edibles lounge to open in the United States. All Chef Jeff needed to do now was start dreaming up his menu.

21
THE BIG 420 FINALE

Los Angeles, California
Spring 2019

A FULL MOON ROSE over the hills of L.A.'s Pacific Palisades as star Kate Hudson turned the big four-oh. The daughter of Hollywood legend Goldie Hawn and now a mother of three, Hudson had confided to the tabloids that all she really wanted to ring in the new decade was a low-key birthday. As she noted on Instagram, Good Friday, Passover, and 4/20, the unofficial holiday celebrating marijuana, all auspiciously coincided with her big birthday weekend. Clad in belted skinny jeans and a white high-necked blouse, the actress turned athleisurewear mogul celebrated at home with a brick oven pizza party attended by an intimate A-list crowd that reportedly included Reese Witherspoon and Leonardo DiCaprio, plus her mother and famous stepfather, Kurt Russell. There was a bubblegum-pink birthday cake and a giggly champagne toast. And, to cap off the night: an array of cannabis-infused sweets created by none other than JeffThe420Chef. At first, Jeff and his team were sworn to secrecy. But when *E! News* disclosed that his handcrafted chocolate-covered strawberries and Canna Apple Roses drizzled with infused chocolate were on the dessert menu, he was able to gleefully confirm the high-profile gig. In truth, by 2019 there was nothing really hush-hush about the whole pot thing. Cannabis was already out among the red-carpet set and increasingly featured in the press as just another way for the rich and famous to unwind.

A few weeks later, Chef Jeff was still flying high from the star-studded evening as he worked feverishly from the crowded kitchen of a much more modest ranch house on the other side of Topanga Canyon. With his sous chef, Andre Lujan, at his side and his middle son/business partner, Jared, snapping photos for his robust social media feeds, Jeff was in his element, happily chatting about everything from his eldest son's upcoming wedding, to how his parents were doing, to his latest innovation, one that he believed would take his FreeLeaf technology to the next level.

He had built a new contraption that sounded like something out of *Charlie and the Chocolate Factory*. It was a two-chamber machine that he promised could transfer the essence of a particular food into his flavorless, odorless cannabis. Conjuring images of the late Gene Wilder as Willy Wonka unveiling his "Three-Course Dinner Chewing Gum" to incredulous visitors at his secret laboratory, Jeff explained—without revealing exactly how it was done—that if he put an orange on one side of his device, the cannabis flower would come out tasting like orange. Tonight, he was most excited to show off his version of a pantry staple that looked, smelled, and tasted just like garden-variety dried oregano but was actually ground-up marijuana that packed a punch and could be sprinkled onto pizza or mixed into any recipe. Jeff was planning to launch an entire line of herbs and spices for home cooks, with kitschy names like Rosemary Jane, Hazy Thyme, Blunt Basil, and this one, NOregano. They would all be featured on the menu of the new cannabis café, along with a line of smokable pre-rolled joints in lavender, clove, and even chamomile varieties. The irony about the spices, he chuckled, was that when he was caught with a bag of weed back when he was in his teens, he told his mom it was oregano. Now he had made something that was both!

He talked about his big plans, politely offering tastes of his dishes as he popped back and forth from an electric frying pan—where he checked on the dozen chicken wings coated in a batter of cornstarch, flour, salt, and pepper—to the oven to peek at colorful slices of purple and orange cauliflower roasting at 400 degrees. On the opposite counter, his rose-colored watermelon gazpacho had been pureed in a blender and was just about ready to be enhanced with one teaspoon—or 10 milligrams—of his THC-infused olive oil to make twenty individual portions. The oil tasted like a plain old extra virgin variety, just as Jeff had promised, and its exact potency, he explained, had been measured using a beta version of a digital calculator app he had created to determine precisely how much THC was in each of his special ingredients. As he prepared the meal, arriving guests were invited to sip on a choice of either a spritzer featuring a dark cherry syrup made with liquid FreeLeaf and mixed with lime seltzer, or a peach iced tea that had also been embellished with his proprietary ingredient. Each cup contained 2.5 milligrams of THC. Tonight, he was preparing a casual feast for a small private party at the home of his two new business partners, millennial restaurateurs Patrick Fogarty and Jon Locarni, to celebrate the future opening of their joint venture.

Los Angeles transplants who originally hailed from the Midwest, Pat and Jon were getting ready to open America's inaugural edibles lounge. Chef Jeff and his cannabis creations would be the main dish.

"The cannabis space is very, very overwhelming for a lot of people . . . So we wanted something bubbly, fun, still slightly sophisticated but memorable. And we wanted it to appeal to some of the older demographics and women instead of kind of going back towards what was currently in the market," explained Pat, a broad-shouldered former swimmer whose wholesome blue eyes and professional demeanor defied stoner stereotypes from the moment he extended a firm handshake.

Pat and his equally earnest business partner, Jon, embodied the new guard of professionals barreling into the industry with graduate degrees, white-collar résumés, and a fresh take on the cannabis lifestyle based on their expertise from outside fields. They both gave off a charming aw-shucks vibe when asked how the licensing and fundraising had played out so far. They had raised and spent more than $100,000 throughout the application process, and were continuing to work with city and state officials on the evolving regulations for the maiden fleet of cannabis consumption establishments that had never before existed. West Hollywood, with its trendy shops and vibrant gay community, was a world away from Lincoln, Nebraska, and the rowdy college bar near the Huskers stadium where they first met in 2012. Back then, Pat was running the day-to-day operations and Jon was working the bar at night while finishing up his business degree. The two quickly became friends and stayed in touch long after Jon moved to L.A. to work as a CPA in the entertainment world and Pat moved back to St. Louis to oversee a 10,000-square-foot downtown party spot called the Wheelhouse. Pat's college girlfriend, Maddy Gruber, a vivacious blonde from Missouri, had always dreamed of living in California. So when Pat got the call from Jon telling them there might be some lucrative opportunities in cannabis now that adult use was coming to California, he and Maddy left their jobs and moved out West to find their fortunes.

At first, the friends set their sights on applying to open a dispensary in Long Beach or Culver City, but quickly turned their attention to West Hollywood when the city announced in 2017 it would be seeking applications for the first-ever marijuana restaurants and bars, otherwise known as "consumption lounges." The opportunity seemed like a perfect fit for Pat's hospitality background, and they could see themselves opening an inviting neighborhood spot, the kind of place that would cater to the new cannabis consumer—someone who would feel at home at the bar sipping a glass of sparkling cannabis rosé on a warm L.A. night. If anything embodied the new Chardonnay, this was it.

But from the outset, beyond the concept and initial fundraising, what they really needed was to find a talented chef—someone who would help them stand out among the hundreds of applicants they expected to compete against for a chance to open one of the first weed bistros in the country. When Jon spotted JeffThe420Chef's Instagram feed, a veritable portfolio of mouthwatering shots of his dishes, Jon direct-messaged Jeff immediately.

After a few calls and meetings, it was time to sit down for a tasting. The two friends were a bit nervous. They liked Jeff's sense of humor and warm personality, but honestly, they weren't sure what to expect of his food. Everything sure looked delicious in the pictures. But would it actually taste good in real life? Was he really able to erase the cannabis taste?

They were not disappointed.

"He had me at the mimosa because it was just mind-blowing to me to be able to drink a mimosa that tasted just like a mimosa, but it was nonalcoholic and there was zero cannabis taste to it. All of the drinks on the market that I've had, have a distinct tang to it, a distinct flavor to it. So, the moment I had the mimosa, I was kind of just riding high from there, both literally and figuratively. It was amazing," Pat said with a laugh.

But they weren't just there to vet the flavors; they also wanted to experience Jeff's "layered microdosing" in action. Over eggs and French toast at a private home in Playa Vista, they were pleasantly surprised to see how he was able to layer tiny doses of the high-inducing components throughout the brunch. It wasn't overpowering. It felt accessible and fun—especially by the end, when the effects kicked in. They were duly impressed. And this was before they even learned about FreeLeaf and Jeff's other crazy new inventions.

"It felt like we had the missing piece of the puzzle," says Jon of the first meal with Chef Jeff. After eighteen months of planning, pitching, and waiting, the city of West Hollywood awarded Pat, Jon, and Jeff permission, along with fifteen other operators, to open their doors in a move that would truly bring pot consumption smack into the center of the public square. Even with the new breed of upscale retail pot shops, with their Apple Store–like décor and friendly sales associates helping customers shop for cannabis and navigate all of the new ways to consume it, weed was still very much a product that people used in private, behind closed doors. There were a couple of pot shops in San Francisco, and one in Denver, that featured separate properties next door where customers could walk over to ingest their purchases on-site. But in the spring of 2019, nothing really existed yet that resembled a modern-day *Cheers*-like tavern where people could gather out in the open to enjoy marijuana while socializing, just as they would a cocktail or a beer.

For West Hollywood, these new establishments would of course be good for economic development, but the move was also an attempt to address remnants of the racial and class bias of the War on Drugs, according to John Leonard, the city policymaker who helped draft the ordinance to permit the new cafés.

Racial minorities and low-income citizens were more likely to be renters, for whom consuming cannabis at home potentially came with the risk of being evicted. And even in the age of legalization, lighting up on the street, in a car, or in a public park could still get one arrested, explained Leonard. Opening up public places where it was legal to consume weed, officials hoped, would cut down on the punitive measures that disproportionately affected the already disadvantaged.

Social justice had long been woven into the fabric of this lively community of 1.9 square miles enveloped by the city of Los Angeles. Draped in rainbow flags at every turn, West Hollywood was a bastion of LGBTQ activism and had been on the front lines of medical marijuana advocacy for decades. The movement for California to become the first state in the nation to allow medicinal cannabis had been born in San Francisco's Castro district at the height of the AIDS epidemic; early on, West Hollywood took its own stand to ensure AIDS and HIV patients had access to medical cannabis, allowing a cluster of dispensaries to open and even helping to buy a building for one of the first collectives when the owner couldn't find a space to rent. When this defiance of federal law spurred multiple DEA crackdowns, West Hollywood's local officials railed against the incursions by the Feds.

As it happened, these clashes unfolded just a mile or two from Fairfax, the Orthodox Jewish neighborhood where Jeff had kept his own sexual orientation hidden until he was forty years old. So it seemed fitting that now, with this next chapter, he had come out of the closet on two fronts, stepping into the spotlight as a gay dad and a cannabis chef all at once. West Hollywood was not only a historically meaningful spot to open a new frontier of marijuana hospitality; for Jeff, it truly was the perfect place to live his truth to the fullest.

"It's a blessing to be opening this lounge here," he told *Civilized*, the digital cannabis magazine, just after the project was announced. "I'm a gay father of three amazing kids, and West Hollywood has always served as a safe haven for me and my family . . . and for so many others like us."

Their lounge was initially going to be called "Budberry," but after a trademark dispute with the U.K. fashion conglomerate Burberry, it was being rebranded as "Monica's House," a reference to L.A. lore about a mysterious woman named Monica who threw secret parties at her beach house in the 1940s and served her glamorous guests the finest weed around. Her namesake was to be a coffeehouse by day and wine bar by night, and would reside in a trendy indoor-outdoor space complete with a Zen garden and a koi pond, off of busy Santa Monica Boulevard. The oasis had previously belonged to interior designer and artist Thomas Schoos, the creator of the TAO chain of hip Asian-themed nightclubs, who had become an adviser to the project.

Just like every aspect of the emerging cannabis landscape in California and elsewhere, however, nothing about the opening was straightforward or predictable. Shifting local and state regulations on cannabis made for a Rubik's Cube of public health and safety puzzles to solve, as Jeff and his partners learned they would need to have not only two separate menus, but two separate serving areas to distinguish the pot-infused food from the virgin items. And all THC edibles would have to be prepackaged and lab tested for contaminants and potency, which meant that nothing could be freshly infused on the spot the way Jeff dosed his private dinners. So for now, the lounge was set to serve light bites that diners could order from a virgin menu first, and then separately choose to enhance with accoutrements like 2.5-milligram portions of NOregano flakes to top the fresh-baked flatbreads, FreeLeaf olive oil to drizzle on hummus, THC creamers to stir into coffees, or sweet syrups and honey for teas.

"The reason that has to work that way is because the salad dressing, or the sauce, or whatever it is, has been tested already, and it's in final-form packaging. Those products have all been tested and have the same labeling requirements that an edible would that you would go and buy from a retail location," describes Leonard, in reference to the strict testing California now required of all commercial cannabis products across the entire supply chain.

To expand the options, the plan was to partner with restaurants in the neighborhood, including Norah, which resided next door and could unobtrusively deliver dishes like its fried chicken sandwich and garlic herb fries through a back patio doorway that connected the two venues. Once the food arrived, patrons would be able to sprinkle on Jeff's special condiments themselves. But the menu hurdles weren't the only challenge these hospitality entrepreneurs would face. This new type of dining experience would also require a highly trained set of servers in the front of the house, who could speak intelligently on both the regular and 420 menus and advise on intended effects. (To head off the long onset time, the partners planned to offer an array of pot-infused beverages at the bar, like Rebel Coast Sauvignon Blanc and Saka Sparkling Rosé, which were said to kick in just fifteen minutes after consuming.) All this while keeping a watchful eye to ensure diners didn't overindulge and that they were not getting behind the wheel. And they would need avid security to check IDs, to ensure no one under twenty-one was served, but in a stealthy way that was still inviting and friendly.

Regardless of all of the kinks to work out before opening day, the one constant in Patrick and Jon's plans was to build a gleaming windowed production area in the center of the lounge to showcase the Julia Child of Weed at work. They envisioned customers looking in and observing Chef Jeff utilizing state-of-the-art equipment to create his tasteless, odorless cannabis bud, plus his new device to infuse the flower with a cornucopia of savory and sweet flavors—while still retaining a bit of mystery, of course. After all, this wizard of weed wasn't about to give away his trade secrets, even as he put on a good show.

But Jeff, a natural performer, would relish the chance to don his chef's coat with the marijuana leaf on the pocket to show that here, just as with LGBTQ identity, marijuana use wasn't simply out of the closet, it was something to be celebrated like a fine wine. For him, it was a symbol of pride in himself and how far he had come in his enduring and sometimes painful journey to be the man and the chef he was today. Cannabis had helped him come into his own. As he looked ahead to opening the new lounge and his next big chapter, he was bursting with excitement to share that feeling of belonging with his future patrons. To him, it was actually quite simple, he said with a knowing smile. "I want someone to walk in and say, 'Oh, I'm finally home.'"

AS CHEF JEFF worked with Jon and Pat to prepare for the lounge's anticipated opening in the summer of 2020, two of their very first investors were hard at work a few miles away in a sunny WeWork office hunting down new deals for Casa Verde Capital, Snoop Dogg's expanding cannabis portfolio. Even as the business press was reporting that the pot bubble had officially burst, Karan Wadhera and Yoni Meyer spent most of their time looking for new private investment opportunities for the fund founded by Snoop and Ted. Theirs was a counterintuitive strategy that had paid off with growing valuations—and credibility—in four short years. While lots of prospectors had run toward cultivation or retail, Ted Chung and his cannabis think tank took a step back and looked at the bigger picture. They quietly went after the unsexy but essential businesses that would end up facilitating the new legal industry, like software solutions for payments, compliance systems, and hiring. These were startups that touched the entire ecosystem and could scale quickly and expand into new markets without having to apply for cannabis licenses or deal with the red tape and potential risk of directly selling a federally unlawful product. This strategy had attracted so much excitement that the Snoop-backed fund had nearly doubled in size to $45 million, and was no longer accepting new money by early 2018. It had grown so fast that it necessitated two professional managers to run it full-time.

That was when Karan, a Goldman Sachs alum and the younger brother of one of Ted's closest UPenn buddies, and Yoni, who cut his teeth at Citigroup, had stepped in. There was so much interest in their approach, Karan and Yoni were on their way to raising a much-larger fund, which would invest in emerging brands.

When the two financiers weren't on the road doing diligence on potential investments or pitching new investors on fund two, they were mulling over a deluge of incoming opportunities while nurturing the young companies they had gambled on. Eaze, the software company that facilitated delivery service across California—and Casa Verde's maiden investment in 2015—was just the beginning. There was Metrc, a tech company that made popular "track and trace" software for state regulators to keep strict tabs on cannabis inventories and the origins of raw materials; and Vangst, the female-founded recruitment and hiring platform that addressed the increasing demand for highly skilled workers, as well as the need for part-time employees like trimmers across the cannabis and hemp industries. They had taken a chance on Oxford Cannabinoid Technologies, a U.K. research lab exploring the therapeutic benefits of dozens of phytochemicals in the cannabis plant, beyond THC and CBD; and on *Miss Grass*, the digital magazine and e-commerce shop aspiring to be "the goop of cannabis." To boot, they had increasingly enticed cautious institutional investors into these deals, like when Casa Verde partnered with the multibillion-dollar hedge fund Tiger Global Management to invest in cannabis software startup Green Bits and, later, Metrc. Snoop and Ted occasionally met with starry-eyed founders, but it was Karan and Yoni who vetted the companies and fielded pitches from startups yearning for an invaluable endorsement from marijuana's top dogg.

Ted was multitasking more than ever. And on top of it, he wasn't getting much sleep now that he had become a dad to an adorable curly-haired baby girl. On a swing through Manhattan via Chicago, he rose bleary-eyed after arriving late the night before, craving a glass of freshly pressed celery juice. A small fruit plate and some herbal tea would have to do as he sat back in his hotel room and shared what was on his mind these days since the pot stock bubble had burst. As he nibbled on berries, Ted explained why the future for this fast-growing market was brighter than ever in his mind, even as stock prices for publicly traded pot companies got hammered. By the fall of 2019, the top five Canadian pot stocks had lost $10 billion in value in response to concerns over continued competition from the underground cannabis suppliers (only 28 percent of Canadians were buying weed from the legal market, according to government reports), concerns over the sharp rise in teen vaping of THC, and the ongoing investigation into faulty e-cigarette devices that had claimed the lives of more than fifty people.

Ted took the long view. From his vantage point, there were continued signs that the demand for cannabis was flourishing. He was heartened by the fact that most of the 2020 Democratic presidential front-runners were talking about marijuana both on the campaign trail and on the debate stage. He was more optimistic than ever that legalization across America and the world was coming soon. Congressional committees had held multiple hearings on banking reform, and, in a landmark vote, the House had passed the SAFE Banking Act, which would open up financial services to cannabis companies, including much-needed loans. (In a historic vote, when the U.S. House of Representatives passed the Secure and Fair Enforcement (SAFE) Banking Act in September 2019, it was hailed as a step forward for small business owners and the industry as a whole—but the bill stalled before it was taken up in the Senate.)

Colorado had been the ultimate test case and based on the data the state had put out five years after recreational use became legal, the sky had not fallen. A report by the Colorado Department of Public Safety to lawmakers flagged drugged driving as a concern but noted that it was difficult to track because roadside technology for police officers to measure the presence of THC was still in development, and often the presence of alcohol contributed to impairment. There was a rise in hospitalizations related to cannabis, but researchers pointed out that with legalization, people were also more open about their usage. And pot use among teens, according to a state survey cited in the report, appeared to remain nearly unchanged. Even though the illicit market was still in business, overall state policymakers and even former governor John Hickenlooper, who had once called the experiment "reckless," agreed that critics' worst fears had not come to pass. By 2019, the state had collected a billion dollars in tax revenue from pot sales and the industry had created more than 200,000 jobs.

And the opportunities today spread far beyond Colorado. Ted observed how quickly the U.S. market had grown. "You turn around in a month, and in one month a group that was only in one state has now been acquired and is now in seven states . . . The market has its players, its fulfillment providers, its agricultural experts, its farmers and then its retail experts and its CPG, product innovation teams . . . The science, the emulsifying technology for beverages, the lattice, if you will, of areas of expertise is now being defined, whereas before it was just in one box," he explained in a professorial tone.

The Chardonnay moms would continue to be a target market as the Leafs By Snoop team looked for partners to develop new microdose products and creative ways to communicate marijuana's story to new demographics. Through Merry Jane, the cannabis information and entertainment site he had founded with Snoop and unveiled at TechCrunch Disrupt, Ted was quickly proving that with the right marketing, even mainstream brands could safely capitalize on the new cannabis lifestyle. Case in point: Jack in the Box's "Merry Munchie Meal." This tongue-in-cheek campaign, conceived by Ted's team (and endorsed by Snoop), was the first time a major company had attempted such a blatant reference to weed in its marketing. With two tacos, three chicken strips, half servings of both curly fries and onion rings, mini churros, and a small drink all for the price of (what else?) $4.20, the Merry Munchie meal was indeed a late-night snack no stoner could resist, as well as an overt nod to times a-changin'. Offered for only two weeks in three Southern California drive-throughs, the stunt garnered a 3 percent bump in sales across Jack in the Box franchises—and earned Ted and Merry Jane high praise from *Adweek*. Other brands, like the food delivery service Postmates, suddenly wanted in, too, and Ted had quickly spun off a new marketing agency, Gram by Gram, to focus exclusively on companies trying to reach the canna-curious. He would soon open offices in Los Angeles, Toronto, Mexico City, and London, in preparation for new lawful marijuana markets to open up across the globe. Attitudes toward weed were shifting everywhere, he observed, from the European Union to South Africa to Thailand to even South Korea.

"This industry moves so fast and you have to be willing to run through walls and think about seven things, all the time, at the same time," he said, describing the fast pace of change.

But Ted and Snoop were still concerned about social justice and who was being left out of this promising new sector. "Now it is like, what are you putting on the table? How do you ensure that, especially for Snoop and myself and those around us, black, brown, and female entrepreneurs are all involved in the cannabis economy?" Ted asked rhetorically.

At least the issue was emerging as a talking point in Washington, with the House Judiciary Committee's passage of the MORE Act in the fall of 2019, as well as in state capitols as lawmakers wrestled with how best to ensure that the communities hurt by the War on Drugs did not lose out on opportunities to cash in on this new industry. The question of how best to address these inequities was complicated and fraught with debate. In Colorado, while the number of arrests for marijuana-related offenses had gone down, blacks were still being charged at double the rates of whites, according to a 2018 report by Colorado's Division of Criminal Justice. Elsewhere, efforts to award licenses to minorities and people from zip codes unfairly targeted by law enforcement had fallen flat. A June 2019 study by *Marijuana Business Daily* analyzing progress for minorities in Ohio and Massachusetts found that despite initiatives to give black and brown entrepreneurs an advantage in the scoring process by which licenses were awarded, only 16.4 percent of cannabis businesses in Ohio were owned by minorities, and just 1.5 percent in Massachusetts.

"This is still an industry that is still very dominated by males and non-minorities," commented *MJBizDaily* research editor Eli McVey in the summer of 2019, noting that the bulk of plant-touching businesses rely on the personal wealth of founders to cover the potentially millions of dollars in startup costs, given that the federally illegal status of the plant made it nearly impossible for many cannabis business owners to access loans or other financial services from banks.

Beyond the fundraising challenges, there were whispers that some of the biggest, most well-financed companies had found stealthy workarounds to take advantage of programs that incentivized diversity, paying minority "straw men" to front their applications for licenses so that they could qualify for an advantage.

"So somebody comes in and says, 'Hey look, maybe we'll pay you $10,000 or we'll give you $2,000 a month to make it look like you're an owner of this business . . .' It's definitely a problem and it certainly will be as long as the incentives for applying as a minority-owned business or a woman-owned businessare high enough. You're going to get these straw-man agreements in every market," said McVey.

The diversity problem was a big part of why, in 2019, legalization efforts hit snags in New Jersey and New York. Even with outspoken governors pushing for reform, the measures were mired in statehouse squabbles over how much funding should be set aside to help minority entrepreneurs and communities hurt by biased policing, whether citizens should be allowed to grow plants at home, or how states would go about expunging the records of people jailed for weed offenses. When Illinois lawmakers wrote social justice provisions into that state's new adult use law, which passed in June 2019, Ted, Snoop, and others held out hope that it might lead the nation on workable solutions to achieve equity. The much-anticipated program would provide a $20 million no-interest loan program for minority entrepreneurs, priority for applicants who live in zip codes disproportionately harmed by drug enforcement, application fee waivers, a marijuana conviction expungement program, and economic development grants to communities that had suffered the most "because of discriminatory drug policies." With 12.6 million people, Illinois would be the second-largest marijuana market after California and a bellwether for the next wave of states to legalize.

It seemed to Ted and Snoop as if the world had caught up to what they had always believed about the power of the plant. The rapper who made a career out of flaunting his blunt-smoking pastime was taking stock of just how much he and the stigma of smoking weed had changed over his enduring two-decade chart-topping career. After all, this was the man who was once wanted for murder, convicted of marijuana possession, and portrayed by the media as public enemy number one when he first burst onto the scene in the 1990s. But with Ted as his manager, he had managed to transcend this gangsta image and his personal brand had evolved into an avuncular figure loved by tens of millions of fans across the globe. Inhaling was part of his charm.

"I love the fact that I used to be a bad guy known for smoking weed like you used to read about me . . . Now it's all love and it's all peace and all understanding. I love the fact that you can be on the wrong side and get on the right side and you can be forgiven and you can fix yourself or you can get things right," the star reflected onstage in September 2019 as he spoke to cannabis scientists, farmers, and activists at a retreat in Mendocino County hosted by the marijuana company Flow Kana.

There was no question that Snoop had reintroduced reefer to Middle America in a way no one else could have. All you had to do was turn on the television to see Uncle Snoop and his buddy Martha Stewart quizzing their smiling talk show guests on their "High Q" or cooking up mac-and-cheese-waffle sandwiches in the epic 4/20 "Munchie Snackdown" to understand Snoop's far-reaching impact and how he had helped to bring cannabis into the zeitgeist.

"Cannabis connects people of all walks . . . Having cannabis in my life, it helped me to be a better person and a better individual," the lanky artist told the crowd packed into the open-air amphitheater.

Now the Doggfather was about to take that message on the road yet again, and would soon be performing in sold-out stadiums and clubs across the country to promote his nineteenth album. The tour and what it stood for were in many ways a crowning moment for both music and marijuana.

Ted had watched with pride as his business partner and friend Calvin Broadus received his star on the Hollywood Walk of Fame. As the multiplatinum-selling and Grammy-winning artist, in a smart camel hair topcoat, sunglasses, and a Gucci turtleneck sweater, took the podium to graciously accept his award, he summed it up like only he could: "I wanna thank me for being me at all times. Snoop Dogg, you're a bad motherfucker."

INDEED. *Martha & Snoop's Potluck Dinner Party* on VH-1 was going strong, attracting celebs ranging from Method Man to Nick Jonas to Paris Hilton to Jimmy Kimmel. In fact, by Season 3, all the talk of weed on the set seemed to have finally convinced Martha that it was time she explore some new business opportunities in the industry. So it was no surprise that the hip-hop legend and his manager introduced Martha to their friend and colleague Bruce Linton, the founder of the largest and highest-valued weed company in the world, a publicly traded Canadian colossus that had just debuted on the New York Stock Exchange. With Ted and Tim Saunders, Canopy's CFO, at the table, Stewart listened intently to what Bruce had to say about the potential for CBD to help aging dogs with pain and mobility. He told her the scientific research into the efficacy of CBD for animals was still underway, but that he believed the non-intoxicating compound held promise for helping furry friends.

"We're not just going to throw in CBD and stop," he assured the famed tastemaker. "We're going to actually have to know it works, to make the claims true, know the dosage so we don't hurt the dog. We also don't want to rip off the owner."

As a well-known animal lover and master gardener, Stewart had heard enough to want to see the operation for herself, and soon made her way to Eastern Ontario to visit tiny Smiths Falls and the former chocolate factory that had brought the town back to life. In the end, they agreed that Stewart would come on board as a strategic adviser to the company to help it develop a line of CBD food, cosmetics, and pet treats that would be produced from hemp. In fact, Canopy would later reveal the $150 million purchase of an industrial park on forty-eight acres in Kirkwood, New York, that would source hemp from local farmers to begin producing CBD capsules, tinctures, and consumables for the United States. Pet products were still in development, but the company had plans to invest heavily in hemp-derived CBD and open seven other hemp manufacturing plants across America within a year, according to a Bloomberg report.

Stewart had no problem lending her name and likeness to the brand.

"No one has canceled a subscription to my magazine because of my relationship with Snoop. Some partners looked askance when my connection to Canopy Growth was revealed, but now those same partners are selling CBD products in their stores," Stewart told the World Cannabis Congress in a June 2019 keynote address.

Bruce, for his part, was riding high having just finessed the potential future acquisition of Acreage Holdings, one of the largest multistate operators in the United States. The historic transcontinental deal was valued at $3.4 billion, and hinged on Congress reforming federal banking laws and clarifying states' rights so that weed businesses in the country could proceed without intervention. Acreage Holdings was run by Kevin Murphy, a conservative Republican from Connecticut who played one season in the United States Football League (USFL). The affable former linebacker was raised in a strict Catholic home and spent his college football career at Holy Cross. He ultimately made his way to Wall Street (where he crossed paths with Beth Stavola for a time) and later made millions from hedge funds.

"Murph," as everyone called him, had moved stealthily under the radar since 2011, when he first put some money behind a medical marijuana operation in Maine. But when he wooed one of the most notorious marijuana opponents to join his board, his company was suddenly thrust into the spotlight. Heads turned at the news in April 2018 that former Speaker of the House John Boehner would lend his name and political clout to Murph's team. The deal with Bruce made international headlines and, by media accounts, made Boehner very rich: the stock package was reportedly worth $12 million and would increase to $20 million if and when the Canopy deal closed. Murph, an aspiring politician in his own right who one day hoped to run for governor of Connecticut, had recruited Boehner over a power lunch in Naples, Florida, one sunny afternoon. By the time Murph met Bruce Linton at the World Economic Conference in Davos, Switzerland, he had former Massachusetts governor William Weld on his board, too. The future Canopy-Acreage marriage looked like a harbinger for the de facto end of Prohibition in the United States. It was only a question of when and how, in Bruce's eyes.

At the same time, after several years of expensive trial and error, Bruce's team had finally done it: they had perfected his version of Wonka's top secret Everlasting Gobstopper—the zero-calorie, hangover-free, clear cannabis elixir. They called it Tweed Distilled Cannabis, and there were plans for it to be bottled and sold like top-shelf liquor. It would also be mixed into thirteen ready-to-drink canned beverages meant to appeal to everyone from Chardonnay moms to millennial hipsters to boomers. For the health-conscious crowd, marketers would unveil a series of sparkling drinks containing CBD only, and a low-dose combination of THC and CBD, in flavors like cucumber and ginger with lime.

"We're doing about a hundred miles an hour down the road, and then what we're going to do is, at the last second, touch the brakes, slide sideways, and go right into the parking spot," Bruce said of the race to get everything ready for when the Canadian government finally waved them to the starting line. The hope was that the libations and an array of new edibles and vaporizers would hit store shelves in time for Christmas.

If it went as planned, Bruce believed the drinks would usher in a whole new healthier way of socializing, celebrating, and taking the edge off. But despite his unflagging enthusiasm, a shadow loomed. Canopy Growth was spending heavily on acquisitions and expanding its global footprint. In Canada alone, the corporation had gone from 600,000 to 4.8 million square feet in just eighteen months, including retrofitting towering greenhouses in British Columbia. Research and science had always been core to Bruce's mission, and the company now held ninety patents and had just launched sixty clinical trials aimed at studying new cannabinoid therapies for its medical arm. Yet losses were piling up fast and furiously and investors were getting impatient for higher profit margins. Constellation Brands, the alcohol giant that had wagered nearly $4 billion on the cannabis corporation and now owned 35.8 percent of the company, was getting especially antsy. And after Canopy told investors on a June 2019 earnings call that its losses for the fiscal year had ballooned to $257 million (more than seven times the previous year's), Constellation's CEO, Bill Newlands, let it be known that the Corona beer and Mondavi wine maker was "not pleased with Canopy's reported year-end results." The ominous comments sent Canopy's stock tumbling.

Still, Bruce remained optimistic. In his own earnings presentation to Canopy shareholders, he underscored that this was all part of the plan to build scale. He was running this company like a Silicon Valley tech startup, building something disruptive, something no one had ever done before. And you had to spend money to make money.

But a week later, Bruce heard that a board meeting had been called for the following Tuesday—a meeting that he, the CEO and chairman of the board, had not called. Something was up.

The following week, on July 3 at 8:02 A.M., Canopy sent out a press release blast stating that Bruce was stepping down. Within minutes, he called up CNBC to clarify that no, he was not willingly relinquishing his role. He had been fired. "I was terminated," he said over the phone to the surprised TV anchors. It had been six years. Bruce had grown the company to four thousand people in fifteen countries with a market capitalization that at one point totaled $20 billion. And in an instant, it was no longer his to lead.

"Our board was uniform," Bill Newlands later told the press in responding to questions about the CEO's ouster. "We needed a different leader to take us to the next phase of growth." Constellation would later install David Klein, its CFO, as the new CEO of Canopy.

It was a punch in the gut to the mayor of Smiths Falls. The community had not seen it coming. Plans for a new hotel and convention center, all fueled by its largest employer, were in the works. The small town had even gotten its very first fast-food franchise and had put out a sharp brochure touting the area's miraculous growth. New single-family homes were being built for the first time in a decade. Mayor Pankow was assured by the interim CEO, Mark Zekulin, that Canopy wasn't going anywhere and would move forward with Bruce's plans to revamp the water treatment plant, and the post office renovation was still on track. But he and the citizens would sorely miss the man who had brought their economy back to life.

"Bruce has been such a leader, such an ally to the community, such a visionary, and the individual probably more than anyone who has completely turned around the fortunes and future of our community," said Pankow two weeks after the news broke.

For his part, the high-energy founder wasn't sitting home in Ottawa licking his wounds or even putting away the black Canopy Growth T-shirts he was known to wear on TV. Not by a long shot. Within days of the bruising turn of events, the former hockey player with the sharp elbows was already in New York City entertaining new offers. He had a non-compete clause that prevented him only from going to work for a Canadian rival, and within hours of his announced departure, his phone was ringing off the hook with prospects in the United States.

The Willy Wonka of Weed wouldn't be leaving the world of cannabis any time soon. He would simply take his vision elsewhere.

BETH STAVOLA COULD not believe that the man she called the "godfather" of cannabis had been shown the door. She respected Bruce immensely for going on TV to set the record straight about his departure. "I'd never let anyone get away with lying about me," she said. She didn't know Linton personally at the time, but as an entrepreneur who had rolled up her sleeves and gotten her hands dirty building her own cannabis empire without a net, she was a kindred spirit. It took guts and grit to do what she had done over seven years. There were so many times she feared she would lose everything, but she kept going.

She still shuddered at one of her worst memories. In March 2018, Beth had arrived at the Toronto airport two hours early for a flight home to New Jersey. She was excited to get home; she missed her kids and was eager to spend the weekend with them. She'd never had a problem going through customs, but this time, when she presented her passport, a U.S. Customs agent asked her more pointed questions than usual. She started to get nervous. There had been stories about people working in legal cannabis who had faced trouble at the border, even some Canadians who were barred from entering the United States because of their marijuana business dealings. She knew she had done nothing wrong, but her hands were shaking. Suddenly, she was being escorted to a back room for secondary questioning, and the agent began rummaging through her designer purse. He then dumped out her wallet, keys, and cosmetics onto a steel table and began probing her about each and every item and what it contained. When he spied Beth's expensive La Mer eye cream, he insisted on testing it for narcotics. Nothing turned up but the whole experience was scary and demoralizing. She wondered if she was somehow on the U.S. government's radar. Even though she strictly complied with state and local laws where she ran her marijuana ventures, the fact was that selling weed was a federal crime, and her bank accounts had gotten shut down because of her business more times than she could count.

After two and a half hours of questioning, she was finally released. As soon as she walked out and through the metal detectors, she burst out crying. This was not a woman who shed tears very often (her mom would tell stories about how she wondered if Beth's tear ducts worked properly as a child, because she almost never saw her cry), but this experience had made Beth feel unusually vulnerable. She was so distraught, she remembers two kind women in the terminal coming up to her to ask if she was okay and if she needed to call someone. Yes, she sniffled, as she wiped at her smudged mascara, she did have someone to call. She immediately dialed her old friend and Arizona attorney Mel McDonald.

Mel, the former U.S. Attorney who first helped Beth disentangle herself from Vince Diorio when she caught him stealing from her Arizona dispensaries five years before, was able to calm her down, and she rebooked her flight to Newark. But the typically unflappable businesswoman was spooked. She told her colleagues this was it. She wouldn't get on a plane to Canada again until America lifted its federal prohibition on pot. Period.

It was a strange time, though, she says, looking back. A flurry of U.S. businesses were heading north to raise the capital they needed to keep expanding, since they were barred from American stock exchanges. The biggest at the time was MedMen, the California-based company known as "the Apple Store of Pot," whose brash CEO, Adam Bierman, once bragged about his goal of creating "the Standard Oil" of cannabis. MedMen and its competitors not only needed cash to keep running their expensive operations, they also needed millions to fund war chests to pay for the high-priced lobbyists and applications to compete in new medical marijuana markets in places like Florida, Ohio, and Pennsylvania (not to mention money to help bankroll legalization initiatives). On the East Coast, where states restricted the number of medical licenses they would hand out, and where owners of medical marijuana businesses would likely have the first shot at doing business if and when states allowed for recreational use, the licenses became so valuable that they were known as "super licenses." Those who didn't win any would wrestle each other to buy them up. In one of the most striking examples, MedMen signed a whopping $53 million deal to buy Treadwell Nursery, a company that owned one of Florida's coveted thirteen medical licenses, and with it, the right to open twenty-five of its glossy dispensaries across the Sunshine State.

"The business has gone from a hundred miles an hour to a thousand miles an hour. I remember this . . . during the early stages of the Internet, there was a lot of this going on. There were big players at that time like AOL just gobbling everybody up, so there's a lot of similarities," explained Beth. "The mergers and acquisition market is insanity. I think it's a huge land grab to see who can become the Canopy Growth of the U.S. the soonest."

She believed that, in the end, there would only be a handful of national cannabis conglomerates dominating the entire U.S. marijuana market. And she hadn't come this far not to run one of them. By the summer of 2018, she and MPX were looking at teaming up with other national players and had become a sought-after prospect for a merger. But it was hard to know who was a serious suitor.

"Nobody wants to sign an exclusive letter of intent right now, because everybody seems to be negotiating with five different people and it's really a race to be the absolute biggest and best," she said.

There was one CEO, though, who she and her board thought might make for a good match. Hadley Ford had founded a multistate marijuana company in 2014 called iAnthus. His brother, who ran a medical marijuana business in New Mexico, had come up with the name, which means "full of flower" in Latin. At first glance, Ford looked like a typical Wall Street banker with his horn-rimmed glasses and expensive ties. But his personality was anything but staid. You had to get to know him to learn he wasn't just another suit. The Stanford MBA had actually spent five years living off the grid and earning what he could as a street performer, juggling and doing magic tricks to get by as he hitchhiked across America and Europe. Tall, loquacious, and charismatic, Ford had been looking to join forces with another multistate company for a while, and from the moment he met Beth Stavola, he was intrigued.

"When we met each other, it made all the sense in the world. From personalities to our footprint in the country, really, we had virtually no overlap," she said of why combining their fiefdoms might work.

If they united, they could cover eleven states with sixty-three dispensaries and have access to an estimated 121 million potential customers. Hadley especially liked the idea that Beth had built her empire from the ground up. She was a true operator who knew all the ins and outs and had learned hard lessons firsthand—the only way you could in a business where there was certainly no playbook. She had endured it all—from pot harvests ruined by powder mold and spider mites, to crushing revelations about backstabbing "friends," to being forced to recall faulty vaporizers made in China.

Further, she and her brain trust had created a line of well-packaged products to appeal to the new cannabis consumer—women, professionals, and the aging—all of whom were interested in the potential health and wellness benefits of weed. She was even in the midst of developing new creations based on the emerging research about cannabinoids like THCV, which early studies suggested might be an appetite suppressant. Beth's grower in Maryland was trying to harvest a strain high in the compound that could be marketed as "marijuana without the munchies." Beth, already, even had a working name and packaging for a disposable vape pen she referred to as the "Lean Leaf." She had inviting stores with a Southwestern flair that she had carefully designed to be places where even her mom, Big Nanny, would want to browse. Her dispensaries in Arizona, Nevada, and now Maryland were staffed with well-dressed professionals, many of them college educated. All were subjected to rigorous training in the law and local regulations, and received constant education in person and online about the flood of new products coming out constantly. If this merger worked out, she envisioned that she and Hadley could build a house of brands that would one day be as familiar as Budweiser.

After a few false starts and some tense negotiations, they had a deal. The first marriage between two publicly traded cannabis companies would be valued at $1.6 billion. And Beth had swallowed her fears of crossing the border in order to fly to Toronto and make it official, face-to-face.

The next morning, on the heels of the big announcement, the new business partners strolled triumphantly into the Canaccord Cannabis Conference to applause and cheers from even their fiercest rivals. It was the best day of Beth's professional life, she would say the following week when she confidently strutted—in a deep purple dress and sky-high Valentino heels—into the inaugural New Jersey Cannabis Media Summit to address a roomful of mostly male investors and entrepreneurs, all hoping the legislature would pass a bill to approve recreational pot in the upcoming 2019 session. Hadley introduced Beth, the new chief strategy officer and board director of iAnthus, to the packed banquet hall as "the $850 million woman" (referring to MPX's value of the merger in Canadian dollars).

A decade before, a psychic had predicted that the thirty-nine-year-old Beth would one day start a business bigger than Stavola Companies, her husband's family's massive New Jersey–based construction corporation. The clairvoyant had put her hands on Beth's forehead and uttered, "It's like Prohibition. It's like the Kennedys. You're going to do a lot of interviews. You're going to get into politics." And Beth remembered laughing it off: "I am the woman in the shoe with eight million kids. There is no way this is going to happen."

And yet, she and her husband had literally bet it all on marijuana and won. Now she was sipping a cool cocktail in the bar of the chic London Hotel in West Hollywood looking like a movie star. In an hour, she would be named one of the top "Women of Weed" by *High Times* at a festive ceremony. She had flown in her tight-knit team from all over the country to share in the celebration. Michele Fiore, now Las Vegas mayor pro tem, chatted up Beth's newest business partner, Hadley Ford. There was Jack, in his dark sunglasses, stoically taking in the scene as Beth's sister Julie and Big Nanny, ever the proud mama, arrived dressed to the nines to walk the red carpet with her. And the icing on the cake: iAnthus had just announced it was going to buy the beauty and wellness company she and her sister had started—as a side hustle—for nearly $14 million. There were already plans to sell CBD For Life products in mainstream retail chains like Dillard's and Urban Outfitters, and new retail pot shops incorporating Beth's style were on the horizon, including a high-profile storefront next to the Barclays Center in Brooklyn.

Beth bubbled with all kinds of ideas for the future, too. If marijuana was turning out to be the new Chardonnay, maybe she would get into the marijuana lounge business, like Chef Jeff, as soon as the opportunities opened up in new cities. She often thought about what it would be like to open a trendy pot café and e-sports parlor on the boardwalk in Atlantic City, or some other type of upscale social club in Las Vegas.

Tonight, though, Beth would simply savor the moment. This was a long way from her *Wolf of Wall Street* days, but she had never lost her edge.

She was "the Queen of Marijuana," as rapper Flavor Flav had crowned her when he introduced her at a recent event. Beth grinned as she looked around the room and thought of a text message from Julie that captured it all:

> *You are the fucking rock star of all rock stars. Don't [let] anyone make you feel less than that because the ones who try want to be you . . . Go crush them like you've always done your whole life.*

ACKNOWLEDGMENTS

The New Chardonnay is based on tireless, old-fashioned shoe-leather reporting, a dream come true for an old-schooler like me. It required hundreds of interviews over three years; countless trips to observe grows, retail shops, and manufacturing operations; and being a fly on the wall at all kinds of gatherings large and small across the United States and Canada. I could not have wrapped my head around such a complex topic without the insights of so many people in the space who generously offered to share their firsthand experiences and granted access to their businesses and, in some cases, their personal lives. Some of those key sources include Gia Morón, Jeanne Sullivan, Alicia Syrett, Aliza Sherman, Joanne Wilson, Lilach Mazor Power (who also introduced me to Drs. Raphael Mechoulam and Yossi Tam and gave me my very first behind-the-scenes tour of her vertically integrated business, the Giving Tree in Arizona), Nancy Whiteman, Jamie Evans, Mitch Baruchowitz, Troy Dayton, Daniel Yi, Roy Bingham, Liz Stahura, Pamela Hadfield, Andrea Brooks, Amanda Denz, Amy Wasserman, Cassandra Farrington, Tess Woods, Chris Walsh, Carrie Tice, Tiffany Chin, Jim Baudino, Karan Wadhera, Yoni Meyer, Jason Gully, Mel and Cindy McDonald, Tenisha Victor, Dale Edwards, Julie Winter, Kathie Beggans, Mollie Twining, Kimberly Wagner, Kimberly Dillon, Kandice Haws, Cynthia Salarizadeh, Rosie Mattio, Shawna McGregor, Dennis Hunter, Sunshine Lencho, Sheena Shiravi, Cam and Shannon Hattan, Erin Gore, Karli Warner, Kyra Reed, and, of course, Ted Chung, who first introduced me to Bruce Linton in the fall of 2017. Thank you to

Ted, Bruce, Jeff, and Beth for sharing your stories with me and letting me peek behind the curtain of your worlds.

This project could not have been possible without the help of so many people who believed that these stories needed to be told and encouraged me, the most unlikely person in the world to write a book about marijuana, to go for it. Thank you to Currency editor Talia Krohn for recognizing the potential of this book, supporting me wholeheartedly through the process of reporting, crafting the narrative over many months, and offering smart and thoughtful editorial guidance. Thank you to deputy editor Erin Little for your passion for this project and lending your creativity and enthusiasm along the way. I want to express my deep gratitude to my literary agent and dear friend, Lisa Leshne of The Leshne Agency, who understood the kind of book I aspired to write and made it happen from the moment we started discussing it, and who went to bat for me to bring it to life. Thanks to attorney Candice Cook, who helped secure legal permissions from sources for me to report the book, web designer Nadine Gilden for lending her creative talents to all things digital, and research assistants Patrick Ralph and Melissa Cabot, who pitched in to cover events when I couldn't be there myself. A special thanks goes to the amazingly talented Kristy Dobkin, who shared her film and TV screenwriting techniques for "breaking story" to help me organize my research and narrative themes. And to all of my mom friends who now know more about pot than they ever wanted to, thank you for listening to me rattle on at the gym, on walks and hikes, and on countless evenings, and for being a de facto focus group as I worked through how I wanted to tell this story.

To my children, Ian and Sam, thank you for understanding all those months I was either on a plane out West or holed up in my office staring at my laptop. Your curiosity about my journalistic endeavors and the really important conversations we had about mass incarceration and substance use kept me on my toes. Thank you, Ian, for making sure I had the correct ice hockey lingo for Bruce's section, and Sam, for patiently listening and offering notes as I practiced my first keynote speech on cannabis. You two are my greatest inspirations and I love you so much.

To my siblings and my parents, thank you for being my West Coast bureaus, providing a place to crash on my crazy trips to your cities, and cheering me on as I embarked on this adventure. I couldn't have done it without your love and support.

And finally, thank you to the most dedicated partner, best friend, and greatest in-house editor in the world: my husband, Neeraj Khemlani. There are too many times to count when you helped me think through early ahas, sketched outlines with me at our kitchen table, gave me no-holds-barred notes on drafts, and helped me think through how I was going to attack this unwieldy, fast-moving tornado of a story that literally changed from day to day. In many ways, the idea for the book sprouted from your early work with Peter Jennings on the 1997 ABC News special "Pot of Gold," in which marijuana was first named "America's number one cash crop." The underground cannabis growers you reported on for that show were in the back of my mind two decades later when I first started hearing about mainstream investors suddenly wagering on legal pot startups. The contradiction piqued my curiosity about this new era, and you encouraged me to chase it down.

I could not have reached the finish line without your constant, patient push for me to just sit and write and rewrite and rewrite. Thank you for talking things through with me as I wrestled with story lines and plot twists. You keenly understood the pressures and anxieties of following a story like this over months and years, not knowing what the conclusion would be. You helped me stay calm and realize that I would eventually figure it out and it would all be okay on the page and in life. I love you. You are my whole world and I can't wait for our next chapter.

SOURCES

Except where noted, the narrative in *The New Chardonnay* was culled from original on-the-ground reporting and interviews conducted by the author, which were (in most cases) recorded and transcribed via Rev Transcription services from July 2017 through January 2020.

Cannabis is a complicated and controversial topic that required extensive reading of books with multiple points of view on the issue of legalization. I could not have completed this project without the following books, which provided helpful background in understanding the history of cannabis prohibition, plant science, and the evolving business landscape with all of its nuances:

Brave New Weed: Adventures into the Uncharted World of Cannabis by Joe Dolce

Cannabis & CBD for Health and Wellness by Aliza Sherman and Dr. Junella Chin

The Cannabis Manifesto: A New Paradigm for Wellness by Steve DeAngelo

Edibles: Small Bites for the Modern Cannabis Kitchen by Stephanie Hua and Coreen Carroll

The 420 Gourmet: The Elevated Art of Cannabis Cuisine by Jeff The420Chef

Grass Roots: The Rise and Fall and Rise of Marijuana in America by Emily Dufton

Last Call: The Rise and Fall of Prohibition by Daniel Okrent

The Least Likely Criminal by Cindy McDonald with Jeni Grossman

Marijuana: A Short History by John Hudak

Marijuana Is Safer: So Why Are We Driving People to Drink? by Steve Fox, Paul Armentano, and Mason Tvert

The New Jim Crow: Mass Incarceration in the Age of Colorblindness by Michelle Alexander

A New Leaf: The End of Cannabis Prohibition by Alyson Martin and Nushin Rashidian
Reefer Sanity: Seven Great Myths About Marijuana by Kevin Sabet
The Two-Edged Sword by Donald W. Tucker
Weed, Inc.: The Truth About the Pot Lobby, THC, and the Commercial Marijuana Industry by Ben Cort
Weed the People: The Future of Legal Marijuana in America by Bruce Barcott

The following daily and weekly digital newsletters and publications provided up-to-the-minute news coverage, which, given the constant state of flux in the industry, offered valuable context and background during the course of reporting and constructing the narrative:

Cannabis Wire
Marijuana Business Daily
Marijuana Moment
Merry Jane
New Cannabis Ventures
New Frontier Data
This Week in Weed
WeedWeek

NOTES

INTRODUCTION

xiii **Goop would curate:** Katie Shapiro, "Gwyneth Paltrow's Goop Gets into the Cannabis Game with MedMen Dispensary Collaboration," *Forbes,* June 6, 2018; Ingrid Schmidt, "10 Things We Learned at Gwyneth Paltrow's Goop Health Event," *The Hollywood Reporter,* June 6, 2018; Jenni Avins, *Quartz,* "Cannabis Has Officially Arrived in the Realm of Luxury Wellness," June 11, 2018.

xiv **encased in a $50,000 Daniela Villegas:** Ingrid Schmidt, "Jurassic Park Inspires Jewelry Collection by Hollywood Designer Daniela Villegas," *The Hollywood Reporter,* May 23, 2018.

xiv **The room buzzed:** Cabot recording and transcription of June 6, 2018, "In goop Health" summit "Future of Cannabis" panel, hosted by Lake Bell, video link no longer available.

xiv **"high as a kite":** Ryme Chikhoune, "In Its Second Year, Goop Health Summit Gets More Grounded," *Fashionista,* June 11, 2018.

xv **one in five:** Bloomberg, "The Marijuana Industry's Newest Spokesman? Former House Speaker John Boehner," *Fortune,* April 11, 2018.

xv **$12 billion in 2019:** Eli McVey, John Schroyer, and Jenel Stelton-Holtmeier, "U.S. Cannabis Retail Sales Estimates: 2017–2022" chart, *Marijuana Business Daily,* May 9, 2018, https://mjbizdaily.com/exclusive-marijuana-sales-may-reach-10-billion-this-year-22-billion-by-2022/.

xvi **Cynthia Nixon:** Vivian Wang, "Cynthia Nixon Puts Legalization Front and Center of Campaign," *The New York Times,* April 11, 2018.

xvi **This argument was so persuasive:** Jon Campbell, "Andrew Cuomo's Changing Position on Marijuana: A Timeline," *Rochester Democrat and Chronicle,* May 25, 2018.

xvii **In his 2020 State of the State:** Jesse McKinley and Luis Ferré-Sadurní, "Marijuana Will Be Legalized in New York in 2020, Cuomo Vows," *The New York Times,* January 8, 2020.

xvii **They had watched as:** David McKay Wilson, "Recreational Pot a Beacon for New Yorkers Flocking to Massachusetts," *The Journal News* (Rockland/Westchester), January 10, 2019.

xvii **Oklahoma, one of the reddest:** Polly Washburn, "Oklahoma Medical Marijuana Campaign Reports Show Grassroots Can Trump Big Money," *Marijuana Moment,* August 3, 2018.

xvii **by six to one:** Ibid.

xvii **U.S. Navy veteran:** Meg Wingerter, "He Was Taught Marijuana Was Evil. Now Veteran with PTSD Says Cannabis Surprised Him and Will Help Oklahomans Like Him," *The Oklahoman,* July 26, 2018; Taylor Newcomb, "Oklahoma Veteran Says Medical Marijuana Better Than Pain Pills," News On 6, KOTV, January 5, 2018, https://www.newson6.com/story/37196987/green-country-veteran-says-medical-marijuana-better-alternative-than-pain-pills.

xviii ***O: The Oprah Magazine*:** Molly Sims, "Welcome to 'High Tea': Why Moms Are Getting Mellow with Cannabis Laced Tea," *O: The Oprah Magazine,* April 2018.

xviii **CNBC's Jim Cramer:** Lizzy Gurdus, "Cramer: 'Legal Marijuana Might Be the Most Disruptive Force Since Amazon' for Pharma and Beverage Industries," CNBC, October 16, 2018.

xviii **even one of the most ardent:** Bloomberg, "The Marijuana Industry's Newest Spokesman?"

xxi **Companies like MedMen:** Alicia Wallace, "CEO of Cannabis Retailer MedMen Steps Down," January 21, 2020.

1: THE QUEEN OF CANNABIS

4 **The news about the licenses:** Chris Kudialis, "Most of New Recreational Marijuana Licenses Awarded to Few Vendors," *Las Vegas Sun,* December 14, 2018.

5 **zealous enforcement of tough:** John Hudak, *Marijuana: A Short History* (Washington, D.C.: The Brookings Institution, 2016), 151.

6 **According to Gallup:** Jeffrey M. Jones, "U.S. Support for Legal Marijuana Steady in Past Year," Gallup, October 23, 2019, https://news.gallup.com/poll/267698/support-legal-marijuana-steady-past-year.aspx.

6 **"godfather of the drug world":** Don Winslow, "The Dirty Secret of El Chapo," *Vanity Fair,* February 1, 2019.

6 **diamond-encrusted pistol:** Associated Press, "El Chapo Trial: Accused Drug Lord Used Diamond Encrusted Pistol, Former Cartel Member Testifies," NBCNews.com, November 8, 2018.

6 **he and his Sinaloa cartel:** Don Winslow, "El Chapo and the Secret History of the Heroin Crisis," *Esquire,* August 9, 2016.

6 **$14 billion don:** Alan Feuer, "El Chapo Found Guilty on All Counts; Faces Life in Prison," *The New York Times,* February 12, 2019.

6 **Manhattan's Metropolitan Correctional Center:** Joseph Goldstein, "Manhattan Jail That Holds El Chapo Called Tougher Than Guantanamo," *The New York Times,* January 23, 2017.

7 **secretly install spyware:** Alan Feuer, "How El Chapo Escaped in a Sewer, Naked with His Mistress," *The New York Times*, January 17, 2019.
13 **Murphy was seen on camera:** David Cruz, "Eyeing Expansion, Governor Orders Review of State's Medical Marijuana Program," NJTV News, video, January 23, 2018, https://www.njtvonline.org/news/video/eyeing-expansion-governor-orders-review-states-medical-marijuana-program/.

2: PLAYING TO WIN

15 **The Rocky Mountain State:** Michael Roberts, "Medical Marijuana Revenues in Colorado for 2012: $199 Million-Plus," *Westword*, June 4, 2013.
15 **Hard-line opponents led by:** Ray Stern, "Governor Jan Brewer's Lawsuit Against Medical Marijuana Law Dismissed by Federal Judge," *Phoenix New Times*, January 4, 2012.
16 **the number of patients registered:** Arizona Department of Health Services, Bureau of Public Health Statistics, and University of Arizona Mel & Enid Zuckerman College of Public Health, *Report to Arizona Department of Health Services: First Annual Medical Marijuana Report A.R.S. 36-2809*, pp. 1, 18, https://www.procon.org/sourcefiles/arizona-department-health-services-medical-mj-report.pdf.
17 **Arizona actually held:** Michael Gossie, "Arizona Medical Marijuana Drawings Use Bingo Balls," AZ Big Media, August 8, 2012.
17 **At 9:00 A.M. on August 7:** "Medical Marijuana Dispensary Selection (Part 4)" Arizona Department of Health Services, August 7, 2012, YouTube, https://www.youtube.com/watch?v=3E6GLZU15qo; "Lottery to Determine Who Opens Pot Dispensaries in Arizona," ABC15 Arizona, YouTube, https://www.youtube.com/watch?v=RRbhR1EDVfU.
17 **Atomic Table Top Bingo Blower:** *Report to Arizona Department of Health Services*, 9.
20 **About six weeks later:** "Claire Elizabeth Noland and Joseph A. Beggans, Jr.," *The Arkansas Democrat-Gazette*, March 3, 2013.
21 **dispensaries in California and Washington:** Tim Dickenson, "Obama's War on Pot," *Rolling Stone*, February 16, 2012; Mike Riggs, "Obama's War on Pot," *The Nation*, October 30, 2013.
23 **including the Poland brothers:** Joe Enea, "Death Row Diaries: Poland Brothers Impersonated Officers, Robbed Guards, Dumped Bodies in Lake Mead," ABC15 Arizona, February 27, 2016.

3: SNOOP AND TED'S EXCELLENT ADVENTURES

25 **His was a formidable run:** Riley Wallace, "Dr. Dre & Snoop Dogg's Classic Record 'Deep Cover' Celebrates 25th Anniversary," HipHopDX, April 9, 2017.

26 **It came out just twenty days:** CNN Library, "Los Angeles Riots Fast Facts," CNN.com, April 22, 2019, https://www.cnn.com/2013/09/18/us/los-angeles-riots-fast-facts/index.html.

26 **"broken window" policing:** Michelle Alexander, *The New Jim Crow: Mass Incarceration in the Age of Colorblindness* (New York: The New Press, 2010), 77, 124, 132; George Kelling, "Don't Blame My 'Broken Windows' Theory for Poor Policing," *Politico,* August 11, 2015.

26 **a certified Bollywood star:** Byron Perry, "Snoop Dogg's Bollywood Cameo," *Variety,* August 8, 2008; Heather Timmons, "Snoop Dogg Brings U.S. Hip-Hop to Bollywood," *The New York Times,* July 28, 2008; "Snoop Gets Bhangra—Singh Is King Exclusive Clip," Cashmere Agency, YouTube, July 28, 2008, https://www.youtube.com/watch?v=oc5mPYnwflo.

27 **the storied performer graciously:** "Snoop Dogg's First Time in India," Cashmere Agency, YouTube, February 14, 2013, https://www.youtube.com/watch?v=2w6mZwEG3ng.

27 **"emotional roller coaster":** "My Gigs in India Will Be an Emotional Roller-Coaster: Snoop Dogg," NDTV interview, YouTube, January 10, 2013, https://www.youtube.com/watch?v=NPcv-fP3jho.

30 **"the burning weed with roots in hell":** *Reefer Madness* 1936 trailer, Warner Bros., YouTube Movies, January 30, 2014, https://www.youtube.com/watch?v=aYHDzrdXHEA.

30 **every forty-two seconds:** Steve Nelson, "Police Made One Marijuana Arrest Every 42 Seconds in 2012," *U.S. News & World Report,* September 16, 2013.

31 **"The war on marijuana is a war on people of color":** *The War on Marijuana in Black and White,* American Civil Liberties Union, June 2013, p. 10, https://www.aclu.org/files/assets/aclu-thewaronmarijuana-rel2.pdf.

31 **Between 1998 and 2012:** "Drug Offenders in Federal Prison: Estimates of Characteristics Based on Linked Data," Bureau of Justice Statistics, NCJ 248648, October 2015, https://www.bjs.gov/content/pub/pdf/dofp12_sum.pdf.

31 **record-expungement initiatives:** Alexander Lektman, "Marijuana Record Expungement Movement Growing Rapidly, Report Shows," *Marijuana Moment,* January 17, 2020.

32 **"Way back in the days":** Andrew Whalen, "'Grass Is Greener' Netflix: Snoop Dogg Shares Story of First Cannabis Toke in 420 Documentary," *Newsweek,* April 20, 2019.

32 **From Louis Armstrong:** John Hudak, *Marijuana: A Short History* (Washington, D.C.: The Brookings Institution, 2016), 102.

33 **"With my mind on my money":** "Gin and Juice," copyright © Death Row Records, Interscope Records, 1994.

4: A CHEF IS BORN

38 **U.S. scientists who wanted:** Alyson Martin and Nushin Rashidian, *A New Leaf: The End of Cannabis Prohibition* (New York: The New Press, 2014), 29.

38 **Dr. Raphael Mechoulam:** *Prescribed Grass,* documentary, produced by Zack Klein, Israeli Television, first aired 2009; *The Scientist,* documentary, produced by Fundacion CANNA, 2015 (follow-up to *Prescribed Grass*), http://mechoulamthescientist.com/.

5: THE WILLY WONKA OF WEED

42 **Canada's "Chocolate Capital":** "Hershey Confirms Smiths Falls Plant Will Close," CBC News, February 22, 2007; "Smiths Falls Will Fight to Keep Hershey Plant Open, Mayor Vows," CBC News, February 16, 2007.

42 **in Arnprior:** Arnprior Chronicle-Guide, "No Medical Marijuana Plant for Arnprior," *Inside Ottawa Valley,* October 3, 2013.

42 **the Canadian government was preparing:** *High Time: The Legalization and Regulation of Cannabis in Canada,* edited by Andrew Potter and Daniel Weinstock, McGill Institute for Health and Social Policy (Montreal and Kingston, Ontario: McGill–Queen's University Press, 2019), 81.

44 **backlash from Canadian police chiefs:** Adam Bluestein, "How Canopy Growth Became the Jolly Green Giant of Cannabis," *Fast Company,* January 24, 2019; Canadian Press, "Ottawa's Move on Medical Marijuana Sparks Flurry of Reaction," *iPolitics,* December 16, 2012; CTVNews.ca Staff, "Health Canada Proposes Changes to Medical Marijuana System," CTV News, December 16, 2012; Josh Wingrove, "Ottawa Considers Softening Marijuana Laws," *The Globe and Mail,* March 5, 2014, updated May 12, 2018.

44 **At CA$7.69:** Marie Ouellet, Mitch Macdonald, Martin Bouchard, Carlo Morselli, and Richard Frank, *The Price of Cannabis in Canada* (Ottawa: Public Safety Canada, 2017), 24, https://www.publicsafety.gc.ca/cnt/rsrcs/pblctns/2017-r005/index-en.aspx#tab4.

47 **66 percent of Canadians:** Ian Vandaelle, "Majority of Canadians Support Legalizing of Decriminalizing Marijuana, New Poll Suggests," *National Post,* January 17, 2012.

47 **Justin Trudeau:** *High Times,* eds. Potter and Weinstock, 16.

47 **It had been five long years:** James Bagnall, "The Day Smiths Falls' Luck Finally Turned: The Story of a Marijuana Boom Town," *Ottawa Citizen,* September 21, 2018.

49 **"Spliff Falls":** Erika Tucker, "Smiths Falls Becoming 'Spliff' Falls'? Residents React to Marijuana Plant Application," *Global News,* October 1, 2013; Michael Aubry, "Former Hershey Factory Set to Transform into

Medical Marijuana Grow Op," *Ottawa Sun,* September 25, 2013; Sarah Harris, "Yes, That Is Marijuana Growing in Smiths Falls' Old Hershey's Factory," North Country Public Radio, February 18, 2014.

CHAPTER 6: WHAT'S BOOZE GOT TO DO WITH IT?

50 **President Barack Obama had just:** Tim Dickenson, "Obama's War on Pot," *Rolling Stone,* February 16, 2012.

52 **Coors Brewing Company:** "History of Coors Brewing Company," Miller Coors website, https://www.millercoors.com/breweries/coors-brewing-company/history.

52 **beer in an aluminum can:** "Generations of Brewing," Coors website, https://www.coors.com/heritage.

52 **first craft brewpub:** Jonathan Shikes, "How Wynkoop Brewing Almost Wasn't the Oldest Brewpub in Colorado," *Westword,* July 18, 2012.

52 **Samantha "Sam" Spady:** Kevin Duggan, "Pain of Drinking Death Not Forgotten," *Coloradoan,* September 5, 2014.

53 **Lynn Gordon "Gordie" Bailey, Jr.:** "Gordie's Story," The Gordie Center, https://gordie.studenthealth.virginia.edu/gordies-story.

54 **the very college campuses:** Janet Bishop, Interviewer, CSU Amendment 64 Oral History Project, Part 2, recorded October 2, 2015, https://mountainscholar.org/bitstream/handle/10217/176472/AMNT_OralHistoryTranscript_Tverk-part2.pdf.

56 **"gateway drug":** Kyle Jaeger, "Where Presidential Candidate John Hickenlooper Stands on Marijuana," *Marijuana Moment,* March 5, 2019.

56 **unfurled a red-and-white banner:** Christopher Osher, "Where There's Toke, There's Ire," *The Denver Post,* October 26, 2005; "SAFER: 5 Years of Marijuana Reform with Attitude," *Good Morning Colorado,* YouTube (1:21), May 18, 2010, https://www.youtube.com/watch?v=Uhpq6mcDkpo.

57 **"deceptive and misleading":** Mike McPhee, "Pot Pitch Called Smoke, Mirrors," *The Denver Post,* October 12, 2005.

57 **Denver passed a bill:** Stephanie Simon, "Denver Is First to Legalize Small Amounts of Pot," *Los Angeles Times,* November 3, 2005.

57 **with 87 percent of the vote:** Zach Patton, "John Hickenlooper: The Man in the Middle," *Governing,* August 2014.

57 **Denver and its mayor:** Jordan Smith, "Hickenlooper vs. Chickenlooper," *Austin Chronicle,* April 13, 2007.

58 **Damien LaGoy:** Associated Press, "Medical Marijuana User Sues State over Policy," *The Denver Post,* June 23, 2007; Michael Roberts, "Damien LaGoy, R.I.P.: Medical Marijuana Patient and Activist Dies at 53," *Westword,* March 26, 2013.

59 **Deputy Attorney General David Ogden:** David Stout and Solomon

Moore, "U.S. Won't Prosecute in States That Allow Medical Marijuana," *The New York Times,* October 19, 2009.

59 **"Entrepreneurs came out of the shadows":** David Blake and Jack Finlaw, *Harvard Policy and Law Review* 8, 2014, p. 364, https://harvardlpr.com/wp-content/uploads/sites/20/2014/08/HLP204.pdf.

60 **federal mandatory-minimum sentences:** Criminal Justice Reform Foundation, "Mandatory Minimums and Sentencing Reform," https://www.cjpf.org/mandatory-minimums.

60 **Wanda James, a respected:** Lydia Dishman, "This Weed Warrior Is Breaking Barriers in the Marijuana Movement," *Fast Company,* October 18, 2017.

62 **Colorado's largest teachers' union:** Michael Roberts, "Marijuana: Colorado Education Association Opposing Amendment 64," *Westword,* September 19, 2012.

63 **no Breathalyzer:** Alicia Wallace, "Testing Drivers for Cannabis Is Hard: Here's Why," CNN Business, January 2, 2020.

63 **Amendment 64 passed:** Michael Roberts, "Amendment 64 Is Now Law: Governor John Hickenlooper Quietly Signs Measure," *Westword,* December 10, 2012.

63 **"break out the Cheetos":** "Hold Off on the Cheetos, Colorado Gov Tells Potheads After Voters Back Marijuana Measure," Fox News, November 7, 2012.

7: MORMONS FOR MARIJUANA

64 **state assembly member from Fountain Hills:** Mike Sunnucks, "Anti-Drug Group Backed by Cardinals," *Phoenix Business Journal,* January 8, 2013.

64 **Approved (albeit narrowly) in 2010:** "2020 Legislative Session Begins as Ballot Effort Continues," Marijuana Policy Project, updated January 13, 2020, https://www.mpp.org/states/arizona/.

65 **Ed Gogek:** Sunnucks, "Anti-Drug Group Backed by Cardinals."

66 **an elderly neighbor:** Cindy McDonald with Jeni Grossman, *The Least Likely Criminal,* (Chandler, AZ: Panoply Publishing, 2018), 58.

69 **Ryan Hurley:** Callan Smith, "Ryan Hurley, Rose Law Group Partner and Director of Medical Marijuana Department, Wins Prestigious Cannaward," Rose Law Group website, https://www.roselawgroup.com/ryan-hurley-rose-law-group-partner-director-medical-marijuana-department-wins-prestigious-cannaward/.

69 **at a state capitol hearing:** Jim Cross, "Battle Lines Redrawn in Arizona's Medical Marijuana Fight," KT-R radio via Rose Law Group Reporter website, January 24, 2013, https://roselawgroupreporter.com/2013/01/battle-lines-redrawn-in-arizonas-medical-marijuana-fight/.

69 **370-mile border:** Derek Staahl, "Arizona's Border Fencing by the Num-

bers," *The Arizona Republic,* November 22, 2016, https://www.azfamily.com/archives/arizona-s-border-fencing-by-the-numbers/article_4821b055-59aa-5cf6-8fc3-b358e023d8fe.html.

69 **"Just Say No":** "Just Say No," History.com, May 31, 2017, https://www.history.com/topics/1980s/just-say-no.

70 **"casual drug users ought to be shot":** Ronald J. Ostrow, "Casual Drug Users Should Be Shot, Gates Says," *Los Angeles Times,* September 6, 1990.

70 **Rodney King's beating:** Keith Schneider, "Daryl F. Gates, L.A.P.D. Chief in Rodney King Era, Dies at 83," *The New York Times,* April 16, 2010.

70 **75 percent of America's high schools:** Amy Nordrum, "The New D.A.R.E. Program—This One Works," *Scientific American,* September 10, 2014.

70 **Laurie Roberts:** Laurie Roberts, "An Unlikely Plea in Support of Medical Marijuana," *The Arizona Republic,* February 2, 2013.

71 **Sheriff Joe Arpaio:** Melissa Etehad, "Joe Arpaio, Former Sheriff in Arizona, Is Found Guilty of Criminal Contempt," *Los Angeles Times,* July 31, 2017.

71 **"There are plenty of folks":** Mel McDonald, "As a Former U.S. Attorney, Here's Why I Support the Medical Marijuana Law," *Arizona Capitol Times,* February 15, 2013.

8: THE NEW CANNA CONSUMER

77 **female-led design team:** "Brand Identity, Packaging, and Website Design for Snoop Dogg's Line of Medical and Recreational Marijuana Products," case study, Pentagram website, https://www.pentagram.com/work/leafs-by-snoop-1/story; "Saturday Night Live Season 44," Pentagram website, https://www.pentagram.com/work/saturday-night-live-season-44/story.

78 **John Desmond Lord:** Lord testimony, "Challenges for Cannabis and Banking: Outside Perspectives," Senate Committee on Banking, Housing, and Urban Affairs, July 23, 2019, https://www.banking.senate.gov/imo/media/doc/Lord%20Testimony%207-23-19.pdf; Burt Hubbard, "Among Colorado's Marijuana Barons, 4 Groups Rise Above the Rest," *The Gazette* (Colorado Springs), November 20, 2018.

80 **Maureen Dowd:** Maureen Dowd, "Don't Harsh Our Mellow, Dude," *The New York Times,* June 3, 2014.

80 **Associated Press:** CBS/AP, "Colorado Wants Most Edible Marijuana Banned," CBSNews.com, October 21, 2014.

80 **"the proposal had not gained much traction":** Jack Healy, "New Scrutiny on Sweets with Ascent of Marijuana in Colorado," *The New York Times,* October 29, 2014.

80 **edibles were big business:** Jordan Steffen, "Pot Edibles Were Big Sur-

prise in First Year of Recreational Sales," *The Denver Post,* December 19, 2014.

80 **spike in ER visits:** John Ingold, "Kids' Emergency Room Visits for Marijuana Increased in Colorado After Legalization, Study Finds," *The Denver Post,* July 25, 2016; Amanda Paulson, "Colorado Wrestles with How to Keep Edible Marijuana Away From Kids," *The Christian Science Monitor,* March 18, 2014; Katie Steinmetiz, "Colorado Kids Are Accidentally Ingesting Pot," *Time,* May 21, 2014.

80 **the pristine white packages:** Katharine Schwab, "The Art of Pot Packaging," *The Atlantic,* November 18, 2015; Merry Jane website featuring Leafs By Snoop, https://merryjane.com/brands/leafs-by-snoop.

82 **LBS finally made its public debut:** Ricardo Baca, "Leafs By Snoop: The Scoop on Snoop Dogg's New Weed Line in Colorado," *The Cannabist,* June 23, 2016; "Leafs By Snoop Launch Party Recap," Merry Jane, YouTube, November 10, 2015, https://www.youtube.com/watch?v=Z2VW9ovhAFY.

83 **"Let's medicate, elevate":** Baca, "Leafs By Snoop: The Scoop on Snoop Dogg's New Weed Line in Colorado."

83 **"Smoke weed every daaaay!":** "The Next Episode," Dr. Dre featuring Snoop Dogg, Aftermath Entertainment, Interscope Records, 2000.

9: THE MAGIC SEEDS

85 **founders of Tweed Marijuana:** Benjamin A. Smith, "Canopy Growth Corp (TSE: WEED) Celebrates Five Years on the Public Markets," *The Midas Letter,* April 3, 2019; Bloomberg News, "First Publicly Traded Canadian Marijuana Stock Pays Off for Early Investors," *Financial Post,* April 4, 2014.

85 **the home growers across the nation:** Noah Rayman, "Canada Rolls Out a '$1 Billion' Privatized Medical Marijuana Industry," *Time,* October 2, 2013.

87 **unaudited reports:** LW Capital Pool, Inc., press release, "Tweed Inc. and LW Capital Pool Inc. Enter into Definitive Agreement Relating to Reverse Takeover Transaction," Cision, March 18, 2014.

89 **interview on the CBC:** Interview with Kevin O'Leary, "Growing Medical Marijuana," CBC, https://www.cbc.ca/player/play/2440819139.

90 **educate patients and doctors:** Interview with Amber Kanwar, "Tweed's Growth Story: Canadian Medical Marijuana Company's Debut on TSX," BNN Bloomberg, https://www.bnnbloomberg.ca/video/tweed-s-growth-story-canadian-medical-marijuana-company-s-debut-on-tsx~319720.

91 **valued at $89 million:** Bloomberg News, "First Publicly Traded Canadian Marijuana Stock Pays Off for Early Investors."

91 **struggling to produce enough:** James Bagnall, "Home Grown: How

Tweed Marijuana Inc. Could Be the Next Big Thing," *Ottawa Citizen*, May 25, 2014.

91 **Expenses were mounting:** "Management's Discussion and Analysis of the Financial Condition and Results of Operations," Tweed Marijuana Inc., September 30, 2014, p. 8, https://cdn.shopify.com/s/files/1/0266/0901/files/MD_A_for_Q3_2014_1.pdf.

91 **Royal Canadian Mounted Police:** Douglas Qwan, "RCMP Went Silent About Massive Pot Bust over Concern for Marijuana Producer's Stock Price, Documents Reveal," *National Post*, May 31, 2019.

91 **a reported clash:** James Bagnall, "Growing Pains: Tale of Smiths Falls Marijuana Startup," *Ottawa Citizen*, October 9, 2019.

92 **their lawsuits:** Kyle Duggan, "Former Liberal Treasurer Suing Marijuana Company for 'Wrongful Dismissal,'" *iPolitics*, May 1, 2017.

92 **The telegenic Justin Trudeau:** Ian Austen, "Justin Trudeau and Liberal Party Prevail with Stunning Rout in Canada," *The New York Times*, October 19, 2015.

10: NEW SHERIFF IN TOWN

94 **Sheriff William Owen "Buckey" O'Neill:** Terry McGahey, American Cowboy Chronicles website, January 4, 2017, http://www.americancowboychronicles.com/2017/01/william-owen-buckey-oneill.html.

94 **On July 14, 1900:** Prescott Chamber of Commerce website, "History of Prescott, Arizona," https://www.prescott.org/history.html; Scott Craven, "Whiskey Row: Arizona's Most Legendary Block," *The Arizona Republic*, February 22, 2018.

98 **60 percent of America's illegal marijuana:** Rene Chun, "Ending Weed Prohibition Hasn't Stopped Drug Crimes," *The Atlantic*, January/February 2019.

99 **Donald W. Tucker:** Donald W. Tucker, *The Two-Edged Sword* (Indianapolis: Dog Ear Publishing, 2010).

100 **Fu Manchu mustache:** Ibid., 51, 54.

100 **Federal Bureau of Narcotics:** Ibid., 86–87.

100 **racialized drug policy:** Alyson Martin and Nushin Rashidian, *A New Leaf: The End of Cannabis Prohibition* (New York: The New Press, 2014), 40; John Hudak, *Marijuana: A Short History* (Washington, D.C.: The Brookings Institution Press, 2016), 25–26.

100 **Marihuana Tax Act:** Martin and Rashidian, *A New Leaf*, 41.

100 **"reefer madness":** Drug Enforcement Administration History, "The Early Years," p. 17, https://www.dea.gov/sites/default/files/2018-05/Early%20Years%20p%2012-29.pdf.

100 **Boggs Act:** Ibid., 42.

100 **Nixon administration's:** Ibid., 46.

101 **Armed with neither:** Tucker, *The Two-Edged Sword*, 54.

102 **Douglas, Arizona:** Robert Reingold, "Arizona Town Is a Casualty in the Border War on Drugs," *The New York Times,* March 9, 1985; Rafael Carranza, "Threats and Extortion: Migrants Come Face to Face with Cartels Near Arizona-Mexican Border," *The Arizona Republic,* April 1, 2019; Rafael Carranza, "Multiple Deaths Reported in Second Round of Shootings Near the Arizona Border," *The Arizona Republic,* June 14, 2019.

103 **"James Bond" tunnel:** Douglas Jehl, "$1-Million Drug Tunnel Found at Mexico Border," *Los Angeles Times,* May 19, 1990.

103 **It was the first:** Monte Reel, "Underworld," *The New Yorker,* July 27, 2015.

107 **turning to an oil:** Saundra Young, "Marijuana Stops Child's Severe Seizures," CNN, August 7, 2013.

107 **Dr. Sanjay Gupta:** Dr. Sanjay Gupta, "Why I Changed My Mind on Weed," CNN, August 8, 2013.

11: 420 GOURMET

110 **Andrea Drummer and Holden Jagger:** Ed Murrieta, "America's Top 10 Cannabis Chefs," *GreenState,* November 22, 2017.

113 **legendary marijuana and gay rights:** Bruce Barcott, *Weed the People: The Future of Legal Cannabis in America* (New York: Time Books, 2015), 297–302.

113 **Emerald Triangle:** Emily Witt, "How Legalization Changed Humboldt County," *The New Yorker,* May 20, 2019.

114 **blanching it:** JeffThe420Chef, *The 420 Gourmet: The Elevated Art of Cannabis Cuisine* (New York: Harper Wave, 2016), 21.

12: CANNABIS CULTURE FOR ALL

118 **inside Pier 70:** Pier 70 San Francisco website, "History of Portrero Point Shipyards and Industry, http://www.pier70sf.org/history/p70_history.html.

118 **$100 million facelift:** Matt Burns, "Disrupt SF 2015 Lands at the Historic Pier 70," TechCrunch, June 4, 2015.

118 **It was TechCrunch Disrupt:** TechCrunch press release, "TechCrunch Disrupt San Francisco 2015 Announces Startup Battlefield Competitors," September 21, 2015.

119 **"a serious celebrity VC":** Rebecca Greenfield, "Snoop Dogg, Investor," *Fast Company,* October 31, 2014.

119 **fireside chat:** TechCrunch video of Snoop Dogg and Ted Chung at Disrupt: "Snoop Dogg's Mind's on His Money," YouTube, September 21, 2015, https://www.youtube.com/watch?v=pH2bIDqHdQc.

120 **Peter Thiel, the legendary:** Jonathan Sheiber, "New Funding for Privateer Highlights Marijuana's Massive Market in the U.S.," TechCrunch, January 8, 2015; Alyson Shontell, "Peter Thiel's Fund Eyes a Major In-

vestment in a $425 Million Marijuana Startup, Privateer," *Business Insider*, December 16, 2014; Kim-Mal Cutler, "The End of the War on Drugs and the Emergence of the Venture-Backed Cannabis Industry," TechCrunch, May 4, 2014.

120 **one of the most celebrated IPOs:** Jen Wieczner, "The Marijuana Billionaire Who Doesn't Smoke Weed," *Fortune*, January 16, 2019.

120 **estimated valuation of $4.1 billion:** Ibid.

120 **The stock price:** Nichola Saminather, "More Pain in Store for Canadian Marijuana Companies After Aurora Cannabis, Tilray Cut Jobs," Reuters, February 7, 2020.

121 **he also contributed:** Christopher Cadelago, "Peter Thiel Opens Wallet for Pot Legalization in California," *The Sacramento Bee*, November 5, 2016.

123 **"Uber of weed":** Josh Kosman, "Uber of Weed Wants to Raise 100M Despite App Store Bans," *New York Post*, May 29, 2019.

123 **$166 million:** Ingrid Lunden and Josh Constine, "Marijuana Delivery Giant Eaze May Go Up in Smoke," TechCrunch, January 16, 2020.

123 **Eaze laid off:** Shwanika Narayan, "Pot Delivery Company Eaze Lays Off 36 Workers, Replaces CEO," *San Francisco Chronicle*, October 4, 2019.

123 **snapped up by Microsoft:** Nat Berman, "10 Things You Didn't Know About Eaze Founder Kevin McCarty," Money Inc.

124 **"Nearly two decades":** Martin and Rashidian, *A New Leaf*, 69.

125 **Eaze found that most customers:** "Eaze Insights: Marijuana Consumption for California 2014," slides 5–7, https://2015.eazeup.com/#1.

126 **"Chardonnay moms—those affluent":** "Eaze Insights: 2018 State of Cannabis," January 2018, https://www.dropbox.com/sh/la1g7ptizrend9m/AACAAcTH15OFOAP_9LFaYbNRa/Eaze%20Insights%20Reports?dl=0&preview=2018+State+of+cannabis.pdf&subfolder_nav_tracking=1.

126 **"Modern Marijuana Consumer" report:** "Eaze Insights: The Modern Marijuana Consumer," January 2017, pp. 2–6, https://www.greenmarketreport.com/wp-content/uploads/2017/10/The-Modern-Marijuana-Consumer.pdf.

126 **very first investment:** Charlotte Alter, "Snoop Dogg Just Invested in a Weed Delivery Startup," *Time*, April 14, 2015.

128 **"It gives me proud honor":** TechCrunch, "Snoop Dogg's Mind's on His Money."

129 **"Julia Child of Weed":** Justin Jones, "Meet the Julia Child of Weed," *The Daily Beast*, November 13, 2014.

13: IN BUBBE'S KITCHEN

133 **into his cookbook:** JeffThe420Chef, *The 420 Gourmet: The Elevated Art of Cannabis Cuisine* (New York: Harper Wave, 2016).

133 **AARP/University of Michigan survey:** "National Poll on Healthy Aging," University of Michigan, Institute for Healthcare Policy and Innovation, April 2018, p. 2, https://www.healthyagingpoll.org/sites/default/files/2018-04/NPHA%20Marijuana%20Report.pdf; Barbara A. Gabriel, "Most Older Americans Support Medical Marijuana," AARP, April 4, 2018, https://www.aarp.org/health/drugs-supplements/info-2018/medical-marijuana-pain-prescription-fd.html.

14: DOUBLE OR NOTHING

140 **Nevada's legislature:** Matt Woolbright, Associated Press, "Sandoval Signs Medical Marijuana Law, Allowing Dispensaries in Nevada," *Las Vegas Sun,* June 12, 2013.

141 **Nevada Gaming Commission:** "Nevada Legalizing Marijuana, but the Casinos Are Not Feeling It," Casino.org, November 9, 2016, https://www.casino.org/news/nevada-votes-legalizes-recreational-marijuana/.

141 **Sig Rogich:** David Ferrara-Journal, "Vegas Heavy Hitters Vie for Medical Pot Licenses," KSL.com, May 4, 2018.

142 **sold a pinup calendar of herself:** Christopher Hooks, "The Lady Is a Trump," *Politico,* June 14, 2016; Lauren Fox and Tierney Sneed, "Trump Has Nothing on These Wacky GOP Candidates Running in 2016," Talking Points Memo, June 1, 2016.

142 **standoff against federal law enforcement:** Dan Good, "Nevada Assemblywoman Michele Fiore Wouldn't Point a Gun at Law Enforcement—Only Bureau of Land Management Agents," *New York Daily News,* May 10, 2016; Julie Carrie Wong, "Who Is Michele Fiore? What We Know About the Oregon Standoff Negotiator," *The Guardian,* February 11, 2016.

143 **A *Politico* profile:** Hooks, "The Lady Is a Trump."

146 **Louis J. Spina:** Andrew Ford: "How a Good Stockbroker Became a Bad Bank Robber," *Asbury Park Press/USA Today,* August 15, 2016; United States Attorney's Office, District of New Jersey, press release, "Monmouth County, New Jersey Man Sentenced to 79 Months in Prison for Operating $20 Million Ponzi Scheme," June 5, 2015, https://www.justice.gov/usao-nj/pr/monmouth-county-new-jersey-man-sentenced-79-months-prison-operating-20-million-ponzi.

148 **MPX wax was the top-selling non-vape:** "iAnthus Reports Fiscal Third Quarter 2019 Financial Results," earnings call, November 20, 2019, https://d1io3yog0oux5.cloudfront.net/_b6a8f9e0cb9c7013501f478a150a2005/ianthuscapital/news/2019-11-20_iAnthus_Reports_Fiscal_Third_Quarter_2019_141.pdf.

150 **$25 million for the two:** Alan Brochstein, "Wall Street Veteran Sells Cannabis Operations Stake in $25mm Deal," *New Cannabis Ventures,* January 23, 2017; "Canadian Company Partners with AZ Medical Mari-

juana Dispensaries," *Marijuana Business Daily,* February 1, 2017; Ray Stern, "For-Profit Canadian Firm Acquires 'Highly Profitable' Arizona Medical Marijuana Businesses," *Phoenix New Times,* January 25, 2017; MPX Bioceutical Corporation press release via Glove Newswire, "MPX Bioceutical Completes $17.8 Million Nevada Acquisition," *New Cannabis Ventures,* December 11. 2017, https://www.newcannabisventures.com/23886-2/.

15: POT ON PRIME TIME

152 **"Just to clarify":** "Martha & Snoop's Potluck Party Challenge," promo, YouTube, https://www.youtube.com/watch?v=IgY2ZADQGyw&list=PLQoOx3TviFqVYW9o8NhW6Gi3_TNVMSWS5&index=80.

152 ***Will & Grace*:** Reid Nakamura, "How 'Will & Grace' Had a Real-Life Political Impact on Marriage Equality," *The Wrap,* September 28, 2017; Barney Frank, "How Gay Marriage Is Like Legalizing Pot," *Politico,* August 19, 2015.

152 **marriage equality:** Justin McCarthy, "Record High Support for Legalizing Marijuana Use in the U.S.," Gallup, October 25, 2017, https://news.gallup.com/poll/221018/record-high-support-legalizing-marijuana.aspx.

153 **Baby-faced Michael Brown:** Brittany Packnett, "How Ferguson Woke Us Up," *Time,* August 8, 2019; Timothy Williams, "Five Years After Michael Brown's Death, His Father Wants a New Investigation," *The New York Times,* August 15, 2019; Amy Davidson Sorkin, "Why Did Michael Brown Die in Ferguson?," *The New Yorker,* August 11, 2014.

153 **Among the tearstained throngs:** Ruth Manuel-Logan, "Celebrities, Activists and Thousands of Others Mourn Michael Brown at Funeral," https://foxync.com/3395173/celebrities-activists-and-thousands-of-others-mourn-michael-brown-at-funeral/amp/.

154 **Reverend Al Sharpton:** Elisa Crouch, "Sharpton at Michael Brown Funeral: 'We Are Required to Leave Here Today and Change Things,'" *St. Louis Dispatch,* August 25, 2014.

154 **"No Guns Allowed" summit:** "Snoop Dogg Meets Mike Brown's Parents at No Guns Allowed Anti-gun Violence Breakfast," SnoopDoggTV, YouTube, October 1, 2014, https://www.youtube.com/watch?v=JuKx_QO9dTc.

155 **Roast of Justin Bieber:** Daniel D'Addario, "Martha Stewart's Performance at the Justin Bieber Roast Was Worth Celebrating," *Time,* March 31, 2015.

155 **"Ask Me Anything":** McKenzie Jean-Phillippe, "How Snoop Dogg and Martha Became the Ultimate Celebrity Best Friends," *O, The Oprah Magazine,* April 8, 2019.

155 **The two first met in 2008:** "Snoop Dogg on Martha Stewart Pt. 1,"

Cashmere Agency, YouTube, November 21, 2008, https://www.youtube.com/watch?v=kXhnCCLPjQA.

156 **Reviewers lauded:** "That Time Martha Stewart Delivered the Sickest Burns at Justin Bieber's Roast," *Fast Company,* March 31, 2013; Bryan Alexander, "Martha Stewart Kills with Justin Bieber Prison Tips," *USA Today,* March 31, 2015.

156 **Seth Meyers:** "Martha Stewart Got a Contact High from Snoop Dogg—Late Night with Seth Myers," *Late Night with Seth Myers,* YouTube, June 15, 2015, https://www.youtube.com/watch?v=K8wOs1Onopk.

156 **SallyAnn Salsano:** David Hinckley, "How Snoop Dogg and Martha Stewart Changed Perception of TV Demographics," *New York Daily News,* October 12, 2017.

156 **she later told *The Hollywood Reporter:*** Marc Malkin, "Martha Stewart, Snoop Dogg Talk Food, Friendship and Marijuana," *The Hollywood Reporter,* June 8, 2018.

157 **"The underlying message":** " 'Snoop & Martha's Potluck Dinner Party' Unifying Message: 'Just Come and Have Some Dinner with Some Friends,' " Reality TV Roundtable video via *Hollywood Reporter,* https://www.hollywoodreporter.com/news/martha-stewart-snoop-dogg-food-friendship-pot-1116774.

157 **2.3 million people:** Sami Main, "The Creator of Martha Stewart and Snoop Dogg's New Show Explains Why It Works" *AdWeek,* November 21, 2016.

158 **"The melding of cultures":** Malkin, "Martha Stewart, Snoop Dogg Talk Food, Friendship and Marijuana."

158 **Gallup poll:** Art Swift, "Support for Legal Marijuana Use up to 60% in US," Gallup, Social Policy and Issues, October 19, 2016, https://news.gallup.com/poll/196550/support-legal-marijuana.aspx.

158 **"So someone smokes marijuana?":** Malkin, "Martha Stewart, Snoop Dogg Talk Food, Friendship and Marijuana."

158 **Emmy nomination:** Ibid.

16: SNOOP'S STAR POWER

160 **greatest business idols:** Emily Popp, "Trendsetters at Work: Cashmere Agency," *E! News Online,* October 14, 2014.

162 **seven times the size of Colorado's:** "Recreational Marijuana: Insights and Opportunities," Deloitte report, Spring 2016, 5.

163 **Deloitte predicted:** Ibid.

164 **studious attorney:** Daniel Fish, "Meet the Lawyer Whose Office Sits Above a Grow-Op," *Precedent,* September 1, 2015, https://lawandstyle.ca/career/career-meet-the-lawyer-whose-office-sits-above-a-grow-op-2/.

164 **thirteenth studio album, *Bush:*** "Snoop Dogg's Pharrell-Produced

'Bush' Is a Half-Baked Effort: Album Review," *Billboard*, May 12, 2015.

166 **potential licensing deal:** Allison Tierney, "Alpha-Capitalist Snoop Dogg Signs Contract with Major Marijuana Company in Canada," Vice.com, February 12, 2016; Alexandra Posadzki, "Snoop Dogg Signs Exclusive Deal with Canadian Pot Grower Tweed," Canadian Press via *HuffPost*, February 11, 2016.

166 **ban on recreational marijuana:** Kurtis Lee, "Q&A: Canada Is About to Legalize Marijuana. How Did That Happen? Justin Trudeau for Starters," *Los Angeles Times*, October 4, 2018.

167 **NBA All-Star Game:** Colum Slingerland, "Snoop Dogg and 2 Chainz to Host Celebrity Basketball Game During NBA All-Star Weekend," Exclaim.ca, February 5, 2016.

167 **the pot farm of the future:** Scott Rosts, "Snoop Dogg Tours Tweed's NOTL Greenhouse," *Niagara-on-the-Lake Town Crier*, November 1, 2016; Nancy Sanders, "Snoop Dogg Inspects Weed at Tweed Farms," WIVB-TV (Buffalo), November 4, 2016; "Rap Icon Snoop Dogg Visited Tweed Farms in Niagara," *Niagara Falls Review*, November 2, 2016; Canopy Growth Corporation press release, "Tweed and Snoop Dogg Launch Leafs By Snoop for Canadian Market," Cision, October 6, 2016.

168 **hadn't happened overnight:** Thomas Suh Lauder and Jon Schluess, "The Last Time California Tried to Legalize Weed, It Failed. What Happened?," *Los Angeles Times*, November 4, 2016.

168 **57.1 percent of the vote:** "California Proposition 64—Legalize Marijuana—Results: Approved," *The New York Times*, November 8, 2016, https://www.nytimes.com/elections/2016/results/california-ballot-measure-64-legalize-marijuana.

169 **first marijuana "unicorn":** Melia Robinson, "The Marijuana Industry's First $1 Billion 'Unicorn' Is a Canadian Company You've Probably Never Heard Of," *Business Insider*, February 2, 2017.

17: DRINKING SALAD DRESSING

171 **potential dealer's license:** "Canopy Growth's Tweed Receives Valuable Dealers License," *Daily Marijuana Observer*, December 12, 2016, https://www.dailymarijuanaobserver.com/single-post/2016/12/12/canada-marijuana-stocks-news-TWMJF-Canopy-Growths-Tweed-Receives-Valuable-Dealers-License.

172 **"*Smith* decision":** "Medical Marijuana Activist Owen Smith 'Vindicated on Highest Level,'" CBC News, June 11, 2015.

172 **cannabis oil was first introduced:** "Canadian Marijuana Industry & Market Snapshot Report," *Marijuana Business Daily*, Fall 2017, 7.

172 **between US$2.3 and $4.5 billion:** Ibid., 14.

174 **1 percent of the entire cannabis market:** Cabot interview with Roy Bingham, CEO BDS Analytics, June 1, 2018.

174 **"like drinking salad dressing":** Jonathan Bloom, "Drink Your Weed: Is Cannabis the Beverage Industry's Next Big Thing?," NBC Bay Area, August 5, 2019.

175 **accounting for only 15 percent:** Cabot interview with Roy Bingham.

176 **Rob Sands:** Jennifer Kaplan, "Cannabis Cocktails? Constellation Sees Opening as Pot Laws Ease," Bloomberg, November 10, 2016.

176 **Cowen & Company:** Jennifer Kaplan, "Cannabis Industry Expected to Be Worth $50 Billion by 2026," Bloomberg, September 12, 2016.

176 **"Why wouldn't big business":** Kaplan, "Cannabis Cocktails?"

176 **the story about Constellation Brands:** Marina Strauss, "Beer to Bud: Inside Alcohol Giant Constellation's Big Gamble on Pot," *The Globe and Mail,* January 26, 2019.

177 **"We think that it's highly likely":** Jennifer Maloney and David George-Cosh, "Big Brewer Makes a Play for Marijuana Beverages," *The Wall Street Journal,* October 29, 2017.

178 **Ebbu:** Adam Smith, "Canopy Growth to Buy Pot Research Company Ebbu in $19.2 Million Deal," TheStreet, October 15, 2018.

179 **the alcohol giant doubled down:** Michael Sheetz, "Corona Beer Maker Constellation Ups Bet on Cannabis with $4 Billion Investment in Canopy Growth," CNBC, August 15, 2018.

180 **Canadian unit of Molson Coors:** "Molson Coors Canada Signs Deal to Make Non-alcoholic Marijuana Drinks," Reuters, August 11, 2018.

180 **Anheuser-Busch's InBev:** Max A. Cherney, "Tilray and Budweiser Maker Will Partner to Research Weed Drinks; Tilray Stock Jumps," MarketWatch, December 22, 2018.

180 **Altria, invested $1.8 billion:** Harry Brumpton and Uday Sampath Kumar, "Altria to Marry Pot with Big Tobacco in $1.8 Billion Cronos Deal," Reuters, December 7, 2018.

181 **The annual shindig:** Desmond Devoy, "Snoop Dogg All Up in Smiths Falls," *Smiths Falls Record News,* August 26, 2018.

182 **The Old Post Office:** Evelyn Harford, "What's Going On Here? Old Post Office in Smiths Falls Undergoing Renovations," *Smiths Falls Record News,* May 7, 2019.

183 **"Young and Wild and Free":** Snoop Dogg Tweed, "So What We Get High," YouTube, August 26, 2018, https://www.youtube.com/watch?v=RUPg7_EGsu8.

18: THE END OF PROHIBITION

184 **NorCal CannaCuisine Gala:** "NorCal Canna Cuisine Recap," KPIX-TV via YouTube, July 24, 2017, https://www.youtube.com/watch?time_continue=1&v=aYb65NwndOA&feature=emb_logo; Rebecca Flint

Marx, "Sonoma's Cannabis Culture Goes Boutique," *San Francisco Chronicle,* December 10, 2017.

189 **The emphasis on terroir:** Matt Simon, "The Quest to Make California's Weed the Champagne of Cannabis Growers," October 10, 2018, https://www.wired.com/story/the-quest-to-make-californias-weed-the-champagne-of-cannabis/.

190 **$4.72 billion by 2025:** "California Legal Cannabis Projections," New Frontier Data, May 20, 2018, https://newfrontierdata.com/marijuana-insights/california-legal-cannabis-projections/; "California's Marijuana Market Is Poised for Huge Growth," *Marijuana Business Daily,* August 15, 2019, https://mjbizdaily.com/california-cannabis-market-poised-for-growth/.

190 **$11 billion:** Patrick McGreevy, "California Now Has the Biggest Legal Marijuana Market in the World," *Los Angeles Times,* August 15, 2019.

190 **Appellations for growing regions:** CalCannabis Appellations Project, California Department of Food & Agriculture website, https://www.cdfa.ca.gov/calcannabis/appellations.html.

190 **bigger even than the state's almond:** "California Agricultural Production Statistics, 2018 Crop Year—Top 10 Commodities for California Agriculture," California Department of Food & Agriculture website, https://www.cdfa.ca.gov/statistics/.

192 **Dennis Hunter:** James Dunn, "Sonoma Co. Cannabis Entrepreneur Dennis Hunter Bounces Back from Prison to Become Model CEO," *The North Bay Business Journal,* June 12, 2017.

194 **"putting together something really classy":** Marx, "Sonoma's Cannabis Culture Goes Boutique."

194 **"This is the end of Prohibition":** "NorCal Canna Cuisine Recap."

19: CBD SISTER ACT

198 **Dr. Sanjay Gupta explained:** Dr. Sanjay Gupta, "Why I Changed My Mind on Weed," CNN, August 8, 2013.

200 **Republican senator Mitch McConnell:** James Higdon, "Mitch McConnell's Love Affair with Hemp," *Politico,* March 2, 2015.

201 **worth $4.2 trillion:** Global Wellness Institute, *Global Wellness Economy Monitor,* October 2018, pp. iii–iv, https://globalwellnessinstitute.org/wp-content/uploads/2019/04/GWIWellnessEconomyMonitor2018_042019.pdf.

203 **rise in consumer spending:** Eve Wiseman, "Feel Better Now? The Rise and Rise of the Anxiety Economy," *The Guardian,* March 10, 2019.

204 **Lord Jones:** Bee Shapiro, "Olivia Wilde Doesn't Do a Painted-On Face," *The New York Times,* January 2, 2018.

205 **Epidiolex:** FDA news release, "FDA Approves First Drug Comprised of an Active Ingredient Derived from Marijuana to Treat Forms of Epi-

lepsy," June 25, 2019, https://www.fda.gov/news-events/press-announcements/fda-approves-first-drug-comprised-active-ingredient-derived-marijuana-treat-rare-severe-forms.

205 **2018 Farm Bill:** John Hudak, "The Farm Bill, Legalization and the Status of CBD: An Explainer," The Brookings Institution, December 14, 2018, https://www.brookings.edu/blog/fixgov/2018/12/14/the-farm-bill-hemp-and-cbd-explainer/.

205 **"For far too long":** Office of Majority Leader Mitch McConnell press release, "Senate Passes Farm Bill, Which Includes Senator McConnell's Hemp Farming Act," June 28, 2018, https://www.mcconnell.senate.gov/public/index.cfm/2018/6/senate-passes-farm-bill-which-includes-senator-mcconnell-s-hemp-farming-act.

206 **outgoing FDA commissioner:** FDA press release, "Statement from FDA Commissioner Scott Gottlieb, M.D., on New Steps to Advance Agency's Continued Evaluation of Potential Regulatory Pathways for Cannabis-Containing and Cannabis-Derived Products," April 2, 2019, https://www.fda.gov/news-events/press-announcements/statement-fda-commissioner-scott-gottlieb-md-new-steps-advance-agencys-continued-evaluation.

206 **Google searches for "CBD":** Eric Leas, Mician Nobles, and Theodore Caputi, "Trends in Internet Searches for Cannabidiol (CBD) in the United States," JAMA Network, October 23, 2019, https://jamanetwork.com/journals/jamanetworkopen/fullarticle/2753393?utm_source=For_The_Media&utm_medium=referral&utm_campaign=ftm_links&utm_term=102319.

206 **Gallup survey:** Kyle Jaeger, "One-in-Seven Americans Use CBD, According to a New Gallup Survey," *Marijuana Moment,* August 7, 2019.

206 **Kim Kardashian:** Opheli Garcia Lawler, "Kim Kardashian's CBD-Themed Baby Shower Seemed Really Chill," *New York,* April 28, 2019.

206 **Megan Rapinoe:** Nick Dimengo, "Megan Rapinoe Joins the CBD Craze," *Green Entrepreneur,* December 23, 2019.

207 **Rob "Gronk" Gronkowski:** Tom Huddleston, Jr., "Ex NFL Star Rob Gronkowski on CBD, His Biggest Money Splurge and Mark Cuban," CNBC, September 2, 2019.

207 **Carl's Jr.:** Danielle Wiener-Bronner, "Why Carl's Junior Is Testing Out a CBD Burger," CNN Business, April 17, 2019.

207 **fresh&co:** Alexis Benveniste, "New Yorkers Get Cannabis with Their Lunch for 4/20 Day," Bloomberg, April 18, 2019.

207 **New York City Department of Health:** Amanda Mull, "The CBD Crackdown Has Begun," *The Atlantic,* February 6, 2019.

207 **A CNBC report:** Angela LaVito, "Pets Are the Hot New Cannabis Customer as Owners Use CBD to Ease Pain and Thunderstorm Anxiety," CNBC, May 5, 2019.

207 **partnering with a Harvard clinician:** Lydia Ramsey and Jeremy Burke,

"Women Have Been Saying It Works for 10,000 Years: 400 Women Will Use Marijuana-Infused Inserts in a Groundbreaking Study from a Harvard Medical School Professor," *Business Insider,* October 9, 2018.

208 **CBD would amount to:** Cannabis Intelligence Briefing, *CBD: Cannabinoids Escape the Dispensary,* Arcview in partnership with BDS Analytics, 2018, 6.

209 **Leafly investigation:** Bruce Barcott, Ian Chant, and David Downs, "Are You Getting the CBD You Paid For? We Put 47 Products to the Test," Leafly, November 18, 2019.

209 **Scott Gottlieb of the FDA:** Scott Gottlieb and Kyle Jaeger, "FDA Chief Warns CBD Rulemaking Could Take Years Without Congressional Action," *Marijuana Moment,* March 20, 2019; Scott Gottlieb, "The CBD Craze Is Getting Out of Hand, the FDA Needs to Act," *The Washington Post,* July 30, 2019; @ScottGottliebMD, Twitter, November 8, 2019, https://twitter.com/scottgottliebmd/status/1192806869586329602?lang=en.

209 **sent a warning to Curaleaf:** Angelica LeVito, "FDA Issues Warning to Curaleaf for 'Illegally Selling' CBD Products with 'Unsubstantiated Claims,'" CNBC, July 23, 2019.

210 **$750,000 to $3 million annually:** Rob Meagher, "The C$845 Million-Dollar Woman: Ianthus' New Director and Chief Strategy Officer, Beth Stavola," *Cannabis Business Executive,* February 12, 2019.

210 **Governor Phil Murphy:** Tom Angell, "New Jersey Governor Promises Legal Marijuana in Inauguration Speech," *Marijuana Moment,* January 16, 2018.

20: GREEN GOLD

212 **more than $9 billion:** Eli McVey, *6th Annual Marijuana Business Daily Factbook 2018,* executive summary (Newport, RI: Anne Holland Ventures, Inc., 2018), 1.

213 **attended by 27,600:** MJBizCon 2018 Recap, website, https://mjbizconference.com/mjbizcon-2018-recap/.

214 **California officially opening up:** Thomas Fuller, "Recreational Pot Is Officially Legal in California," *The New York Times,* January 1, 2018.

214 **Cole Memo:** "AG Sessions Rescinds Cole Memo, Roiling Marijuana Industry," *Marijuana Business Daily,* January 4, 2018.

214 **John Boehner:** John Boehner, "Washington Needs to Legalize Cannabis," *The Wall Street Journal,* November 4, 2018.

214 **U.S. companies were going public:** Chloe Aiello, "US Cannabis Companies Look to Canada When Going Public," CNBC, January 24, 2018.

215 **$21 billion by 2021:** McVey, *6th Annual Marijuana Business Daily Factbook 2018,* 4.

218 **first edibles lounge to open:** Mona Holmes, "West Hollywood Ap-

proves Edibles-Only Cannabis Consumption Café," *Eater LA*, October 1, 2019.

21: THE BIG 420 FINALE

219 **Kate Hudson:** Corinne Heller, "Kate Hudson Celebrates 40th Birthday and a Whole Lotta Stars," *E! News*, April 20, 2019.

219 **As she noted:** @katehudson Instagram post "Full moon rising, Good Friday, Passover, my birthday . . . do you know what that means? Neither do I but it sounds groovy," April 19, 2019, https://www.instagram.com/p/BwdesU2HhG3/.

220 **entire line of herbs and spices:** Press release, "Float Technologies Set to Launch the World's First and Only Flavored Odorless Smokable Cannabis Flower and Edible Culinary Herbs," *Businesswire*, September 11, 2019.

224 **Social justice had long been:** Alex Bynn, "West Hollywood's Queer and 420-Friendly History Come Together in Budberry Cannabis," *Civilized*, 2019.

225 **DEA crackdowns:** Tami Abdollah, "DEA Raids Marijuana Outlets," *Los Angeles Times*, January 18, 2007; NORML press release, "Feds Raid Eleven Los Angeles Medi-Pot Dispensaries," January 18, 2007, https://norml.org/news/2007/01/18/feds-raid-eleven-los-angeles-medi-pot-dispensaries.

225 **"It's a blessing to be":** Bynn, "West Hollywood's Queer and 420-Friendly History Come Together in Budberry Cannabis."

229 **top five Canadian pot stocks:** Sergei Kiebnikov, "Top Cannabis Companies Have Lost Almost $10 Billion in Market Value Since Vaping Crisis Began," *Forbes*, October 11, 2019.

229 **28 percent of Canadians:** Ian Austen, "From Canada's Legal High, a Business Letdown," *The New York Times*, December 17, 2019.

229 **sharp rise in teen vaping:** National Institutes of Health press release, "Vaping of Marijuana on the Rise Among Teens," December 18, 2019, https://www.nih.gov/news-events/news-releases/vaping-marijuana-rise-among-teens.

229 **faulty e-cigarette devices:** Jonathan Corum, "Vaping Illness Tracker: 2,506 Cases and 54 Deaths," *The New York Times*, December 23, 2019.

229 **Democratic presidential front-runners:** Charlotte Alter, "The Democratic Presidential Candidates Mostly Agree on Marijuana Legalization. The Exception? Joe Biden," *Time*, June 7, 2019.

230 **passed the SAFE Banking Act:** Lisa Gora and Anthony Osbourne, "The SAFE Banking Act: High Hopes for the Cannabis Industry," *New Jersey Law Journal*, November 11, 2019, https://www.law.com/njlawjournal/2019/11/11/the-safe-banking-act-high-hopes-for-the-cannabis-industry/?slreturn=20200022100912.

230 **five years after recreational use:** Sam Tabachnik, "Colorado's Anticipated Marijuana Report Details Youth Usage, Driving and Crime over the Last 5 Years," *The Denver Post,* October 26, 2018.

230 **drugged driving:** *Impacts of Marijuana Legalization in Colorado: A Report Pursuant to Senate Bill 13-283,* Colorado Department of Public Safety, 2018, p. 33, https://cdpsdocs.state.co.us/ors/docs/reports/2018-SB13-283_Rpt.pdf.

230 **rise in hospitalizations:** Ibid., 78.

230 **pot use among teens:** Ibid., 101.

230 **a billion dollars in tax revenue:** Bart Schaneman, "Top Business Lessons from 5 Years of Legal Recreational Cannabis in Colorado," *Marijuana Business Daily,* January 15, 2019.

231 **"Merry Munchie Meal":** Zlati Meyer, "Fast-Food Chain Tests 'Merry Munchie Meals' for Marijuana Smokers," *USA Today,* December 28, 2017.

231 **Gram by Gram:** Jeff Beer, "Snoop Dogg's Weed Media Company Launches New Ad Agency with Ex-Vice Execs," *Fast Company,* May 21, 2019.

232 **MORE Act:** Anna Gunther, "Bill That Would Federally Decriminalize Marijuana Passes House Committee," CBS News, November 21, 2019.

232 **blacks were still being charged:** Ibid., 20.

232 **progress for minorities:** Eli McVey, "Women and Minorities in the Cannabis Industry 2019," *Marijuana Business Daily,* July 28, 2019. 4.

233 **"straw men":** Jackie Borchardt, "Medical Marijuana Company Misled Ohio About Ownership, State Regulators Say in Document," *Cincinnati Enquirer,* July 31, 2019; Todd Wallack and Dan Adams, "Massachusetts Marijuana Regulators Investigating Whether Companies Violated License Limits," *The Boston Globe,* March 27, 2019.

233 **Illinois lawmakers wrote:** "Illinois Releases Timeline, Social Equity Plans for Legalizing Marijuana," *Marijuana Moment* via Weedmaps, May 6, 2019, https://weedmaps.com/news/2019/05/illinois-releases-timeline-social-equity-plans-for-legalizing-marijuana/; Nick Thomas, "Will Illinois Change the Social Equity Landscape for the Marijuana Industry?," *Marijuana Business Daily,* October 9, 2019; "Illinois Releases Social Equity Map for Adult-Use Licensing," *Marijuana Business Daily,* September 30, 2019.

234 **"Munchie Snackdown":** *Martha & Snoop's Potluck Party Challenge,* "4/20 Munchie Snackdown" VH-1 video, April 3, 2019, http://www.vh1.com/episodes/20hl80/martha-and-snoops-potluck-party-challenge-4-20-munchie-snackdown-season-3-ep-301.

235 **"I wanna thank me":** "Snoop Dogg Gets Star on Hollywood Walk of Fame," ET Canada, YouTube, November 19, 2018, https://www.youtube.com/watch?v=GvpZ2mcUJWc.

236 **Stewart would come on board:** Maureen Judkis, "The Buzz Is True: Martha Stewart Partners with Canadian Cannabis Company," *The Washington Post,* March 1, 2019.

236 **$150 million purchase:** "Canopy Breaks Ground on Industrial Park in New York," *Hemp Industry Daily,* July 29, 2019.

236 **seven other hemp manufacturing plants:** Kristine Owram, "Canopy Wants Hemp Operations in 7 States Within 12 Months," Bloomberg, June 4, 2018.

236 **"No one has canceled":** Sara Ritchie, "Martha Stewart on Cannabis, Women in Business and Why She Wants to Put a Leash on Elon Musk," *Civilized,* June 2019.

236 **potential future acquisition of Acreage Holdings:** Kristine Owram and Craig Giammons, "Canopy Buys Acreage for $3.4 Billion in Bet on U.S. Market," Bloomberg, April 18, 2019.

236 **Kevin Murphy:** Alex Halperin, "Acreage CEO Kevin Murphy: The Weed Week Interview," *Weed Week,* July 9, 2018.

237 **Boehner very rich:** Elizabeth Wiseman, "John Boehner: From Speaker of the House to Cannabis Pitchman," *The New York Times,* June 3, 2019.

237 **Tweed Distilled Cannabis:** Peter Hum, "Tweed Targets Cannabis Novices with Unveiling of 13 Drinks and Three Chocolates," *Ottawa Citizen,* October 31, 2019.

238 **600,000 to 4.8 million square feet in just eighteen months:** Edited transcript of CGC.TO earnings call, via Yahoo Finance, https://finance.yahoo.com/news/edited-transcript-cgc-earnings-conference-122952442.html.

238 **ninety patents:** Canopy Growth press release, "Canopy Growth Outlines 'Cannabis 2.0' Portfolio," November 28, 2019, https://www.canopygrowth.com/investors/news-releases/canopy-growth-outlines-cannabis-2-0-portfolio/?mc_cid=70c14a2e0b&mc_eid=c299d96f.

238 **June 2019 earnings call:** Max Cherney, "Canopy Co-CEO Defends Large Losses as a Deserved Reward for Pot Company's Employees," MarketWatch, June 24, 2019.

238 **Constellation's CEO, Bill Newlands:** Max A. Cherney, "Constellation CEO 'Not Pleased' with Pot Investment Canopy Growth's Recent Earnings," MarketWatch, June 29, 2019.

239 **He had been fired:** Angelica LaVito and Matthew Belvedere, "Bruce Linton Says He Was Fired as Co-CEO of Canadian Pot Company Canopy Growth," CNBC, July 3, 2019.

239 **"Our board was uniform":** Carmen Reinecke, "The CEO of Constellation Brands Throws Cold Water on the Idea That Former Canopy Growth Chief Bruce Linton Was Fired for Financial Reasons (CGC, STZ)," Markets Insider, July 9, 2019.

242 **MedMen signed a whopping:** MedMen press release, "MedMen Announces Acquisition of Florida Marijuana License and Cultivation Facility," June 6, 2018, https://investors.medmen.com/press-releases/press-release-details/2018/MedMen-Announces-Acquisition-of-Florida-Marijuana-License-and-Cultivation-Facility/default.aspx.

244 **The first marriage:** iAnthus Capital Holdings press release, "iAnthus and MPX Bioceutical Announce Closing of Transformational $1.6 Billion Business Combination," February 5, 2019, https://www.prnewswire.com/news-releases/ianthus-and-mpx-bioceutical-announce-closing-of-transformational-1-6-billion-business-combination-300790408.html.

245 **"Women of Weed":** "High Times Celebrates the Women of Weed Honorees," Green Market Report, April 1, 2019, https://www.greenmarketreport.com/high-times-celebrates-the-women-of-weed-honorees/.

INDEX

ABOUT THE AUTHOR

HEATHER CABOT is the co-author of *Geek Girl Rising: Inside the Sisterhood Shaking Up Tech*. She is a former ABC News correspondent and anchor, and an award-winning local TV news veteran. Cabot serves on the alumni board of Columbia University Graduate School of Journalism and resides outside New York City with her husband and twins.

ABOUT THE TYPE

This book was set in Caledonia, a typeface designed in 1939 by W. A. Dwiggins (1880–1956) for the Merganthaler Linotype Company. Its name is the ancient Roman term for Scotland, because the face was intended to have a Scottish-Roman flavor. Caledonia is considered to be a well-proportioned, businesslike face with little contrast between its thick and thin lines.